HEARTS OF THE MATTER

Heart of the Matter

An Introduction to Eighteen South Australian Poets

Edited by
Ioana Petrescu and Naomi Brewer
with Tully Bates, Jane Bettoney, Demelza Gers,
Nathan Gogoll, Lauren Phillips, Gill Ratcliff, Lisa Solomon

CONTRIBUTORS

E.L. Benn, Robert Bloomfield, Megan Boyd, Naomi Brewer,
Brad Cameron, Kelly Campbell, Samantha Crosley, Ian Furness,
Nathan Gogoll, Carly Gange, Hilde Haraldseid, Nina Higgs,
Fleur Holmes, Clay Hunter, Elizabeth Kidd, Alison Kiesau,
Maria Kiland, Margaret Klopper, Lauren Kourtidis, Kirsty Lubcke,
Miki Maricic, Liam Monkhouse, Rebecca Oakey, Caryn Rogers,
Dorothy Shorne, Lisa Solomon, Iain Spalding, Andre Starr,
Brett Steel, Ben Taylor, Adriana Timpano, Linda Uphill,
Christy Van Stralen

LYTHRUM PRESS
Adelaide

First published by
Lythrum Press
128 Hindley Street
Adelaide
South Australia 5000

February 2004

The material in this book was researched, written and edited by students of the University of South Australia, who studied Writing and Reading Poetry and Advanced Editing in 2002/2003. The project was initiated and coordinated by Dr Ioana Petrescu, Lecturer in Professional and Creative Writing, School of Communication, Information and New Media, University of South Australia.

Cover artwork by Megan Boyd, University of SA
Designed and typeset in Giovanni by Michael Deves
Printed and bound by Hyde Park Press

ISBN 0 9751260 4 0

The editors would like to thank the Centre for Professional and Public Communication, University of South Australia, and the Australian Awards for University Teaching 2000 for support with the production of this book.

Disclaimer
The views expressed by the interviewees may not necessarily be those of the University of South Australia.

CONTENTS

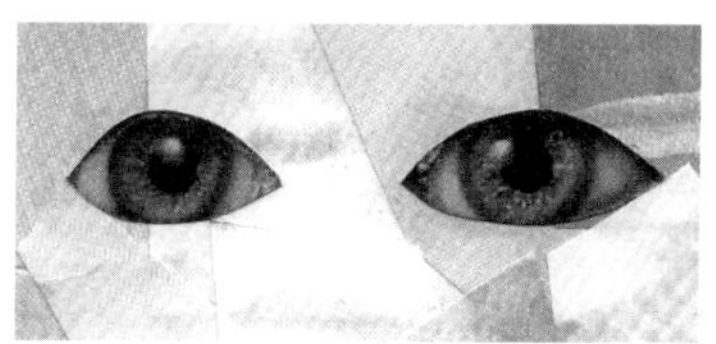

Heart of the Matter: An Introduction to Eighteen South Australian Poets

When Scilling and I, with a clear voice,
raised the song, loud with the harp sounded the melody:
then many a man, exultant in mind those who well knew,
spake and said that they never had heard a better song.

from *Widsith*, late 8th/early 9th century

Poetry is a mode of expression that has elicited much debate both in newer and older times. More than a thousand years ago powerful masters discovered that bards had a need to compose and would produce their poems anyway even if the masters stopped offering them privileges in return for poems that celebrated their heroic feats and exploits. The bards were in trouble—they had to start searching for patrons happy to sponsor their craft. Poetry achieved a higher status several centuries later when noble courtiers took to writing gallant verses and odes of praise for their lords, but a new dimension was added to the picture: the metaphysical poets believed it was below their status to publish their work, which had been written just for the enjoyment of their peers. In the meantime, folk forms of poetry entertained people at fairs. The debate whether poetry on the page was superior to performance poetry or vice versa, and whether it has an important social function or not, was there ... What to do?

One way of sorting this out would be the Leavisite response to literature, i.e. to create a value system that looks down one's creative and/or theoretical nose, and tell others what is value and what isn't. Another approach would be to postmodernly declare that value is in the eye of the beholder. Yet another way would be to look at the kitty, see there isn't much money there for poetry and prioritise according to ... What, really?

This must be a fairly interesting topic otherwise it wouldn't have been discussed both at the 2003 Conference of the Australian Association of Writing Programs in Sydney, and at the meeting of The Australia Council with publishers on 8 December 2003.

The 2003 AAWP Conference was titled *Negotiations. Writing, the*

Academy and Publishing, and academics from Australia, New Zealand and the USA looked at creative writing as it is taught in universities, and also at the chances manuscripts have on the publishing market once they have received recognition from the academy (Honours, Masters, PhD). In Australia university presses are scarce and students have to compete in the market with both new and established writers. The market is not huge and is mostly dominated by non-literary or hybrid forms. A panel that included a literary agent, an editor, a publisher and the director of the Australian Society of Authors offered a realistic view of the market at present. They confirmed what academics had experienced for several years—while writing programs discover and nurture many writers each year, the market will only take up a very select few. Poetry is in the unenviable situation where agents won't accept manuscripts because they would never see much money in return for their work—poetry doesn't sell and ten per cent of nearly nothing is not a sum that could keep going a business such as a literary agency. Publishers have left poetry entirely to small presses, which have recently experienced funding cuts. Speaking of Australia Council grants, Ron Pretty says in the Editorial of the fourth issue of *Blue Dog* that, 'The overall success rate for all applications in the July 2003 round was 62.5%, but for poetry publication it was less than 50%.'[1] In her *Writer's Guide*, Irina Dunn, the Executive Director of the NSW Writers' Centre, says, 'Few book publishers in Australia and New Zealand are interested in publishing poetry. Despite the large numbers of people writing poetry, the market for poetry books is tiny and so the competition to publish a volume of poems is fierce. To achieve this, a poet must first have published many individual poems in periodicals or won prizes in literary competitions.'[2] Is the situation really as bleak as it looks?

There are several answers to this question and they are all related to the fact that poetry has rarely been the producer of bestsellers, and even poets such as T.S. Eliot and W.B. Yeats didn't depend on it for a living. But poetry has always brought to its writers and readers much satisfaction, it is a genre that can take many forms and can be expressed through a diversity of media. What some believe to be its doom, very often is its greatest strength—because it expresses itself in so many ways and is hardly dictated by the market, poetry has a freedom of literary and personal expression that not many other literary genres can boast. While poetry will never sell as many book copies as novels do, poets are invited to festivals and conferences, their work is broadcast on the radio and printed on bus tickets, and whoever wishes to examine society at a given time refers to poetry as one of its most faithful mirrors. The *Macquarie Dictionary* states that 'poetry is the art of rhythmical composition, written or spoken, for exciting pleasure by beautiful, imaginative or elevated thoughts.'[3]

A fact proven by statistics is that students keep enrolling in poetry/creative writing courses. Surely they wouldn't be interested in paying HECS for something that has no value to them or anyone else. In 2003 the University of South Australia undergraduate poetry class had twenty-nine students enrolled and the attendance rate for each class was over eighty per cent. The students were told throughout the semester about the reality of publication but they were still there at the end of the semester, writing their poetry folios, editing each other's work, and assessing their colleagues' performance readings with honesty and professionalism. One student in this class submitted a poetry collection for publication and it was accepted; another student had a poem published and received a cash prize; a student decided to continue poetry study through an Honours degree; a student reads poems in nursing homes; a student is a wedding celebrant and put together a collection of poems that can be read on such occasions; a student already had a business before starting this class—finding poetry on cards too unappealing, the student produced her own cards with poems for all occasions; several students attended Friendly Street Poets, the longest running performance poetry venue in Australia, they enjoyed the experience and went back to read there in an attempt to get integrated in the local poetry scene. And, last but by no means least, all of the UniSA poetry students from the 2002 and 2003 classes were engaged in a poetry project that made this book happen.

About the project

Based on the principle of linking theory with practice, the UniSA poetry course aimed from the beginning at building an awareness of the current poetry scene in which new poets can become involved if they wish to do so. The students hadn't heard of many of the South Australian poets who live and write in the here and now—their previous experience regarding poetry was based on class exercises that often looked at poets of the 'canon'. While looking at the great masters is a valid exercise, an awareness of current poetry adds to the experience. Many students said that they had always thought of poets as being remote, secluded beings that lived on ideas, feelings and metaphors, in times that were not necessarily contemporary. The UniSA poetry course offered the students the possibility of interviewing contemporary South Australian poets and writing about the experience.

The project consisted of several stages: going to local bookshops and publishers, looking at their shelves and choosing a contemporary South Australian poet's work that truly appealed to the student; setting up a flexible structure interview of approximately ten questions and contacting the author; interviewing the author and transcribing the interview; writing a reflective 'meet the author' piece; writing a brief exegetical piece about the entire work, part thereof, or a few poems that would be representative for the poet's work. The students engaged in the project as they do with all of their university work, but in the process the reality of the project took over and they found themselves in new territory. They had to develop and use several skills that I believe will help smooth the transition from the world of the academy to the 'real' world: they had to work in the community in a responsible way, endorsed by the Ethics Committee of the university; they had to develop interviewing skills and then spend long hours transcribing the interviews from tape; they had to reflect upon the experience and realise whether this is a path they would truly be interested to follow; they had to set the South Australian poet's work in a more general context, thus becoming aware of the contemporary Australian and world poetry scene.

Most students engaged with enthusiasm in this project and the quality of the written products induced the Professional Writing team of lecturers to think of ways of promoting student writing, thus creating one more necessary link between the academy and the world of practice—publication. Thus, students who came to the poetry class most probably believing that they would read a bit, write a bit, learn about poetry writing and obtain a grade in a field that many still believe can hardly be assessed, found themselves thrown in the deep end of the industry and actually enjoying it. When asked whether they would like to see their work in print, all of the student authors represented in this book gave their consent and many supported the project even after graduation, offering their input through editing skills, artistic skills (book cover), and organising skills (book launch). The level of their professionalism is attested by their individual publications and employment in the industry as editors.

From the 2002 poetry projects eight chapters were selected for publication. In the first semester of the next academic year, 2003, eight students from the Advanced Editing class chose as their major project to edit these chapters and bring them up to industry publication standards. The editing students set up a house style, had many meetings and collaborated throughout the semester, and by the end of the course half of the book was nearly finished. In the second semester of 2003 ten more chapters produced by the poetry class were added to the book, thus creating a 'real' product to be sent out there in the 'real' world to compete for a place on the shelves. Whether they believed university would do this for them or not, the Professional Writing students found themselves doing exactly what it says on their degree—Professional Writing. The UniSA students chose the authors, wrote the interviews, met the authors, wrote reflective and exegetical pieces and edited their own work.

South Australian poets and their work

In a letter to the editor in the May 2003 issue of *The Adelaide Review*, I stated that Adelaide has a variety of poetic voices to present to the audience, and also that South Australian poetry is alive and well: The Australia Council's Director is an SA poet, ABC Radio National's *PoeticA* is produced from Adelaide, the prestigious national John Bray poetry prize was awarded in 2002 to an SA poet, tents overflow when poets perform at the Writers' Week, all three universities in Adelaide and TAFE institutes offer courses in creative writing/poetry; Friendly Street Poets have met monthly for twenty-seven years, poetry readings happen nearly every week in bookshops, pubs, universities, libraries, and in the last year I have been invited to more poetry book launches than I would ever have the time to go to. Many of these books were published by small presses in rather limited print runs, but they do sell their print runs to poetry lovers at readings and festivals, and if the authors actually reach their audience this is perhaps what truly matters.

UniSA students went to local bookshops and publishers, read the poetry books that were exhibited on shelves and liked what they read. This is where they discovered slim volumes that contained thoughts they could relate to. Very often, after meeting the authors the students felt inspired to read more, write more and find out more about poetry. The feedback received from the interviewed poets was just as positive. They enjoyed talking to students about their work and many encouraged them with their own writing, welcoming the new writers in the industry. The South Australian poets offered their advice, expertise and time, always knowing there were no financial rewards attached to this project, which is totally non-profit. I would like to thank here the poets for their time and dedication to poetry and writing. This book is here due to their support and professional advice.

This book contains chapters produced in 2002 about the work of Tom Shapcott, Peter Goldsworthy, Mike Ladd, Stephen Lawrence, Martin Johnson, Cath Kenneally, Shen and Jules Leigh Koch. In 2003 the book was enriched by chapters about the work of Ken Bolton, Peter Lloyd, Jeri Kroll, Graham Rowlands, Steve Evans, Geoff Goodfellow, Jude Aquilina, Rory Harris, David Adès and Amelia Walker. The students discovered in the bookshops and at publishers the work of long-established poets, but also the more recent work of poets who are rising on the poetry scene, and even debut books of new poets. The book reflects this diversity, which is proof of the healthy state of South Australian poetry—a poetry scene that has well-established names, as well as ascending poets and new poets, cannot but be alive and well.

The interviews have been reproduced in full, with minor editing according to the house style, and also in terms of spelling and punctuation. While all interviewers worked within established parameters, due to the specific personalities of the interviewers and poets no two interviews are alike. They all speak about the poets' love of words, their desire to put these words in print and see whether they can reach out and speak for them. Also, the interviews vary according to the chosen media—some interviewers recorded the interviews on audiotape, others on videotape, and others interviewed the authors by email, always negotiating the interview media with the authors. Depending on the chosen media, the interviews have specific writerly or spoken qualities, adding a new dimension to the portraits of the poets.

Most reflective 'meet the author' pieces and also the exegetical pieces were abridged due to space constraints, but every effort has been made to keep intact the words and opinions of the authors. The voice of the student-author is important because it records the encounter with both the work and the person behind the work, and very often the experience is remarkable and worth reproducing in a book about South Australian poetry and its writers. The chapters have been run by the poets and their approval was sought before publication. This is again a place where thanks need to go to both the student-authors and the South Australian poets for making this book possible.

Why a book about South Australian Poetry?

South Australian poetry is a literary phenomenon in its own right, and, although geographically delimited by borders it is by no means just regional, it belongs to the contemporary poetry space having equal rights and equal claims to a readership and due recognition. Both Aristotle and Wilde's Lady Bracknell would have been appalled if they could read the above, but facts are facts and poetry does happen on both sides of the 'street', in Felicia just as in Arcadia—although, one has to admit that if readers wish to search for writing about contemporary South Australian poetry the only sources that can be found are the blurbs on the back covers of books and the occasional reviews in literary magazines.

This is where this book comes in, with the hope of providing reference material for poetry lovers in South Australia and interstate by shining a light on this literary phenomenon and bringing information about South Australian poetry to the community of readers.

Bob Perelman, a celebrated language poet, wrote:

> 'The Marginalization of Poetry'—it almost
> goes without saying. Jack Spicer wrote,
>
> 'No one listens to poetry,' but
> the question then becomes, who is
>
> Jack Spicer? Poets for whom he
> matters would know, and their poems

would be written in a world
in which that line was heard,

though they'd scarcely refer to it.[4]

This book about South Australian contemporary poets and their work might help to offer a more optimistic view by showing that poetry is not and cannot be marginalised by anyone, anywhere, for the simple reason that it is ubiquitous—it exists in universities, libraries, pubs, at country fairs, festivals, in the city as well as in the bush, in magazines, books and on the Internet. South Australian poets are part of this literary phenomenon and, with this book, the UniSA Professional and Creative Writing students invite the readers to share the experience.

Dr Ioana Petrescu
Lecturer, Professional and Creative Writing
School of Communication, Information and New Media
University of South Australia

Adelaide, 28 December 2003

Notes

1 Ron Pretty, 'Editorial' in *Blue Dog. Australian Poetry*, vol. 2, no. 4, Poetry Australia Foundation, Wollongong, 2003, pp. 3–4.
2 Irina Dunn, *The Writer's Guide. A Companion to Writing for Pleasure or Publication*, Allen & Unwin, 2002, p. 40.
3 *The Macquarie Dictionary*, eds A. Delbridge et al., revised third edition, The Macquarie Library, Macquarie University, 2001, p. 1470.
4 Bob Perelman, *The Marginalization of Poetry. Language Writing and Literary History*, Princeton University Press, Princeton, New Jersey, 1996, p. 3.

PETER GOLDSWORTHY

Chapter by Nina Higgs

Published poetry books

Readings from Ecclesiastes, Angus & Robertson, Sydney 1982
This Goes with This: Selected Poems 1970–1990, ABC Enterprises, Crows Nest 1988
This Goes with That, Collins/Angus & Robertson, North Ryde 1991
After the Ball, National Library of Australia, Canberra 1992
If Then, Angus & Robertson, Sydney 1996
New Selected Poems, Duffy and Snellgrove, Sydney 2001
This Goes With That: Selected Poems, Leviathan, London 2002

Biographical note

Peter Goldsworthy was born in Minlaton, South Australia in 1951 and grew up in various country towns before finishing his schooling in Darwin. Since graduating in medicine from the University of Adelaide, he has divided his time equally between medicine and writing. His novels have sold more than a quarter of a million copies in Australia alone, and have been translated into most major Asian and European languages. His first collection of poetry, *Readings from Ecclesiastes*, won the Commonwealth Poetry Prize, the Ann Elder Award and the South Australian Premier's Prize. His second collection of poems, *This Goes with This*, won the Australian Bicentennial Poetry Prize in 1998, jointly with Philip Hodgins.

An accomplished and dynamic poet, Peter Goldsworthy has had several of his poems set to music by leading Australian composers, such as Graeme Koehne, Richard Mills and Matthew Hindson. He also wrote the libretti for the Richard Mills operas, *Summer of the Seventeenth Doll* and *Batavia*, the latter winning him the 2002 Robert Helpmann Awards for Best Opera and Best New Australian Work.

Peter Goldsworthy is currently the Chairperson of the Australia Council's Literature Board.

Interview with Peter Goldsworthy

Nina Higgs (NH): How old were you when you started to write poetry and what inspired you to write?

Peter Goldsworthy (PG): I was about seventeen. I used to write a lot of science fiction when I was an adolescent and then, when I was about sixteen or seventeen, I started reading a lot of poetry and really liked it.

NH: So you started reading it first?

PG: Yes, well, sometimes when you read something shattering or fantastic, you think that you wouldn't mind doing that too.

NH: Can you specifically name any of the poets whose writing really inspired you to write yourself?

PG: The *Penguin Modern European Poets Series* came out in the 1960s, including authors such as Zbigniew Herbert, Miroslav Holub, Vasko Popa and Tadeusz Rozewicz. Then, a couple of years later, I started to read Les Murray. He's the best writer this country's ever produced. He encouraged a lot of the early writing that I did.

NH: So it wasn't until you were seventeen that you started writing poetry yourself. Did you start from scratch?

PG: Yes, because I'd mainly written science fiction stories.

NH: How did you go about publishing your material? How long did it take to get published?

PG: When I was at university, poetry was part of the whole political thing. So you'd get published in the university newspapers and a few other magazines. It was all part of the sixties generation.

NH: As a child, did you aspire to become a poet or a writer?

PG: Yes, I always thought I was going to be an author.

NH: How did your parents feel about your ambition?

PG: They were pleased—they thought it was a rather amusing ambition!

NH: I understand that you also work as a GP. Had you always wanted to be a doctor as well?

PG: No ... well, I was always good at science and maths. In Year 12, I thought I might study history, but in the end I opted for medicine, because the medical course looked interesting. Also, there was the idea that I could work part-time in order to write. Even though I studied medicine full-time, I've always worked [as a doctor] part-time.

NH: Did your writing have to take a bit of a backseat while you were at medical school?

PG: I just wrote poetry during those years. Poetry's something you can write in your spare moments. You couldn't write a novel in your spare time. Although, Michael Crichton did—he wrote three or four of them when he was still in medical school. But yes, that suited me—doing poetry and medicine.

NH: Do you feel that you like one profession more than the other?

PG: No, they're complementary. Writing's a very lonely business, but medicine gives you that human contact. It also gives you a lot of stories and a sense of what's really important in the world. So I think the two balance each other very well.

NH: I recently read an interview in which you described medicine as your wife and writing as your mistress.

PG: Chekhov actually said that originally—I pinched it from Chekhov [laughs].

NH: Whilst being a doctor, you've published many books. Do you set aside a specific time to write? Is your writing structured in this respect?

PG: Yes—every morning I write—but not the poetry. I don't think poetry works like that—well, it doesn't for me anyway. Poetry comes to you. However, with the poetry I've written for opera libretti, I've had to set aside specific times, because it's such a big task. You can't do that type of thing just in the gaps.

Poems themselves come to you unbidden—lines can come at any time. Sooner or later you've got to sit down and fit them together—I don't actually plan that. But I do plan novel writing, which I do from 9 am to 1 pm every day.

NH: So with the poetry the ideas will come to you and you'll just jot them down as they come and piece them together later.

PG: Yeah.

NH: You certainly do seem to treat your writing as a separate profession in that it's a lot more than just a hobby.

PG: Oh no, I make more money from writing than I do from medicine!

NH: Please tell me about the writing process for you—how do

you go about it? On average, how long do you take to put a poem together once you've got the ideas?

PG: Generally, lines come to you and you jot them down in your notebook or whatever and sometimes I'll form a whole poem right there and then. However, sometimes over a period of six months, a year or even more, you'll see that certain lines that have come to you over that time actually belong together—and they'll form themselves. They're a bit like plasticine. You gather a poem as it comes, slowly lay it out over however long a time it takes. But for me, there's no hard and fast rule.

NH: Have you ever written songs or lyrics?

PG: I've had poems set to music by different composers. But I didn't write them as songs, I wrote them as poems. I've written two opera libretti. I'm currently writing some cabaret songs and hip-hop lyrics, and having a lot of fun.

NH: Are you putting the music to these?

PG: No, I'm going to work with various composers.

NH: For the type of lyrics that you're writing now—the more contemporary sort of stuff—have you had to study the craft of song writing?

PG: No, not that much. I think it's all in us—rhythm and rhyme are all in us. They're all part of our DNA. I don't think you can really study it that much—I think it is part of our nature. But for the last opera, I had to read a lot of Shakespeare and I had to absorb a lot of the vocabulary. I had to study the verse lines, sonnets and things like that.

NH: That's interesting, I didn't know you were into song writing. I imagine that working as a doctor would provide you with some interesting material. Could you tell me of any specific experiences you've had in your profession that have led to great poems?

PG: I think my best recent poem is called 'Morbid Song' and it comes from a year that I spent in the dissecting room when I was a student. I've only just written it. I've written a few poems about that, but the new one's a good poem I think. Generally, I find that medicine's given me a lot of short stories, but it hasn't really given me as many poems. Actually, I've written a whole book of short stories, called *Little Deaths,* which are about my medical experiences.

NH: Where does the poetry come from?

PG: Oh, you can get poetry anywhere. I mean, I've written a lot of love poems lately.

NH: Would you say that your poems come more from just your general, everyday observations?

PG: Well, yes. I've written animal poems, I've written love poems, I've written a lot of ironic, sarcastic poems, I've written poems about places—about potatoes, tomatoes. I mean, you can find a poem anywhere. I've even written a poem about shaving. For a while, I wrote a series of poems that were very ordinary and obvious. Because I thought, well, the traditional inspirations of poems of things like daffodils etcetera don't really need poems—they're beautiful things in themselves. So I thought, what needs a poem? And I thought, a spud. So I wrote a poem about a potato.

NH: I guess we wouldn't really give much thought to the poor old spud. I read in an on-line interview that you tend to do a lot of work with the terminally ill.

PG: Oh, I guess any doctor does.

NH: I got the impression that you specialised in this area.

PG: No, not really. It's only recently become a specialised area—palliative care.

NH: I was just curious to know if when working with dying patients, you sometimes let the two disciplines cross over and read people a few of your poems in order to brighten them up a bit. Have you ever done anything like that?

PG: No, but many of my patients read my books. Although, you've got to keep track—make sure the person's not in the book they're reading [laughs].

NH: Do your patients quite often ask about your writing?

PG: Yes, especially if there's an article in the paper about something I've written.

NH: In your opinion, what makes a good poem?

PG: I don't think there's one hard and fast rule. But I think poetry should be memorable, so that it sticks in your head.

NH: What about elements such as rhyme, rhythm, metre and metaphors? I mean, do you view them as being important?

PG: Not necessarily—I mean they can be important or they may not. There's wonderful poetry written with rhyme, rhythm and metaphors and there's wonderful poetry written without these things. It's not a crucial thing, but at some level, the poem needs to be memorable—whether it's memorable because of a great line or rhythm or whatever. [Pokey, his dog, jumps up into my lap.]

NH: [referring to Pokey] She's beautiful. Have you written a poem about her?

PG: No, I haven't. Recently, after I'd been in Melbourne doing the opera, *The Advertiser* did an interview with a picture of me and Pokey. And then, the following week, they rang me up and said that people kept ringing in asking what sort of dog Pokey is. You never share the stage with animals! I also had a picture taken with her in *The Age* and people were ringing up asking about her.

NH: You're famous, Pokey!

PG: Yeah, Pokey is much more famous than me.

NH: Have you got one or two poems that you feel are your best work?

PG: Yep—'A Statistician to His Love'—that's got a lot of airplay all around the world now. Then there's a little haiku—the shaving haiku. It's pretty well known. And then there's the 'Morbid Song'. But I don't keep all the poems that I write. If you look at that book [*New and Selected Poems*, 2001], it contains thirty years' worth of poems. And I can tell you that I've written a hell of a lot more poems than that. I like a lot of the poems in that book. Though I'm a great believer in the fish that John West rejects—I take a lot of stuff out.

NH: [laughs] I particularly like the one you wrote about a next-door neighbour.

PG: Oh yeah, I think I scrapped that one from the most recent book. But seeing you like it, I'll put it in the next one.

NH: What advice would you give to someone who'd like to pursue a career as a poet?

PG: Well, don't plan on making any money. Read a lot. Work a lot.

NH: You'd really need to have another career as well, wouldn't you?

PG: Yes, you'd need to have a 'cover job'.

NH: Well, you've got a pretty good 'cover job', haven't you?

PG: I've been very lucky, because I can do it part-time and make a living.

NH: How many days a week do you work?

PG: I work five half-days. I'll have to cut that down, because I'm chairman of the Literature Board of the Australia Council and that's sort of an extra commitment. So, I'll have to readjust things a bit.

NH: Is there anything else that you'd like to discuss, that I haven't already brought up?

PG: Just one thing—you were asking me about what I think is important in a poem. I think metaphor is very important—probably much more important than either rhyme or rhythm. Metaphor is essential. I called a book of my poems *This Goes with That* which is basically what a metaphor is—this is so much like that. That's the thing in poetry that makes that sort of connection. In the end, that's what really moves us. Chimpanzees were taught sign language about twenty years ago. One day, one of them was very cross with the keeper, and called the keeper a 'shit' in sign language. The chimp hadn't been taught to use the sign 'shit' except in its physiological sense, so that's a poem—she created a metaphor. That's the only poem I know that's been created by another species.

We reach for metaphor when we're deeply moved in any way. That gives it immense poetic power.

Talking to Peter Goldsworthy

On learning that I would need to select a South Australian poet to focus on as part of my professional writing studies, I went into a tailspin of panic. Even though I'd written poetry for many years myself, I had not, at that stage, taken the time to explore the 'who's who' of the local poetry scene. So began my search for a well-known South Australian poet. Whilst sifting through the poetry section of Borders bookshop the following day, I came across a poetry anthology written by Peter Goldsworthy. I recognised this author because I had been introduced to several of his science fiction novels in primary school. Eager to see how Goldsworthy shaped up as a poet, I spent the next few hours reading through his latest selection of poetry. What appealed to me most about his work was not his exquisite use of metaphor and imagery, but rather, his dry sense of humour. I also enjoyed poems such as 'A Statistician to His Love' and

'Coast', which were inspired by his real life experiences as a general practitioner. By this stage, I had more than made up my mind that Peter Goldsworthy would be the poet I would focus on.

Arranging an interview with this accomplished author proved to be a relatively painless task. I must admit that I felt a little intimidated by his professional phone manner, as I was expecting to speak to Peter Goldsworthy the poet, as opposed to a very serious Dr Goldsworthy. Nonetheless, he kindly agreed to see me the following day at 4 pm. Feeling somewhat nervous at the prospect of interviewing one of South Australia's foremost poets, I checked my tape recorder one last time before I made my way to the doorstep of his inner city home.

A tall, slim man opened the door. 'Hello! I'm here to see Dr Goldsworthy,' I said. 'Yes, that's me,' said the man, who invited me in. I felt rather embarrassed by my failure to recognise him, but he did look quite different from how he looked in the photograph in his most recent book.

As Peter led me down the hall and into the kitchen, I was greeted by a pint-sized pup named Pokey. I was most grateful that Pokey chose to join us for the interview. Peter Goldsworthy and I spoke about dogs for the next five minutes while he prepared some coffee. With a grin on his face, he told me of how this little Maltese Terrier had recently appeared in both *The Age* and *The Advertiser*.

We sat at the kitchen table, alongside a window which revealed a lovely little courtyard. Overlooking an array of brightly coloured plants, it seemed like an ideal place to write.

Peter Goldsworthy seemed quite different from how I had imagined him to be. Although he was very polite, he came across as being quite serious and a little reserved.

Peter is obviously a very busy man, as he works as a GP five mornings a week and is currently working on several writing projects, including a very demanding piece for an opera. However, the more humorous side of his personality came through later on several occasions. I was very pleased by the manner in which Peter went about answering my questions—he considered each question carefully and provided me with thoughtful and comprehensive responses. In particular, he went into a lot of detail about the theoretical aspects of poetry writing, which I found interesting. I also enjoyed hearing about how he started out as a poet and the ways in which his writing career complements his 'cover job' in medicine.

Whilst it is not my intention to compare myself to a writer of Peter Goldsworthy's calibre, I have to say that we seem to experience the poetry writing process in a similar fashion. For instance, I could relate to a lot of what he said about the ways in which poetry just comes to you—regardless of the time and place. Like Peter, I find that I cannot simply sit down and write a poem at a certain time, whereas other people can. Furthermore, I too believe that a good poem does not have to adhere to any one specific formula but needs to be memorable.

Reading the poems

The range of poetry existing within contemporary Australia is extremely rich, diverse and liberating (Porter 1998). Surely this reflects the changing nature of our society and the impacts of forces such as reconciliation, feminism and multiculturalism. Indeed, Australian poetry now features many fine female poets and is written in various languages aside from just English (Tranter and Mead 1991). Also, with the translation of Aboriginal poetry and song cycles taking place over the past fifty years, Indigenous poetry now assumes a greater place in Australia (Tranter and Mead 1991).

Despite the fact that there still exists a strong love of rhyming verse among Australians, there appears to be a growing trend towards the use of free verse (Haynes 2002). Furthermore, many of our modern poets have left behind the traditional outback themes of early Australia in favour of poetry which is based upon pure ideas and issues of the present day (Porter 1998).

Nonetheless, the bush ballad approach is still seen in contemporary Australian verse and thus remains an important part of our culture (Haynes 2002). While Les Murray stands out as one of the greatest poets that Australia has ever produced, the past few decades have brought forth a wave of new talent—with poets such as Stephen Edgar, John Kinsella, Jan Owen, Judith Wright and John Forbes paving the way to a new poetic era. Each state has its own unique crop of accomplished and up-and-coming poets, along with its own poetry readings, festivals and publications. In South Australia for instance, there is a bustling poetry scene with live readings taking place at various venues and poetry hotspots. The fact that such a strong poetry culture exists within South Australia is further indicated by the amount of interest generated by Writers' Week. This festival, which takes place every second year, attracts some of the finest poets from both within Australia and overseas.

Peter Goldsworthy, who is well known to Australian audiences for his children's fiction literature, is also arguably one of this state's most accomplished poets. Described as 'one of the most skilled and satisfying poets in Australia', Goldsworthy is said to have 'the rare ability to mix seriousness with humour' (Page 1995). Indeed, his poetry collections, which span from 1982 through to the present day, 'offer rueful ironies at the expense of the universe' (Wilde, Hooton & Andrews 1994). At the same time his use of language is elegant and according to Page (1995), 'there is something intellectually or linguistically interesting happening in virtually every line' of his work.

Peter Goldsworthy has published six collections of poetry. His poetry has been featured and reviewed in a myriad of publications, and several of his poems have been set to music.

Perhaps one of the most appealing elements of Peter Goldsworthy's poetry is the fact that it deals with aspects of everyday life in such a way that it relates to people from all walks of life. Indeed, many of his poems are based upon the observations that he makes in his day-to-day living. A well known example is his haiku titled 'Razor', in which he reflects upon the monotonous routine of shaving. The metaphoric element contained in this piece makes it both elegant and thought-provoking:

> Carving this same face
> out of soap, each morning
> slightly less perfectly.

He has written poems about vegetables, insects, colours and other such things that we all encounter and perhaps take for granted in our everyday lives. His decision to work with the simple things in life is reflected in his belief that it is important to give the gift of poetry to things that need it (see interview, p. 13). He believes that, 'Daffodils and those types of things don't really need poems, because they're beautiful in themselves'. It is for this reason that he chose to dedicate poems to things such as tomatoes and potatoes. 'Ode to the Potato' stands out as one of his most well-known poems. With its clever use of similes and personification, one could convincingly argue that

Goldsworthy does this vegetable justice.

In much the same way his poem 'Bees' opens our eyes to another aspect of nature that tends to be overlooked and even feared by some. In this particular piece, Goldsworthy describes these insects by mixing subtle ironies with intricate details, whilst at the same time, evoking some exquisite pieces of imagery,

> Bees
> have small furry pelts
> hard to keep from getting sticky.
> Their languages
> are dance and telepathy.
> Inside each bee
> is delicate machinery
> a noisy watch mechanism.

Apart from capturing fragments of everyday life in his poetry, Goldsworthy's work also reflects his experiences as both a medical student and as a general practitioner. 'A Statistician to His Love'—the poem that he regards as his own personal favourite—is based on a year that he spent working in a laboratory as a student. It is easy to see why Goldsworthy is so fond of this poem, as it is unique in the way in which it presents factual information about fatalities such as homicides and suicides in an interesting and ironic fashion.

Without being unnecessarily disrespectful, Goldsworthy frequently chooses to tackle religion with sarcasm, as in his haiku, 'Is There a God':

> I needed to pray but felt
> embarrassed: what if
> Someone was listening?

Stylistically, Peter Goldsworthy appears to have a preference for free verse, as the majority of his poems are not constrained by rhyme nor are they confined to any specific pattern or form. However, in recent years he has made some use of rhyme—with poems such as 'Mermaid's Song' appearing in an open quatrain (xaxa) format (Hirsch 1999). Certain lines of this poem contain rhymes occurring midstream, which serves to complement the playful, lyrical nature of the overall piece. In terms of metre, 'Mermaid's Song' appears to be dominated by couplets, which occasionally alternate with elegant triplets. The repetition of the line, 'Fin and scale, sand and shale' is very effective, as it adds to the rhythm of the poem.

Although Goldsworthy has incorporated rhyme into some of his other more recent poems, the rhyming schemes contained in these are at times inconsistent. For instance, from the outset, 'Pelsaert on His Sickbed' appears to take the form of a closed quatrain (abba). However, it quickly falls out of this scheme and seems to jump back and forth between rhyming and non-rhyming stanzas. This inconsistency does not seem to detract from his work. Indeed, as Roberts (2000) points out, using rhyme in a deliberate and frequent fashion can result in the reader becoming preoccupied with predicting the rhymes rather than focusing on the content.

Goldsworthy regards metaphor as the most essential element of a poem. According to Goldsworthy, metaphor 'is probably much more important than either rhyme or rhythm' (see interview, p. 15). Several of his poems contain very effective and at times, quite elaborate metaphors. For instance, in his poem 'Music', which could be considered an extended metaphor, he describes rain through various rhythms and musical terms.

Whilst Goldsworthy's poetry exhibits a dry sense of humour, it exudes elegance and sophistication. Even though Goldsworthy has received numerous poetry awards, he continues to explore new horizons.

References

Goldsworthy, P. (2001) *New Selected Poems*. Sydney: Duffy and Snellgrove.

Goldsworthy, P. (2002) 'Death and the Comedian',[viewed 15 August 2002], http://www.mja.com.au/public/issues/17311041200/goldsworthy/goldsworthy.html.

Haynes, J. (2002) *An Australian Treasury of Popular Verse*. Melbourne: ABC Books.

Hirsch, E. (1999) *How to Read a Poem and Fall in Love with Poetry*. New York: A Harvest Book, Harcourt Inc.

Page, G. (1995) *A Reader's Guide to Contemporary Australian Poetry*. Queensland: University of Queensland Press.

Porter, P. (1998) *The Oxford Book of Modern Australian Verse*. Melbourne: Oxford University Press.

Roberts, P. (2000) *How Poetry Works*. London: Penguin.

Tranter, J. and Mead, P. (1991) *The Penguin Book of Modern Australian Poetry*. Sydney: Penguin.

Wilde, W.H., Hooton, J. and Andrews, B. (1994) *The Oxford Companion to Australian Literature*, 2nd edn. Melbourne: Oxford University Press.

JERI KROLL

Published poetry books
Death as Mr Right, Friendly Street Poets, Adelaide 1982
Indian Movies, Hyland House, Melbourne 1984
Monster Love, Wakefield Press, Adelaide 1990
House Arrest, Wakefield Press, Adelaide 1993
The Mother Workshops, Five Islands Press, Wollongong, forthcoming 2004

Biographical note
Jeri Kroll is Associate Professor of English at Flinders University and Program Coordinator of Creative Writing. She moved to Adelaide in 1978 after growing up in New York City, and now lives in Adelaide with her husband and son. As well as poetry, Jeri writes fiction for young adults and 'middle-aged' children. In addition, she has also published six picture books. Jeri has recently completed two new books: *Mickey's Little Book of Letters,* a novel for older readers, and *The Mother Workshops,* a collection of poems for adults, which will both be available in 2004.

(Compiled by Brett Steel)

Interview with Jeri Kroll

by Brett Steel and Samantha Crosley

Brett Steel (BS): Your last individual poetry book, *House Arrest,* was published in 1993. What is it that has drawn you back to publishing poetry nearly ten years later?

Jeri Kroll (JK): The situation is that I have been writing a lot of young adult fiction, as well as picture books and older reader novels. When I'm writing a lot of fiction I tend not to write poetry. As well, one only has a certain amount of time in one's life, so I've really been putting my energy into that. I've still been writing poems, and about a year ago I realised that I certainly had enough for another collection. Some of the poems actually come out of a mixed-genre work—prose and poetry—that I've been working on. I decided I might as well just take some of the poems out of that and put them into a book and I'd certainly have enough for a full-length collection. I sent it off to Ron Pretty at Five Islands Press and he accepted it, so that's coming out at Writers' Week 2004. It's going to be launched along with Steve Evans's and Jeff Guess's books, so there will be a triple launch at Writers' Week of Five Islands Press books.

It's not as if I started writing again, I haven't stopped. It's just that I wasn't writing a lot of poetry. I like to produce integrated poetry collections. My other books are integrated around themes except for the first one. Most people's first books tend to be a bit of a hotch-potch. As you can see, *Monster Love* is a theme book. *House Arrest* is as well, but in a slightly different way. The first section in *House Arrest* is a long sequence about family, but then the book moves into questions of responsibility for other young people and ends with ideas about responsibility for the planet. *House Arrest* begins at home and ends in space. The last few poems are about outer space, so as I've said, there's progression. *The Mother Workshops* is the book that's coming out next year and a lot of it is centred around my mother's Alzheimer's and coming to terms with that. The book opens with a sequence, 'A Coastal Grammar', which is actually about family as well as landscape, and the main part of it is *The Mother Workshops* poems, which are all written as if they were exercises about certain issues. There's a villanelle, a sonnet, prose poems, and other forms as well. Most of the book is free verse but there are some poems that are in particular forms. There is some prose too.

BS: Some poems are in traditional forms. Is that how you write poetry?

JK: Yes, there are some. I like to do a bit of everything. I've written a couple of sestinas in my life, one won a prize. I've got two poems coming out in *The Australian Book of Sonnets* [2003], which Geoff Page is editing. I've probably written about ten sonnets in my life. I don't write a lot. A couple of villanelles. Most of the poems I write are free verse, but that doesn't mean that there's not a lot of pattern to it.

BS: What is it that you hope people will gain from reading your poetry? Is it a relationship that you're hoping to foster with your reader?

JK: I guess what most writers want is to somehow communicate their vision of the world and you can do that in any number of ways. One way is by revealing things about yourself. With the author in fiction, it's about trying to make people connect with the characters, and also about making readers see things in a particular way by manipulating a book's structure. A lot of it has to do with getting into an audience's head. If I actually knew how to definitely do all of that I wouldn't be here! I'd probably be rich and famous and able to sell the secret for the rest of my life. But I think that's what it is. It's partly communicating the way you see the world, partly making people question the way in which they (and you) see the world, and partly trying to make people connect with your own experiences. I like to share understandings of the way people think and relate and emote as well. I think *Monster Love* is my most popular book partly because parenting changes you irrevocably, and that's one of the things *Monster Love* is about. You'll never be the same again, no matter whether you have a good or bad experience—it changes you irrevocably and it does teach you a lot about yourself, as well as other people. Many readers and live audiences connected with that. When I've given readings from that book, people have come up to me after and said, 'I know just what you mean. This is what happened to me.' Some students in Matric study poems from *Monster Love* and email me about it. They seem to respond too.

BS: Do you find that poetry holds a special connection that adult fiction or children's books sometimes lack, or even films?

JK: The odd thing about poetry is that a lot of people write it who never read it. You've all probably written some poems in your lives before you started studying them, and people who never pick up a book of poetry will often feel moved to sit down and write a poem. This doesn't mean that poems are only about personal issues, but there's something about a short lyric poem that people feel will allow them to express the way they feel on an emotional and psychological level. I think that's one of the reasons why people often respond to poetry. It doesn't mean that they'll then go out and buy books and read it, which is a problem for writers because it's very hard to sell poetry. But certainly, if a writer's work does click with an audience they take it home—internally—in a way that doesn't necessarily parallel their experience reading popular fiction.

Other people's poems I really like, I remember. I read them a couple of times and I can remember them—at least all of the great lines. They don't have to rhyme. I've got that kind of a memory. It's because they resonate, and a lot of that resonance results from the language, not just the meaning but the language. Poetry, as Coleridge said, is the best words in the best order, and so it's the way the lines work that prints them in your memory. A dialogue between two characters in a film, you might remember a couple of the good lines, but most people won't remember a whole sequence. With poems you often do because of the language. I think that's one of the most important things about poetry.

BS: Has your poetry been representative of your changing positions in life, your changing stages?

JK: I think so, in a lot of ways certainly, because I wouldn't have written a book about Alzheimer's twenty-five years ago. I wouldn't have had any experience of it. That disease changes you as well because it certainly brings home, this is a cliché, but it does bring home your own morality. I look a lot like my mother and you can't help but think, 'Is this where I'm going to be in another twenty or twenty-five years?' It's not that people don't do this in fiction; it's just that it's hidden more often because you create other characters. When I've written children's fiction and I've asked my son to read things for me–for his opinion–he'll often read a book and say, 'I know where you got that!' It might simply be a dog's name I've used, or a dog's behaviour or somebody we knew but they're all mixed up, a bit like a jigsaw puzzle. My poems tend to have more of a direct relationship with my experiences. Much of my poetry does follow the stages you go through in life. I think that's because many poets often have more of a direct connection with what they produce than fiction writers. Sometimes fiction is a way of escaping. I'm having great fun being a twelve-year-old girl right now because I've got a novel coming out next year and I'm rewriting it. I've got to become her in a way. I've got to get into her mind.

BS: Where do you think you might be in ten years time and what might you be writing about then?

JK: I'd like to be retired and writing but I don't think that's going to happen. Talking about brains disintegrating and feeling one doesn't have enough time left, I'd like to spend a lot more time writing because there are a lot of things I still want to do. The older you grow the more intense the feeling that the clock is ticking. You don't want to lose the time you have left. There's a lot more books I'd like to write, and novels take time, a lot more than poems. You can't rewrite a novel as many times as you can rewrite a poem.

BS: Iris Murdoch's work touched on that a bit. Do you feel a relationship between that and the Alzheimer's?

JK: I think for intelligent people who live with words, that's one of the greatest terrors—worrying about losing your mind—because that's where you live a lot of the time. It's not that other people won't feel it. For instance, if you haven't had a good memory you don't tend to notice its weakening that much because you don't expect to remember everything. I was actually having this conversation with somebody at a party last month. We both obviously had similar memories. Mine wasn't photographic but it was very, very good, so that I could remember where things were on a page. I could read something for an exam the night before and quote part of it the next day. When you can't do that anymore, you notice. So yes, the whole Iris Murdoch thing is horrible. It's horrible for anyone, but I think it's worse when you rely on being able to call things up. You're sitting there trying to rewrite something and you think, 'What was that word? I used to know that word I wanted. Where is it?' When it doesn't come, it's terrifying.

BS: How do you view the modern poetry scene in Adelaide at the moment?

JK: I was very involved with Friendly Street when it first started. I co-edited *Tuesday Night Live* with Barry Westburg and we wrote the history of Friendly Street for the first fifteen years. It was very, very vibrant in the 80s when a lot of people like Peter Goldsworthy, Andrew Taylor and John Bray were there all the time. Then it went through a period of 'going off the boil'. Now Friendly Street's got a new group of people running it. It's the longest running community poetry reading series in Australia. It's a great venue for people to go and actually find out what else is happening. I think it's very important. Some writers, especially at the beginning of their careers, need to be out and about. They listen to other people and even might feel, 'You're no better than me, I could get up and do that'. Often people are very self-conscious and they think 'I'm no good'. Then, they listen to someone else and they think, 'If they can read, so can I'.

The other point is that if you want to write, you really need to actually perform your stuff. I don't mean in the sense of learning how to act (although a good delivery is a bonus), but because you don't really know what the poem sounds like and what it actually wants to say until you present it to an audience. I tell this to my poetry students; often your voice will correct what your eye can't. By trying to read something to a group you will notice that a line is not working, whereas if you're mumbling to yourself at your desk, you might not. In the middle of a reading I'll sometimes think, 'No, that's not right, I'll have to change that'. If I hadn't read that poem to a live audience I would not have learned that. It is very important for developing writers to have a place to go to read, a friendly, welcoming place. One that's non-judgemental.

BS: Looking at your own poetry, what would you say makes your poems unique? Is there any specific aspect?

JK: I don't know, probably my sense of humour as much as anything, I like to mix tones. I do that a lot in *Monster Love*. I do that in *House Arrest*, as well as in my new book.

BS: Even the title.

JK: That's true. I like being honest. 'On Watching a Sleeping Child' from *Monster Love* is my 'why parents don't murder their children' poem. I've often said that, and anybody who's had a child who's driven them crazy during the day knows exactly what I mean. To be truthful, I think that originally being an American in Australia has caused me some problems. Some of my speech rhythms are different, although they've changed now after twenty-five years. People don't really cut you slack if you're American, whereas they will if you come from another ethnic background (which I actually do, but most people didn't realise this), so it's been a bit strange. I remember somebody saying once about a short story of mine, which they finally accepted for a literary magazine, 'It's too American', but it was set in the States. That was later published again in my first book of short stories, *The Electrolux Man*. Some of the stories in it are set in Australia, some are set in the US. That's my background. It depends what things are uppermost in your mind when you're writing.

BS: We also noticed there seems to be a continual theme of cats running through your poems—is that something you picked up on intentionally? Do you have any pets?

JK: At one point we had three cats and three dogs. We only have two cats and two dogs now. We've always had animals, horses as well. They're just always there and they're always sitting there telling you things. For instance 'Felis domestica' is a poem in *House Arrest*. That's actually travelled very well. It's been published in a number of places. People have pets a lot and so I think that's another universal thing people connect with.

BS: Are you still being published back in the States?

JK: I've got some kids' books there but I haven't actually sent any poems overseas in ages. What I'd like in ten years—my dream—is to have a person to do all these administrative writing chores for me. I'd say, 'Send these out,' because I don't have the time. I've only done a few mailings in the past year and a half, so I've got a couple of things in Australian outlets and in a UK journal. Especially when I'm writing fiction, I just don't think about sending poems out. Any poet would love a secretary to put things together, package them and decide where to send them.

Samantha Crosley (SC): What advice would you have for an emerging poet in South Australia?

JK: Go to Friendly Street or other readings. That is always good. The exposure will not only give you other ideas but also confidence; and it will help you to revise. Try to make yourself write. I think that computers are a trap in a way. I hardly ever write poems on computers. I don't put them on until I've rewritten the draft a number of times because with laser printers and even good bubble jet ones, the printed work looks finished. You need something to remind you that it isn't. Writing poems is an ongoing process. Even when a poem has been published, it doesn't mean it's finished. Some of the poems that are going to be in this new book I'm going to rewrite. More than half of them have been published in magazines, journals and newspapers. I'm still going to rewrite some, even if I just change a word, because nothing's perfect. That's not a thing to depress you. Every writer revises. Remember that the more you write the better you get. Don't be afraid of trying new things. People are often afraid of failing and they think, 'Oh, I've never written a sonnet'. So what? Maybe you come up with a bad sonnet but you would have learned something from the experience. You don't always know at the time what you've learned. Maybe four years down the track you're working on something else and then all of a sudden a line pops into your head, or a structure comes into your head, and it's just right at that time. That is why writers like to have big bottom drawers. I never throw anything away. Don't throw anything away, just get a lot of archive boxes. A writing teacher of mine, an American poet, William Meredith, said to our class a long time ago, that no one gets things right the first time but sometimes you do have 'happy accidents'. I have had poems that have come out and have needed very little change but the people who have the 'happy accidents' are usually the people who write all the time and live with words. You've already done the preparation. It's not like you've never written and you sit down and write a great poem. That won't happen. But you might have written for months and months and done things you think are sort of OK, and then all of a sudden something will come out and it's almost whole. It looks like a gift, and it is in a way, but it's a gift based on a lot of hard work that's actually prepared you to take advantage of the opportunity when it came. You need to put the hard yards in basically, otherwise it doesn't happen.

BS: What do you teach in your poetry course? Do you concentrate on the masters or more contemporary work?

JK: I use a bit of everything. The majority of students these days don't want to buy many books. I compile my own handbook that contains material from all centuries but a majority of it is modern and contemporary. I also use chapters from various textbooks. I don't think that it is useful for poetry students nowadays to spend two weeks studying simply Shakespeare if they're in a writing course. It is very useful to look at perhaps a poem by Shakespeare, and a poem by Keats, and a poem written by three or four other people, and then a couple in translation, if they're all on a similar subject. That's what I tend to do. I collect material around various themes and forms. That's a fairly standard approach. You need a wide range of options and a variety of work to inspire. I don't think that students should read only contemporary work. It's the same thing with fiction. Reading only what is contemporary (or from one's own culture) limits a writer.

Many postmodern and contemporary books and films allude to great works of the past as well as to history. Or are actually set in the past. Take the series *Black Adder*. The Elizabethan and eighteenth-century episodes are my favourites. Audiences find them funny, but if you know anything about literary history they are even funnier. The point is that they wouldn't be as rich and as good if the scriptwriters hadn't been educated, if they hadn't been aware of their literary heritage. Aspiring writers who don't want to read have a very thin foundation. They are not actually going to be able to develop as much as somebody who is open to a range of options, who listens to other voices. It doesn't mean that they are going to write like those other voices, to imitate them (although many begin that way). For instance, Mem Fox has said that good picture books are like poems (and they are). A text is only 300–600 words long, it has rhythm, it has a sense of closure, it's succinct. In fact, she has said that reading a lot of the Bible, Shakespeare and Jane Austen gave her the sense of language that enabled her to write the kinds of picture books she does. The more you read the more useful it is. Don't just read contemporary work. Plenty of writers who never went to university or never studied writing educated themselves.

Talking to Jeri Kroll

by Brett Steel

After exchanging emails a number of times with my fellow students, we met at the Magill Campus bar to finalise our questions and prepare our notes before going to meet Jeri Kroll. I had prepared the questions and was designated as 'interviewer' by the team. We left with plenty of time to spare and drove in convoy down to the Flinders University campus.

Passing through the frenzy that was student elections in the courtyard and much to the dismay of many candidates who discovered we were UniSA students and therefore ineligible to vote, we made our way up the multiple flights of stairs and down the corridor to Jeri's office.

The door was slightly ajar, and peering in I could see a woman with curls of long dark hair running down over her shoulders. She leaned in over a computer keyboard with her back to us, and as I tapped solidly on the wooden door she responded simply in the most teacherly of manners with a well-worn 'come in'. Not bothering to turn away from the monitor or see who had entered her small office. She continued typing until we stood beside her.

A short introduction and polite handshake with the three of us, we all sat down and began the interview. But it was not I who had the advantage of asking the first question. Jeri presented her authority to us with a probing immediate question, asking which of her books we had actually read. Fortunately between the three of us we had most of her work covered and she seemed content that we were now ready to continue. My first question was about her forthcoming book, *The Mother Workshops*, and, proving that we had done our research, we were now granted the respect we might otherwise not have had.

The interview ran smoothly and Jeri proved to be quite grounded in her family life. She spoke of her journey from her earlier work and travels to destinations as broad as India to her now family home in Adelaide, and her love of horses.

We were grateful for her thirty minutes that she allowed us to have in her obviously busy workplace, and as we thanked her and wrapped up our interview, she reminded us of her two books that were coming out next year and we assured her that we would endeavour to look them up.

As we got up to leave her office, even before we had reached her door, the sound of the tapping of the keyboard could again be heard.

Reading the poems

by Margaret Klopper

There was an instant connection on reading the poetry of Jeri Kroll. The subject matter was mostly of everyday happenings, normal life as we know it, and yet written in such an extraordinary way, that one had an immediate sense of identification with the work.

Kroll's free verse has a rhythmic, yet patterned significance. Although she has written a couple of sestinas, some sonnets and a few villanelles during her career as a poet, the majority of her work is in free verse, which makes for easy relaxed reading when alone or reading aloud to someone. Edward Hirsch gives a definition of free form verse in his book *How to Read a Poem and Fall in Love with Poetry*,

> A poetry of organic rhythms, of deliberate irregularity, improvisatory delight. Free verse is a form of non-metrical writing that takes pleasure in a various and emergent verbal music. (Hirsch 1999, p. 282)

Jeri Kroll writes about the things we all experience in life—family and friends, love and lust, divorce and death, growing up and growing old. She writes with a great sense of intimacy, which draws the reader into her world. I have loved, I have had babies, I have stepchildren, and now am learning to live with Alzheimer's disease within my own family. I am also a feminist, so all in all, there is a great empathy there and would be for many other readers. On the subject of feminism, several of her poems show her feelings on the matter. She speaks of women writers in one of her poems titled 'A Subtler Lesson', from her book *Monster Love:*

> When water's been dashed on the fire,
> It's women writers who've sizzled up through the smoke.
> Even those who had success—
> The single scribblers at parlour tables,
> The mothers supporting families as well as fame...
> A whirlwind of anarchic women
> With nothing in common but being women
> And loving writing, haunting the land.

J. Grant in an article in the magazine *Good Reading* (September 2003), claims that:

> Poetry today has been somewhat in the doldrums. A few have caught the attention of the media, reading their own verses on television, but many poets out there are having a great struggle to be recognised. The reader does not enjoy poetry that he [sic] has no empathy with and it has become easier to stick with the old masters who are long time dead. What normal people want to find in poetry is quite simple: a clear expression of recognisable emotion, set in the world we belong to. Ordinary life does not have to be boring and can be written about in an extraordinary way, instantly perceptible to the reader.

I believe also that what readers need from a poem is an honesty emanating from whatever the poet is feeling when he or she writes. Aristotle said that poetry is the most philosophic of all writing. Its object is truth, not individual and local, but general and operative; not standing upon external testimony, but carried alive into the heart by passion; truth, which is its own testimony, which gives competence and confidence to the tribunal to which it appeals, and receives them from the same tribunal. Poetry is the image of man and nature. (cf. Tydeman 1972, p. 160)

Jeri Kroll believes that you have to try to get inside the head of your audience and that is a difficult task at best. (see interview, p. 23) These words gave me the impression that one of the issues that much of contemporary poetry today is missing out on is that it is often written about what is going on inside the writer's head, with very little thought as to connecting with an audience. Certainly poetry writing is an intensely private thing, but one might still wish to have an audience in mind.

Wordsworth said, in a letter to Charles James Fox in 1801, that his poems

> are careful copies from nature; and I hope, whatever effect they may have upon you, you will at least be able to perceive that they may excite profitable sympathies in many kind and good hearts, and may in some small degree enlarge our feelings of reverence for our species, and our knowledge of human nature. (Tydeman 1972, p. 50)

The same desires are as real today as they were two hundred years ago. It is to the credit of Jeri Kroll that she writes poetry that is not only honest and true, but also elicits 'profitable sympathies' from her readers.

In a letter to Wordsworth, John Wilson claimed that,

> if we have ever known the happiness arising from parental or fraternal love; if we have ever known that delightful sympathy of soul connecting persons of different sex; if we have ever dropped a tear at the death of friends, or grieved for the misfortunes of others; if, in short, we have ever felt the more amiable emotions of human nature, it is impossible to read your poems without being greatly interested, and frequently in raptures. Your sentiments, feelings, and thoughts are therefore such as ought to constitute the subject of poetry. (Tydeman 1972, p. 59)

The significance of Kroll's work to a large audience of readers is remarkable—her poetry helps the readers feel that they are not alone with their problems, it helps the readers understand where women are in society today, and it also helps the readers to recognise how deep their own emotions run.

Edward Hirsch says that,

> The reader exists on the horizon of the poem. The message in the bottle may seem to be speaking to the poet alone, or to God, or to nobody, but the reader is the one who finds and overhears it, who unseals the bottle and lets the language emerge. The reader becomes the listener, letting the poem voice and rediscover itself as it is read … and that encounter is active, inquisitive, relentless, disturbing, exuberant, daring and beholden. (Hirsch 1999, p. 30)

I believe that this encounter constitutes the value of the poetry of Jeri Kroll.

References

Grant J. (2003) *Good Reading* 'Views of Ordinary Life', Odana Editions, p. l4.

Hirsch, E. (1999) *How to Read a Poem and Fall in Love with Poetry*. New York: A Harvest Book, Harcourt Inc. (The glossary p. 282, and Ch. 1 p. 30)

Jones A.R., Tydeman W. (eds) (1972) *Wordsworth Lyrical Ballads*. London: Macmillan Press Ltd, pp. 50, 59 and 160.

KEN BOLTON

Published poetry books

Four Poems, Sea Cruise Books, Sydney 1977
Blonde and French, Island Press, Sydney 1978
Christ's Entry into Brussels, Red Press, Sydney 1978
Two Sestinas, beer rhymes with bier press, Wollongong 1980
Talking to You, Rigmarole Books, Melbourne 1983
Blazing Shoes, Open Dammit, Adelaide 1984
Notes for Poems, Shocking Looking Books, Adelaide 1984
Two Poems – A Drawing of the Sky, Experimental Art Foundation, Adelaide 1990
Sestina to the Centre of the Brain, Little Esther, Adelaide 1991
Selected Poems, Penguin, Ringwood 1992
'Untimely meditations' & Other Poems, Wakefield Press, Adelaide 1997
Happy Accidents, Little Esther, Adelaide 1999
August 6th, Little Esther, Adelaide 1999
Horizon, Vagabond, Sydney 2001
With John Jenkins: *Airborne Dogs,* Brunswick Hills, Melbourne 1988
The Ferrara Poems, a Verse Novel, Experimental Art Foundation, Adelaide 1989
The Gutman Variations, Little Esther, Adelaide 1993
The Wallah Group, Little Esther, Adelaide 2001
Nutters without Fetters, PressPress, Berri 2002

Biographical note

Born in Sydney in 1949, Ken Bolton is a poet and an art critic, editor and publisher. His academic background includes an Arts Degree from the University of Sydney, majoring in History and English, and with First Class Honours in Fine Arts, plus some Italian and Anthropology. He has a PhD in English from Adelaide University. He has taught visual arts and communication at a number of universities, schools and tertiary institutions. From 1982 he has lived in Adelaide and is associated with the Experimental Arts Foundation. He has travelled to Paris, Italy and New York as well as London, Dublin and Beijing, and lived for six months in Rome. Along the way, he has met other writers and poets. He has published a number of books of his poetry and work written collaboratively with John Jenkins.

(Source: Ken Bolton)

Interview with Ken Bolton

by Robert Bloomfield, Lisa Solomon and Miki Maricic

Robert Bloomfield (RB): Do you have a manifesto or do you consider yourself to be part of a movement that would have a manifesto?

Ken Bolton (KB): It's not because I am fiercely independent but I wouldn't be part of a group that had a manifesto. People don't trust manifestos very much. They know not to trust groups' accounts of themselves because they're always self-interested. But I think that's a good thing: if you're prepared to publish the poems, you want people to read them—so you might as well be prepared to join a group that says, 'we're all for a certain kind of poetry', if you are agreed about that. It gets more attention to what you're on about. I haven't issued any manifestos at all and not anything close to it. You'll see I identify with people in my book, such as Pam Brown, John Forbes, Laurie Duncan.

RB: You said you were 'worried about your own authenticity in relation to the great art of elsewhere'. Is that something that everyone goes through?

KB: I think it's a fairly common position for people who aren't in the European main centres to feel. If you're writing in Canada or Australia you're just not part of it and just aren't going to be paid attention to. And you think maybe their standards are higher, in ways that you don't even realise, and you're not very good at judging yourself. For those sorts of reasons you think you'll never make the grade. But you've got to learn to ignore that or to think about it logically. There's a huge amount of creditable stuff in England and America that seems to make the grade critically over there, and if you think it's no good that should give you heart if anything. I'm ambivalent about it.

RB: Do you see yourself writing for an international audience?

KB: Well, there's almost no audience out there that I've got. So realistically I don't see myself writing for much of an audience. And I do tend to have that Australian perspective (which mightn't be common to all Australians). So in that sense, it's not for Americans or Londoners. I mean, they just think what is this guy worrying about. So to some degree I am writing for a local audience. But in a way I am writing for myself. I think you are lucky if you get an audience anyway. But I think it's the best way to write in the sense of ethics and stuff. If you're saying things that you wouldn't take seriously yourself, you shouldn't ask other people to take it seriously. That's why I think you need to be your own critic and your own audience.

RB: But if you are saying stuff that you take seriously yourself, wouldn't you want to share that?

KB: Yes, you would. But I think you are the first critic and audience for your stuff yourself and that's the most important audience. You know, if you have that other audience and not yourself in mind you tend to say things that are patronising or you don't really believe in because you tend not to credit them with their own intelligence. That's usually a mistake too.

Miki Maricic (MM): You are also an art critic, how did you get into that?

KB: I studied art history at university as a student and liked it a lot. I started it because I failed at anthropology and they wouldn't let me try it a third time. So, luckily, it forced me into visual arts and I did Honours. So I gave it a lot of thought at the time. Adelaide didn't, and still doesn't, produce enough of its own critics, so there was a way in for me. Whereas in Sydney, it would have been much harder to talk your way in, if you were given a break at all. It would have seemed not terribly serious, or unprofessional. That's why I've been doing it and I've been working at the Experimental Art Foundation ever since I got to Adelaide. So I've been involved in the visual arts. The other thing is, I think it's good for artists of any medium to be interested in other arts. Just because it gives you a way of thinking about aesthetic issues and not being blinded in your judgements by the fact that it's exactly your medium that you are working in and you've got prejudices set already and axes to grind. I'm sure that it has affected my thinking about writing and has probably been good for it.

RB: It must be awkward to express on paper what you see visually?

KB: It's an interesting difficulty. You don't have to describe it, you can just talk about the issues the art raises. But describing it is an interesting exercise, and usually that leads into points that you want to talk about in relation to the description. I enjoy it a great deal and find it more enjoyable than writing literary criticism. Again, because visual arts isn't in words and, therefore, getting it into words is three quarters of the job, and that's enough. Whereas with poetry it's difficult and I'm not sure why really. But also my tastes in poetry are a lot narrower than they are in visual arts. With visual arts there are a lot of things that I like, whereas with poetry I have pretty narrow tastes and don't like a lot of stuff. Quite unreasonably, I agree.

RB: Will you be writing on the surrealist exhibition?

KB: No, probably not, only because the people who publish my criticism won't care about covering it, or if they do, they'll hand it to a more usual suspect to write about it. I write about stuff that's in this gallery, stuff at CAC, more contemporary.

RB: *The stroke of undeserved luck has kept the mental composition of some individuals not quite adjusted to the prevailing norms*. Would you like to explain that one?

KB: Well, I'm probably using it because it sounds pretentious and jokey, as a way of saying some people aren't in touch with the times. And I've forgotten what Adorno would have meant. He's a Marxist. He was young, in his twenties or thirties, and went to America to get away from the Nazis, didn't like it much there and came back to Germany in the late fifties or early sixties. And he's always associated with pessimism. I guess he doesn't have much hope for the Marxist revolution ever happening. So very likely the rest of the sentence or in the next sentence he would have said that this is quite impossible, what I have just said. I can't remember what he was on about.

It's more positive than negative but rather a foolish and brave thing to say, 'I'm marching under this banner'. He's hard to read but he's great to read. He kind of tears your brain about. There's a book called *Minimum Moralia,* that's the easiest one to read. They're all sections about a page long and they're all gloomy and ironic and a bit sad. They're kind of mean and vicious as well. Cranky.

That's the beginning of that long poem, 'Untimely Meditations', because that poem is sort of challenging Australian mainstream traditions. Or some of them. The ones that say Australia is about landscape and the country and values of country folk. And it's not about city slickers who 'know too much about the wrong things'. Not that I'm alone in my position. I mean most poets are born in the city so they would agree with me, or I think they would. Until the seventies those traditions were still dominant—and still could be in terms of entrenched values.

RB: So you're saying that poetry is a city thing then?

KB: Not inherently, but statistically it probably tends to be. I'm not saying that it is or isn't. I think *Australia* is a city thing. People used to say that it has the highest proportion of population in cities of any nation in the world. And yet there are people who are always going on about how Australian paintings should be about landscape, Australian poems should be about the country, tractors and cars. The other 99% should go out there a bit; they might learn something, I guess.

RB: You were playing Ornette Coleman the last time we came in here?

KB: I've only been playing him the last few months. The music I've mostly played all my life, practically ever since I was 17, is blues and R&B. But you can't play it in the shop without disturbing the average punter who is 19 or 20. I mean, some like it when they hear it. But most of them just think that it sounds like the past—which is pretty reasonable, it is from the past. And if you play jazz it doesn't date you as much, it doesn't date the shop as much. So it seems to me that it is bearable and I like it a lot.

Talking to Ken Bolton

by Miki Maricic

At first I was not sure what to expect, when I was told that I was going to have to conduct an interview with a South Australian poet, since I had never really been a poetry enthusiast. Sure I've studied some poetry during my university years, but I have never really been inclined to read much poetry outside of the classroom, let alone write my own. Anyway, when asked to choose a poet that I would like to interview, I was faced with a bit of a conundrum, for all the poetry that I've read was by poets long since gone. So basically I read a couple of Ken Bolton's poems, which I liked, and decided to choose him for the interview.

Thankfully I wasn't alone, for there were two other people who had chosen Ken for their interview: Robert Bloomfield and Lisa Solomon. Luckily a time and place for the interview were sorted out within a few minutes when I spoke with Ken—the interview would take place on the Friday of the very same week that I had asked him for the interview, at about three o'clock in the afternoon at the Dark Horsey Bookshop, of which he was the manager. It struck me as funny because I had often passed the bookshop—it is near the City West Campus, where I have studied for several years, but I had never entered it until that day. It's unusual how things turn out, having passed the bookshop so many times, and never suspecting that one day not only would I be entering it but interviewing the poet who managed it. So with all the details taken care of, there was only one thing left to do, and that was to pen down a few questions, and from reading Ken's poetry, I knew that I couldn't ask such questions as what's his favourite colour, or what colour ink he likes to write with. I had to ask more detailed questions than I had expected, because there were so many images and ideas that I got from reading his poetry, that I knew I needed some questions with substance.

So as the time of the interview drew closer, my quest for some meaningful questions became increasingly difficult, and the only question that I dared ask out of those I had was not exactly earth shattering. I found it difficult to come up with anything meaningful to ask. I had only recently found out that I enjoyed poetry and could write some poems myself, and now I was going to approach a poet who had published a number of books, with nothing more than a few questions to which I might have hopefully received more than a single word response.

Anyway, to my relief, Rob came to the rescue and came up with some dazzling questions of his own, so equipped with his tape recorder and note book of questions, I was confident that the interview would go well. On the Friday afternoon of the interview, Rob, Lisa and I walked into Ken's bookshop, and with Ken sat down and prepared for the interview. There was no particular strategy we used or a set plan that was followed, except that we took turns to ask questions, or one of us would ask if the others had anything to add or ask. Ken answered all our questions in considerable detail, and from him I got the impression that we could talk to him about almost anything.

The bookshop seemed the perfect atmosphere for an interview about poetry. By the end of the interview I was sure that we had enough information to successfully complete the project, and I have to say that it was definitely one of the more interesting assignments that I've had to do as a student. Far from being a difficult task, I found it rather fascinating to sit and listen to the answers of the questions asked. All in all the interview was a task that certainly helped me to appreciate poetry a lot more, and to perhaps get me to write more of my own. From the interview I learnt that there are more things that one can do besides writing, if one chooses to do so, and that I should not limit myself to one aspect of writing.

Reading the poems

by Robert Bloomfield

bloomfield on bolton—commentary on the texts: 'to generalise', 'hot night', and 'lecture'.

I sit with Bolton at a table in *The Baci*
aware, with Aristotle
that this is where
the poetry begins
because
tho' dithyramb may not be
always in his mind

his partner Bacchus
sometimes is
(I sit here quietly stoned)
and Bolton's intellect
awash (this time) with caffeine
hoists up sails
and takes another voyage
in ever-whitening space

he writes of *we* but he means *I*
the real we
(that's us, the audience)
receives impressions
of
someone thinking
not someone talking
as he makes conversation
with himself

a metrically uneven monologue
sans drama

bravely advocating Adelaide

where
the speaker is a poet
who impersonates
nobody
but himself

instead

the indoor table is a springboard
for him as well as me
as images connect inside his head
and migrate into mine
although the table
is not entirely
satisfactory
for some reasons
that matter to him

but not to me
since life, and lunch hours
are too short

and so we both pick up our copies of
The Guardian
and he is suddenly
divided
in two places
at one time
his perspective
is disturbed
and it worries him
and he talks about it
to himself
and anyone that cares
to listen
which I do

and confronted
with the world
he sees in life
a series
of connected incidents
small in themselves
which fit together
in a general picture
the generalisation
of which concerns him

and he wonders
should he care?
are the problems of the world
tangible, graspable, solvable,
metaphorical
local
and I wonder with him
and I share a generous berth
on his metaphysical
voyage

imagination
set in motion
leads (of course)
to many places
but here it leads again
to a metaphor
(an international one, at least)

in which

The Guardian is a weapon
of an ideology
and all around the world
ideological fly swats
in the shape of local news reports
are bashing flies
defenceless fragile flies

(is this comparison more
immediate
than just?[1]

if so, it could be termed a 'conceit', although, admittedly,
it contains no
curious learning)

anyway ... Bolton is concerned that
no one cares

but now
because I'm here
at a table in *The Baci*
and because of
(or maybe despite)
the idea
that my brain and my eye
are one unit

I start to care

and so

I leave the table
and move into the **'Hot night'**

where Bolton is my guide

he falls asleep (some guide)
or runs a mile, depending,
(but on what?)
and speaks in serious tones
annoyed at English verse

from a safe distance

a little tired
perhaps
of art
and of pretence
(must be the heat)

and pulling faces
for the moment
pulling them
for fun
because faces are facades,
figureheads
superficial signals
to implied audiences
and he's suddenly aware that
the audience has arrived

he's cooling off in parkland sprays
contemplating death
by mangled bicycle
and all that death entails
the priests
the music
the expense

and all the time
it's 43 degrees
and that explains

a lot
so
when he writes:

... I can ring Julie tomorrow
& say—

'The cheque is in the mail' *like an Australian businessman*

he doesn't hide the irony

and now we must attend a

'Lecture'

in which more themes
are explored
and
influences revealed
in a tour of Bolton's attitudes
and his attitudes
'to the attitudes of others'
all with brief witty phrases

superadded accessories [2]
(rhythm's pleasures)
and seeds of ideas
planted

in huge white acreages
of philosophically
fertile prairie

humorous of course
tongue in cheek
'if you see a leg pull it'
(or is that a bluff)

all of which
Bolton writes
'to be liked'
(that's *certainly* a bluff)

and as I write
I hear to the words
of René Char
brought into focus
by the sympathetic *soundprompts* (my own word)
of *Pierre*
Boulez

and urgently recall
that Bolton 'studied' Berrigan
(another who is sometimes
labelled a surrealist)
and Ashbery
and the rest

and the styles
have things in common
rooted, as they seem to be
in Whitman
and the American tradition
so beloved
of Australian poets of the sixties
and seventies
visible
in the rejection
of Gautier's 'easy rhythm'[x]
and the insistence
on line conforming to thought
do people buy
anymore to shore up, or vote for, the
national I.D.?

Or just to register their social distinction ('I think this
is cute,' 'I think this is funny,' 'See, this
is my sense of humour.')?

and the personal impulse

I've been bathing in the poem[3] (Berrigan)

I don't have a cruel theory in my body (Bolton)

and the quotes
and the (admittedly instructive) name dropping

Compare this by Lee Harwood:[4]
(coincidentally (?) in the same volume
as John Ashbery)

Today I got very excited when I read some
poems by Mallarmé and Edwin Denby, and later
in the evening, by F.T. Prince ...

... Ted Berrigan has met Edwin Denby.
I don't know anyone who's met F.T. Prince ...

to this by Ken Bolton: (from *poem: live at birdland*)

The books are Kenneth Koch,
Basil Bunting, Meanjin,
the dictionary,
Anna & lyssiotis, Liz Grosz,
& upstairs on the
bed—the loft where I sleep—Ted Berrigan,
who has provided
many of the rewards for
reading poetry
in my life.

Checkpoint

✓ Berigan is clearly
an important inspiration
for this generation of
poets

✓ Naming of other
favoured
poets

is an accepted stylistic device

then there are the
lexical peculiarities
Berrigan (and others) *yr*
Bolton *tho* … (but does he identify with C17th England and Coleridge
and the rest?
and why should he not? the tradition is in the mind of the practitioner)

and
there's **that**
layout
too

(a throwback from New York? or does it help the reader? the latter I suggest … I think I may adopt it … in fact … it seems I already have!)

yet Bolton has no time
for conceit
or 'verbiage'
only for
analogies
[it is like a little tv
where the subtitles arrive (late)
and linger – pointedly]

shades of the imagists … Ezra Pound? (not clearly)

O fan of white silk;
clear as frost on the grass-blade,
you also are laid aside.

no time for obscurity:

Berrigan:

Oh pneumonia in American poetry
Do we have time? well look at Burroughs
7 times been caught and brought back to Mars
uneaten

contrast with Bolton, and be sure that he would never use an 'O'

then talk naturally!

Though theory has taught us
there is no such thing

that even prose
is rhetoric, is untransparent—

though it's mostly prose
it has taught us that in

NEXT
he makes his points about

'modernism, post modernism, various
poetic movements'

by 'theorising about the theory'
in a circular manner
('theory has no monopoly on theory':
does this mean that you can talk about,
better still, refute,
a theory
without a counter-theory?
I guess it does)

but since *modernism*
should always mean
'new thought',
and is a strange word to use,
(even posthumously ... *especially posthumously!*)
for a historical movement,
it is in character
for Bolton to ignore it;
with
('poetry must make its own [theory]')

besides: ignoring modernism
is a good way
to deny post-modernism …
('it was modernity's self criticism merely')

and he would agree, perhaps, with Eliot, that

the forces of deterioration are a large crawling mass,
and the forces of development half a dozen men [5]

which may be why the celebrations of

the Australian landscape, our identity,

are rejected as **colonialist doxa** (Les Murray)

(*Ken's* own word I think, and thus defying criticism)
because

his landscape (Ken's)
is city
and it's the old TS Eliot versus Thomas Hardy debate
again

and even when Les's landscape is urban, maybe

Bolton

doesn't think it worth mentioning that:

something over ten thousand
beer bottles went to build
a house once in Queensland[6]

and besides, **spiritualized emotion** (Adamson) is 'out of context, as far as [he, i.e. Bolton] could see'

certainly Bolton and Adamson
have little in common:
Adamson fishing

on the reef,
Bolton at his table
at Baci's

and Bolton goes
OUT OF HIS WAY

to make these opinions
thoroughly clear
and even when
custom has 'bedimmed all the lustre'[7] (especially when)

he makes it shine
by making it relevant
and modern (in its normal sense)

yet he is not surreal
but suggestive and subjective
and occasionally
sublime

(but so is Ted
and so are all creative minds,
including Les, out ploughing on his tractor.)

so Bolton ploughs on
with monumental momentum
and ideas come
directly to the page

as if he were a medium
or a vessel (more imagism)

(does he make revisions? not too many one would guess)

and tho (!) a reader
chancing on his work
may
'look around for poetry'[8]
it must be said
that Bolton isn't

'chanced on' often

(or as often as, perhaps
he could be)

because

as Hazlitt said of Wordsworth's ballads

'he takes a subject
or a story
merely as pegs or loops
to hang thought and feeling on' [9]

(but isn't that what all writers do, Bill?)

(whatever)

and Bolton hangs
heroically
obliviously
struggling for breath
aware of the size of his audience

while I sit here
in the library
demonstrating Bolton's 'value'
by

reading
in addition to O'Hara, Ashbery (and Bolton)

James Schuyler,

(Bolton's favourite[10] ... his epistemological, juxtapositional irreverent style, and his predilection for filling his poems with friends, everyday activities etc., certainly an influence.)

Schuyler:

another day full of wild beauty
and the timer pings [11]

Berrigan on Schuyler:

"Your work makes up an 'underground movement' all by itself!"

and wishing
that Hazlitt
had put some rhythm
in his prose
instead
of
spoiling mine.

Notes

1. Definition derived from Helen Gardner's introduction to *The Metaphysical Poets.*
2. Paraphrase of Aristotle's conception (p. 230).
3. Berrigan, 'Sonnet lll', from E. Germain (ed.) 1978 (p. 265).
4. From 'The late poem' in *Penguin Modern Poets 19.*
5. Egoist May (1918) *Observations by TS Apteryx.* cited in Stead 1964 p. 114.
6. Les Murray 'The House of Fourex' from *Australian Poetry Now.*
7. Shawcross, 1907, *Biographia Literaria,* Oxford, cited in M. Jacobus (p. 7).
8. Owen, W., & Smyser, J. (eds) Advertisement, *Prose Works of William Wordsworth,* cited in M. Jacobus (p. 8).
9. Hazlitt, W. (1825) *The Spirit of the Age,* cited in Jacobus (p. 10).
10. According to personal communicaton (interview).
11. james schuyler *closed gentian distances* (source plagiarist.com) [viewed 25 September 2003] http://www.plagiarist.com.

x Théophile Gautier, cited in J.M. Cohen 1966 p. 15 *'shame on the easy rhythm, like a shoe that is too large, of a kind that every foot can put on and take off'.*

References

Ashbery, J., Harwood, L. and Raworth, T. (1971) *Penguin Modern Poets 19.* UK: Penguin.

Bolton, K. (1997) *Untimely Meditations.* Adelaide: Wakefield Press.

Bolton, K. 'To generalise', from *Ten Australian Poets Series 5* [viewed 23 September 2003] http:// www.thylazine.org/archive/thyla5/kb.html

Bywater, I. (ed.) (1954) *Aristotle's Rhetoric and Poetics.* New York: Modern Library.

Cohen, J.M. (1966) *Poetry of this Age.* UK: Hutchinson.

Germain, E. (ed.) (1978) *Surrealist Poetry in English.* UK: Penguin.

Gardner, H. (ed.) (1957) *The Metaphysical Poets.* UK: Penguin.

Jacobus, M. (1976) *Tradition and Experiment in Wordsworth's Lyrical Ballads.* Oxford: Oxford University Press.

Shapcott, T.W. (1970) *Australian Poetry Now.* Melbourne: Sun Books.

Bibliography

Furbank, P. and Kettle, A. (1975) *Modernism and Its Origins.* Milton Keynes: Open University Press.

Hirsch, E. (1999) *How to Read a Poem and Fall in Love with Poetry.* New York: A Harvest Book, Harcourt Inc.

Stead, C.K. (1964) *The New Poetic.* UK: Pelican.

STEPHEN LAWRENCE

Chapter by Ian Furness

Published poetry books
Her Mother's Arms, Wakefield Press, Adelaide 1997
Beasts Labial, Wakefield Press, Adelaide 1998
How Not to Kill Government Leaders, Wakefield Press, Adelaide 2002

Biographical note
Stephen Lawrence is an Adelaide poet who works for the South Australian government. His writing has won or been shortlisted for many literary awards, and he has been published internationally in the United States, Denmark, Canada and Romania. He contributed a media page for *The Adelaide Review* for several years, and currently reviews poetry for the *Journal of Australian Studies*. Stephen was a guest author at the Adelaide Festival of Arts Writers' Week 2000. His third collection of poetry was launched at Writers' Week 2002, at which he also judged the Festival Literary Awards.

Interview with Stephen Lawrence

Ian Furness (IF): Some people find a certain environment helpful or even necessary to write their poetry. Do you have a particular environment that you find helps your writing?

Stephen Lawrence (SL): Yes and no. Hm. Better flesh this out. Environment is secondary for me. I used to speculate about writing best creatively when sitting facing east upstairs, and writing my best critical pieces when downstairs facing east. But that's basically bullshit. No distractions is the best environment, whether it's in a noisy club or a sylvan glade. But then even the distractions can sometimes be helpful—or at least jolt the potential poem into another interesting track.

Poems are really contingent, I find: something begun one minute later can produce an entirely different end-product. The main thing is to be able to take down a few notes while the inspiration is hot. I've debated this with writers, such as Dorothy Porter, who, like many writers, thinks you can't just sit down and say, 'I'm going to write a poem now', then write a poem. Actually, I think you can. Or at least, I can. When the idea's been circling for ages in my mind, and my available time is structured and limited, I have little choice but to make myself write on, say, the same half-day off per fortnight (usually Thursday morning). If I waited until the Caspian Terns were hunting lakeside, or the wind was blowing SSE, or the moon was a week past full, I'd get nothing at all written.

IF: For you, what makes a good poem?

SL: A good poem, eh? Shall we say that a 'good' poem for me is something that catches my eye/ear, and succeeds on the terms it sets up for itself? So a good poem can be almost anything at all, from 'Swart-smecked smythes' to Gig Ryan's latest blast. But to answer the question, I'll have to reveal a prejudice or two. A good poem is artful and intelligent. True to itself; unashamed of its learning or lineage or subject-matter.

IF: What would you say has been the greatest source of inspiration for your poetry?

SL: As much as my physical environment and social interactions, my poems can be 'inspired' by other written texts. For example, in recent times—although not possibly the 'greatest' source, but certainly a wonderful source of jargon and bureaucratic discourse—my poems are informed by such publications as the *Australian Dispute Resolution Board* newsletter, *BRW*, *HR Monthly*, *Management Today* and the *Federal House of Representatives* magazine (e.g. 'Meeting With the County Board …', 'Acts' and some new poems).

IF: Humour seems to play an important part in many of your poems. How important a role do you believe humour plays in conveying the message of a poem?

SL: Depends on the poet's intent. Humorous poems are often labelled as 'light poetry'. People might think of, say, Pam Ayres's rhyming trifles. I guess my humour is more mocking than that sort of poetry. My 'jargon' poems began in the early

90s, with a few poetic monologues set in an advertising agency, primarily from my experience in business then as media writer for the *Adelaide Review*. Since being taken up by the public service, I find that the soil for a discourse-sensitive writer is real terra rosa. Humour is important in this kind of writing because it 'leavens' the message and doesn't threaten or put people offside so readily. Those inside the system are just as likely to find it funny as those outside. But I find that I still have to be gentle so that people can more readily laugh at themselves instead of feeling they're being laughed at.

I write other kinds of poetry as well, which don't contain satire or humour. The subject defines the approach, but the 'voice' usually brings them to life and chooses the level of humour once it has decided to assert itself.

IF: Please name three poets that you would say have influenced your poetry.

SL: Ted Hughes. An astonishing nature-poet, and, I think, a much better poet than his wife. Hughes provides obbligatos throughout my writing. Shakespeare. The poet who, as Harold Bloom controversially said, created modern culture and sensibility. Why the hell is he not compulsory in undergraduate English anymore? A third? Better find a living one. Paul Muldoon, perhaps. Active Irish poet living in the US, who unforgivingly sends the reader on a mission searching for the rest of the poem somewhere out in the real world. He makes you work harder, but it's worth it.

IF: What made you decide to start writing poetry?

SL: Nothing really made me decide. I just did it, possibly out of my interest in reading. If there's anything that might have spurred it, it would be being an inward boy with his face in a book at most social occasions, then being mildly brutalised at high school. I'm sure you know the cliché—to bend a quote from Swift, or was it Pope? 'Affliction doth make us all Artists!'

IF: How old were you when you wrote your first poem? What was it about?

SL: My first poem was written at about age 14. With rudimentary alliteration, it juxtaposed the 1969 moonwalk with a Vietnam soldier stepping on a mine, ending 'the step's the same, on the moon or on a mine'. Plagiarised/appropriated shamelessly from a Rigby cartoon. Pleased with myself, I recall telling a classmate that I'd written a poem on my own, for its own sake, without being asked to in an English class or anything. What a strange thing to do.

IF: If you had to pick three poems by poets other than yourself to be your favourites, what would they be and why?

SL: Poems other than my own? I don't think I'd pick one of my own as a personal favourite anyway! A contingent selection rather than a firm Top 3, and chosen for being particularly formative: 'Gaudete'—Ted Hughes. For an explanation, just read it: you'll either find it as bizarrely creative and powerful as I did, or you'll scratch your head and make a mental note not to stand next to me at parties. 'The Prelude'—William Wordsworth. Great rites of passage poem, profoundly examining the development of a poet and the difficult transition from youth to, uh-oh, responsible adulthood. 'Shirt'—Robert Pinsky. A poem that reintroduced me to the power of the definite article (see part one of 'Flesh Made Wisdom'). And how research, and connected vignettes artfully constructed around a theme, can produce most intense and satisfying art. It helps that he's also a brilliant reader of his own work. His voice is Willem Dafoe meets William Burroughs.

IF: How often do you write poetry?

SL: How often? I could write anything between one and three dozen poems a year. Depends on the stimulation and work burden of the year. Most times I finish a poem, I think that maybe I'll never write another one. Then another one insinuates itself.

IF: What advice would you give to an aspiring poet?

SL: Advice to an aspiring poet (apart from to use a good deodorant)? Um. Don't expect to make money out of it. If it helps, I'll give my spiel about it that I gave at Writers' Week in 2000:

> Nowadays, poetry could not be further from mainstream intellectual discourse. It's seen as Writing's poorest, most embarrassing cousin. Poetry has no influence, it has a miniscule readership—and there's no money in it. The fact that poetry's practically ignored, is its great strength. Because poets have no power, they have no paymasters, or restraints on their expression. Versifiers have a freedom that no other writer has.

I'm not sure that I entirely believe this rhetoric. Or, at least, I don't think being unrestrained and powerless is a virtue. I myself am a bit afraid of total freedom, and so should all poets be. I arrogantly think that a poet should have some formal craft under his/her belt before getting past the aspiring part. To call themselves a poet, all poets, I sweepingly state, should have had a go at a villanelle and a sonnet. Divergence into anecdote. A local writer of my acquaintance—when he was still an undergraduate student, and thought himself a bit of a poet—was brought down to earth by his university tutor who told him that, 'no-one can really call themselves a poet if they haven't written a villanelle'. Now, this young poet's testosterone response to his tutor's words was to say to himself, 'Right! I'll prove to him that I'm a poet! I'll write a villanelle'. So he spent some time and effort having a go at writing one—and when he had, he slammed the poem down on his tutor's desk at the end of the semester, saying, 'There! I can write one. I'm a poet'. When I heard this story, I had my own testosterone event, my own pheromonic response to it. I thought, I haven't written a villanelle myself. And so I set about to do so. 'The Baby, The Gun' was the result.

Talking to Stephen Lawrence

From the first poem I read by South Australian poet Stephen Lawrence I could tell I was dealing with a character. Stephen's poetry is both complicated and accessible to a wide audience. His use of words intrigues the reader with their complexity and captures them with their innate rhythm. Working with Stephen was something I looked forward to from the beginning. Like his poetry, Stephen is friendly and unassuming, both in writing and in physical presence, his manner throughout the process was very much that of someone who treats people equally. Stephen could never be a poet resigned to be alone with their poetry and oblivious to the outside world. It is evident in everything that Stephen had to say, that he watches closely the world in which he lives, and in a way revels in its complexity and irony. Stephen is farthest possible from the stereotyped 'high brow' poet who looks at the rest of the people in the world as merely less talented than themselves. His view of the world is unusual, he is a real person in a world filled with characters. From his vantage point in the world of business and public service he is able to see the irony and indeed the humour inherent in a life dedicated to paperwork, computers and due process. Just as he analyses the world around him, it is obvious that he analyses what he says, as he says it. He is both spontaneous and witty in a way that I found engaging. He would begin with a statement very much at home in the 'high brow' school of poetry and then go on to contradict it with a witty counter-statement that relates the process of writing poetry back to the real world. This was obvious in many of his answers during our interview, particularly when I asked him about the environment in which he likes to write.

For a long time the only contact I had with Stephen was via email and this proved an interesting way to get to know him. Throughout our sporadic email chats I was surprised at how much of his personality came through. It became obvious that Stephen communicates via writing in much the same manner as he does in any other way and I was pleasantly surprised upon meeting him to find the image of him I had gradually created through our initial contact was more accurate than I had expected it to be. Stephen was friendly and open about his work and it was a refreshing experience to meet someone who had achieved success within the world of poetry and remained an obviously warm person.

When everything eventually came together I found that Stephen was helpful in any way possible and I suspect spent an amount of time on answering my questions that many poets, or people for that matter, would not. His ideas about poetry were very clear and were somewhat of a combination between traditional literary notions of formal structure, artistic flourishes and realist points of view. He seems to be able to lose himself in the writing process without losing a hold of the sheer practical act of writing. I cannot imagine, for example, Stephen talking about a poem in which he was transported to another world without a mention of something in the real world as an anchor.

In his mention of the poem 'Gaudete' by Ted Hughes he demonstrates this neatly by describing the way in which he found the poem to be 'bizarrely creative' but allows for those with a mind that is not quite so open to innovation by following this statement up with a joke that indicates that, unlike many people, he does not judge others by what they like when it comes to art. It's not about taste, but personal preference.

Within his writing, Stephen displays a wide variety of influences, which he will attest to freely if asked. In actually talking with Stephen I got the feeling that these come easily to him, as he speaks like he writes—cleverly with a touch of a very sharp wit. His use of humour is particularly of note as it parallels his poetry very closely. Stephen uses humour to make his poetry and his writing more accessible and in his own words, allow 'people to laugh at themselves, rather than feel they are being laughed at'. Through his clever use of humour, Stephen seems able to capture an audience that might otherwise overlook him. Humour is a common factor among people, and he uses this to his advantage—after all, if someone can't laugh at the world around them, or at themselves for that matter, then in my opinion they are missing out on a great deal.

Reading the poems

If you go back far enough, poetry is songs, stories, a reason for the complication of language. Through time poets have become more than storytellers. They examine and reflect the world around them using language as a window into their own world. Poets use the very structure of language itself to weave experiences into words on a page or spoken aloud. Contemporary poetry attempts to do this in ways which, in the past, have been dismissed. No longer is poetry bound by syllabic structure or by rhyme, poetry speaks through rhythm and imagery. In modern times, defining what poetry is has become a study in itself. Contemporary poets deal with contemporary issues, the modern world is very different to the world in which well-known poets such as William Shakespeare or Edgar Allen Poe grew up. Poetry, being a reflection of the world, has changed to reflect this.

Australia is a land of contrasts—from the deep desert plains of the sun-bleached outback to the busy cities, 'poetry has shaped our Australian national character' (Department of Communications Information Technology and the Arts 1998). Australian poetry has grown to be as diverse as the landscape in which Australian poets live. The poetry of Australian poets dealing with city life can seem hard to find. One South Australian poet though, by the name of Stephen Lawrence, attempts to tackle the issues inherent in a life dictated by the society of business and public services within a city.

The traditional image of the poet is not that of a businessman. The poet is stereotypically first an artist and second a real person. Stephen Lawrence attempts to bridge this divide with poetry examining what it is to be a businessman, the irony inherent in the business world, and the cold, methodical way in which people can become less important than numbers. His poetry has been described as a 'menagerie of intellectual intrigue' (Braune 1998).

Lawrence writes about issues that are serious to him, but uses humour to attempt to get his point across without causing offence. One of the types of poetry that Lawrence writes forces him to undergo a change in perspective. He creates a hypothetical character—a man of the business world, of which examples are no doubt present in the real world. This character may be described best as a management guru. The character is both the catalyst and director of change within a company. Quick to speak and slow to listen, he bulldozes any opinion that may differ from his own with an arsenal of terms, phrases and colloquial sayings that, when put to the listener at a frighteningly quick pace, cannot but dominate conversation.

Lawrence's poem 'Powerhouseeast Consultants' (Lawrence 2002) is one of the few that he has published featuring this character. The title carries with it an air of professionalism, and in compacting the words *power, house* and *east* together Lawrence begins to convey the hurried nature of the poem. The word *power* is very important because when combined with the word *house* it begins to describe the guru-character himself. In addition to this, the title allows the reader to guess at the character and his motivations from the very first line of the poem. On the surface the poem appears to be a transcript of a meeting between existing employees at a company and the guru-character. On reading the poem, it becomes readily apparent that it is more of a retelling of the guru-character's thought patterns than an actual re-telling of a meeting. The character thinks as he talks, moving quickly from one topic to another, avoiding sticking points and attempting to reverse any complaints back on their speaker through manipulation of words. In a way this allows the reader to be more submerged in the character as everything else begins to seem less important to the direction of the poem. This is a very similar attitude to that held by the guru-character.

His manipulation of speech is subtle and quick, creating a firm image in the mind of the reader of a confident, well-dressed person walking into a room of people he doesn't know and being completely confident that he can control what they are thinking:

> Let me set the table for you:
> Convergence objectives.
> Yes. To modernise. Modernise. Try a few new things.
> Find the signal in the noise.
> To bring this company into the twenty-first century.
> I know we're already there, Damien—
> But some of us are more There than others
> (Much of your thinking here is very '98),
> And we all need to be brought through
> Into the Now
> Together.
> Funky business. Totally business. Mojo business.

Everything he says has a hidden catch, a side-mention at the end. When one of the others present in the meeting notices this, they are quickly turned around by reassurances from the guru-character that so long as they accept the changes proposed and work with them then they need not worry.

The rhythm of 'Powerhouseeast Consultants' is hard to identify. The poem is structured exactly as the reader can imagine the guru-character talking in real life. Initially through the use of shorter lines, Lawrence manages to convey a slow, deliberate measure in the speech of the character. The poem is essentially one stanza, serving to emphasise the speed and sheer willpower evident behind the guru-character. Any breaks within the piece would only serve to create a pause, and the impression that a reader gets from the structure and themes behind the poem is that a pause is not something that is likely to happen in the situation that the poem is set in. As the poem progresses the character's speech speeds up and becomes more complicated, using longer words and longer lines. This momentum that builds up is only slowed when the other members of the meeting query the guru-character. For instance, in one section the character uses an analogy referring to the future as bright. The other members of the meeting begin to try to attack this by adding inclement weather conditions to the analogy. The character is momentarily slowed by this but rolls right over any criticisms by repeating back the criticisms with emphasis on his initial analogy that the future will be bright:

> Now let's get back to the bright future—
> Alright, Paul: *Windy*, but bright.
> Alright, Veronica: *Cold* and windy, but bright.
> Alright, Damien: *Raining* and cold and windy—but still bright.
> I guarantee: you'll be right at home with it.
> No, not at home on the dole, Matthew—
> Unless you *choose*.
> Unless you consistently fail
> To meet new, very reasonable base revenue goals.
> And employers have an extended duty of care,
> To manage the transition out of work.
> Our enacted exit strategy
> Is one of your many safety nets.

Beyond this the poem again gains momentum, moving at a frenetic pace as the character begins to spout catchy words and phrases describing what this future will be like without actually revealing any detail. Because this poem is structured and worded around relatively normal speech patterns, metaphor and imagery are not used in traditional ways. Rather it is the character who uses these as devices to try to convince his audience within the poem of his vision.

The next poem in Lawrence's volume is titled 'Wisdom Statement' and deals with a similar character to 'Powerhouseeast Consultants'. This time the task of the character is to convince people that he has already been working in the restructuring of the company in which they work and this will be to everyone's advantage. There is an almost nervous tone present in this poem and, in contrast to the previous poem, 'Wisdom Statement' is broken up in places to signify a pause in the conversation. In addition to this, the change in direction of the conversation that happens every time there is a pause suggests that the guru-character is heading somewhere and has a plan for the direction of the meeting.

In 'Powerhouseeast Consultants' there is a touch of a theme of aimlessness in the hurried and seemingly directionless talking by the guru-character. In 'Wisdom Statement' there is a notion present that the character is just the messenger in this particular situation and holds less power than he did in the previous poem. The rhythm is similar to the previous poem. There are sections that will fit a particular rhythm and it is obvious to the reader that these are parts of the conversation that were rehearsed in the mind of the character before the inevitable confrontation:

> Look: what about Terry,
> Chief of Information Technology?
> Not any more.
> We're heavily devolving our C-class.
> No CEOs, no Chiefs of anything: too authoritarian.
> No more pointy bits in this organisation.
> Our culture will be all team-based.
> We all went orienteering in the Dandenongs
> With the Attachment and Bonding Consultants;
> Yes. Oh yes, we are ready.
> So Terry is Manager of Information Systems.
> (Answerable to the Director of Intellectual Capital.)
> No, Terry. This isn't downgrading.
> It's an opportunity.

There are many themes common to these two poems but the overriding one is that of the depressive and dissatisfied nature of the business world. Employees of both companies seem constantly worried about their employment and treat any change with doubt and a touch of fear. The workers that are being spoken to are lacking completely in motivation and the failure to have any impact on this only becomes apparent in the speech of the character in 'Wisdom Statement'.

Lawrence's analysis of the business world can, like much of his poetry, seem humorous at first. Under closer observation, woven through the poems is a consistent theme of fear and confusion. Whilst the guru-character is in control at all times, the other characters are without any idea of what the future will be like and are concerned for their own wellbeing. This is a side of the business world that is rarely examined, especially in poetry, and Lawrence's style carries the message along clearly without any notion of preaching. His poetry is both accessible and interesting, and it seems that through this character, Lawrence is able to express some of the frustration that he has encountered in his life as an observer within the business world. Future directions for Lawrence's poetry are as difficult to predict as the poetry itself, but provided the business world does not get any different it is likely that he will continue to write about its particular experiences.

References

'Australian Poetry' (1998) Department of Communications, Information Technology and the Arts,[viewed 26 October 2002], http://www.acn.net.au/articles/1998/08/poetry.htm.

Braune, B. (1998) 'Stephen Lawrence, Beasts Labial', *Cordite*, no. 4, pp. 19–20.

Lawrence, S. (2002) *How Not to Kill Government Leaders*. Adelaide: Wakefield Press.

JULES LEIGH KOCH

Chapter by Kelly Campbell

Published poetry books

A Strip of Negatives, Wakefield Press, Adelaide 1998
Each Goldfish Is Hand Painted, Wakefield Press, Adelaide 2002

Biographical note

Jules Leigh Koch was born in Sydney and raised in suburban Adelaide where he lives, along the tram lines, with his son. He has had a long and active involvement with Housing Co-operatives in South Australia and is employed by Ashford Special School as a school Service Officer. Jules's first collection of poetry, *A Strip of Negatives*, was published in *Friendly Street New Poets 4* (1998). This was followed by the publication of *Each Goldfish Is Hand Painted* in 2002, a collection of seventy-three poems written over sixteen years.

Interview with Jules Leigh Koch

Kelly Campbell (KC): What do you think makes a good poem?

Jules Koch (JK): Atmosphere. That's what I look for. And mood. That's the two elements I like to have when I write and what I like in other people's work. I'm not necessarily looking to affect other people's moods, but a poem has to have a mood for me to have an interest in writing it.

KC: You commented that you like to use imagery in your writing. Why imagery? Why not something else?

JK: I'm more interested in the picture than the language, sound or the words. I actually am more inspired by art galleries—paintings, drawings, art installations—than I am by literature. I don't actually read a lot, and I still haven't actually read a novel. I am dyslexic and reading and spelling have always been difficult. Words on a page are a jigsaw for me. I see things in images. I approach poetry like a camera lens.

KC: Why do you think your poetry is popular?

JK: I think it's fairly uncomplex, it's precise. It's not elitist but I don't think I write for the masses either. I am interested in 'feelings', more so than 'emotions' which I believe makes my poems less indulgent and therefore more popular or accessible.

KC: How much time a week do you spend writing?

JK: It varies. The preparation of the book took a lot of time, maybe some nights two hours. This year, it's two or three hours a week at most. I haven't had the need this year. But in the past I spent a lot of time writing. I'm a very slow writer, in fact I've only written one hundred and twelve poems in twenty three years, so that averages about five a year. I don't really consider myself a writer in that sense. I just happen to have a lot of success in what I do write.

KC: How do you write?

JK: My best thinking is done in the morning, but having to get a child ready for school and myself ready for work I don't have the opportunity to write. So I write usually late at night. I have a notebook with me most of the time and I just take down words every so often. And, when I do read poetry, I take down collections of words and do word charts, and then put those words into my own patterns. I create word lists of a similar mood and landscape and I write them for weeks on end. The mood and atmosphere consumes me, so much so that I only work on one poem at a time. It becomes a love affair and I cannot move on till it is completed to my satisfaction.

KC: Where does your inspiration come from?

JK: My biggest inspirations have been from lyrics, because I was just at the tail end of the poetry era of the Beatles and all that 60s music, and I think there was a lot of good lyrical poetry on the radio, which most people would have listened to.

KC: What advice would you give to a budding writer who wants to be published?

JK: That's two different things. Anyone can write, if they have language and if they can hold a pencil. Getting published is a whole different ball game. That's partly luck, knowing the market. I spent hours in libraries, looking up journals and seeing what their particular focus was. So if it's got photography in there, or paintings or drawings, then I think it'll appeal to the editors because I have an artistic mind, whereas if it's a very literal magazine, they might not like my work. I have a tendency to be published more by females than males, and by younger people rather than older people. So I've worked very hard at being published in the sense of taking in all those considerations. I send a lot of copies off at the same time, and it's a law of averages. So if I send six poems off in a two month period, then maybe one in six will get published, so it's really a law of averages. And I guess the main thing is that I've never been disillusioned about not getting published. I could wallpaper my room with the rejection slips. I think some people get offended by rejection. If the person finds that difficult then maybe it's best not to send work off. I do have belief in myself.

KC: When did you start writing poetry?

JK: When I was 21, I was doing a drama workshop and I had to read a poem for voice work. I didn't do poetry in school. My apprenticeship was listening to poetry on the radio, through songs. I decided it was time to write myself. It was that immediate.

KC: Is there any particular form or type of poem or technique that you really enjoy using?

JK: I'm not too sure that I have a particular technique. Now, as I'm maturing, I like poems to have a little bit more to do with the interior rather than the exterior. I've always been interested in the picture. But I now like to look inside myself a little bit more, to look inside other people. To me, that is a harder type of writing. So I'm just interested in the essence of the human being.

KC: Do you feel that your poetry has been influenced by the imagist poets? Any in particular?

JK: The only poet who has influenced me in this genre is the Australian poet Robert Gray. Notwithstanding I have been drawn to the works of various French imagist poets, and contemporary songwriters such as Bob Dylan and Nick Cave.

KC: Have there been any particular phases in your poetry?

JK: I write in collages rather than phases. Interestingly, much of my writing is associated with coastal imagery although I have not had the luxury of living at the seaside. My interest in observing people rather than landscapes has evolved over the past five years. I now like to focus on my own inner self.

KC: Do you write for any particular audience?

JK: I definitely write for myself, although I am aware of the marketplace. I do not write specifically to be published in a particular journal. Instead, I concern myself with topics that interest me.

KC: What is your opinion about the use of metaphor and simile in poetry? How/when do you use them yourself?

JK: The use of metaphors and simile excites me when well used. I am inspired by examples of these techniques and my usage of them comes naturally to me.

KC: How would you describe both South Australian poetry, and Australian poetry in general?

JK: In my opinion, the primary interest of South Australian poetry is rural not urban based. Martin Johnson, a Gawler poet, is a great supporter of rural poets in the state.

The South Australian Writers' Centre has a specific focus on poets and young writers, as opposed to novelists and scriptwriters as with interstate writing centres. Friendly Street Poets is the longest surviving 'live' poetry reading event in Australia (since 11 November 1975). Mike Ladd, a South Australian poet, has the only national radio poetry show, *PoeticA* on Radio National, which is based in Adelaide. South Australia is great for poets. Also, the 'spoken word' poetry performing groups are becoming a large part of the pub scene throughout Australia, and this can only be healthy for poetry and its audience.

Talking to Jules Leigh Koch

In order to choose a poet to study, I spent some time in Wakefield Press (Rundle Street) looking through its collection of local poetry books, including the Friendly Street publications. I came across two authors whose work I was particularly interested in—Cath Kenneally and Jules Leigh Koch. In the end I chose Jules's work to study because I love the way his poetry is so fresh—often short and to the point. I also really liked his use of imagery. Many of Jules's poems easily conjured up images of people, places or events in my mind, as though he were a painter as well as a poet.

I met with Jules on 9 September 2002. We arranged to meet at the Alfresco Café on Rundle Street. I was a little nervous, but I was also looking forward to meeting Jules. I was a little unsure about what to expect before the meeting, as I didn't know very much about him, though I had heard that he was a very pleasant man, and I found this to be true.

Jules seemed to me to be a fairly shy man, but also very friendly. He was very happy to do the interview, confessing that he had 'never done anything like this before'. He appeared to be a little bit nervous because of this, but it didn't interfere with the interview, and I was pleased with the way he addressed and answered the questions. The more Jules relaxed, the more in depth his answers became.

Jules and I began by talking about the type of poetry we each enjoy, and why we enjoy poetry. Jules also wanted to know a bit about why I was interviewing him and what I was going to be doing with the interview. He told me that he was flattered that I had chosen his poetry to study. Jules was happy for me to record the interview. We then went on to the more formal part and I asked Jules the questions I had designed for the interview, with a few ad-libs thrown in when he brought up points that I was interested in. Jules and I also talked about some general poetry concepts.

Jules did not fit my image of a 'successful poet'. I found it very interesting to discover that he has never read a novel from cover to cover, and that he started writing poetry because he enjoyed song lyrics played over the radio. I also thought it interesting that he has only written just over one hundred poems in his life.

Overall, I got on very well with Jules. I think it would be hard not to. I also thought that the interview was successful. Jules came across as an interesting, friendly and very pleasant man who was easy to talk to and very approachable. I thoroughly enjoyed meeting and interviewing him. I would, however, have liked some of his answers to be a bit more in-depth, but I found that if I teased out his answers a little, he was more than happy to go into a bit more detail.

A few weeks after the initial interview had taken place, I found myself still wanting to know more about his writing, so I contacted him to ask if he would answer a few more questions. He was happy to do so. This time, we didn't meet in person but the questions were asked in writing, delivered to Ashford Special School where Jules works. Jules answered these questions, and also supplied me with an extensive list of publications in which his work has been featured, and a copy of a review of his book *Each Goldfish Is Hand Painted*, titled 'Fragility Is the Poet's Strength', published in *The Bunyip*, 28 August 2002.

I was surprised by how long the list of publications supplied by Jules was—I wasn't aware that he was so successful. Of particular help and interest to me was the information Jules gave me about poetry in South Australia. He supplied me with facts such as that South Australia often has the highest ratio of poets in national anthologies, and that Friendly Street Poets is the longest surviving 'live' poetry reading event in Australia (since 11 November 1975).

Reading Jules's answers to the written questions was an interesting experience. I found that even these interview answers were written with a special talent. I found that Jules wrote about his poetry writing experiences with a passion that was easily visible. It was obvious to me that Jules loves writing.

Reading the poems

Morris and Ribner (1962) write that 'no general definition of poetry can be fully satisfying, for poetry has meant different things in different periods of civilisation, and even in a single period it has offered diverse values to different individuals.' Despite this claim, the questions 'what is poetry?' and 'what is a poem?' have been answered with many long and complicated explanations, indeed there have been whole chapters, even whole books dedicated to this task. But perhaps the best explanation, certainly the simplest, is that of intention and reception. If a poet puts a group of words on a page intending them to be a poem, and the reader interprets these words as a poem, then both a connection and a poem have been formed.

The task of defining what constitutes Australian poetry is a slightly more arduous task. As Taylor (1987) writes, 'it seems that the apparently innocuous and self explanatory term 'Australian poetry' is not only hard, but actually impossible ultimately to pin down'. As Wright (1957) points out, the evolution of Australian poetry had to initially overcome a problem which few other nations faced. It had to create its own background and its own tradition in a new landscape (Wright 1957). However, it overcame these obstacles and has risen to a place where, in terms of quality, it is as good as the poetry of any other English speaking nation (Porter 1996). Despite this, the industry is still not given the full recognition it deserves.

The contemporary poetry scene in South Australia is one which encourages writers, particularly through the SA Writers' Centre, which takes much more of an interest in poets as compared to most interstate centres (see interview, p. 71). Friendly Street Poets is an important association which has the prestige of being the longest surviving 'live' poetry venue in the country (see interview, p. 71). In Jules Leigh Koch's words, 'South Australia is great for poets' (see interview, p. 71).

Jules Leigh Koch is a contemporary South Australian poet who has been published in such prestigious publications as *Overland*, *The Weekend Australian* and *New England Review* and has recently published his first full-length book—*Each Goldfish Is Hand Painted* (Koch 2002). This publication contains a collection of very modern poetry—short, sharp and direct, with a song-like quality about it. Koch writes using an array of literary devices but without any formal metrical schemes or structure (with the exception of some haiku poetry).

Koch's poetry is often simple, but at times with hidden layers. It is poetry which can be understood by the majority of people. It could also be compared to that of the imagists, such as Amy Lowell, Ezra Pound, Hilda Doolittle, James Joyce and William Carlos Williams (Jones 1972). Imagism is the name given to a movement in poetry which began around 1912 and aimed at 'clarity of expression through using precise visual images' (Lowell 1917).

There are six major assumptions of imagist poetry, all of which are illustrated in Koch's poetry. The first is the use of the exact word (National University of Singapore 2002), and Koch's short, sharp poetry certainly does this. The second rule of imagism is to create new rhythms, with a focus on the use of free verse (National University of Singapore 2002). All of Koch's poetry in *Each Goldfish Is Hand Painted* is written using free verse, with the exception of several haikus. Imagist poetry also promises complete freedom in the choice of subject (National University of Singapore 2002). The fourth premise of this type of poetry is the presentation of an image. Jules does this in poems such as 'Street Performance' (Koch 2002), which begins with the lines:

A performer juggles
four fire sticks
her hands busy as a windmill
a ferris wheel of flames

Imagists produce poetry which is hard and clear, as opposed to indefinite or blurred. Jules does this by presenting short, exact definitions and images using a straightforward method of explanation. And lastly, imagism 'insists on concentration as the very essence of poetry' (National University of Singapore 2002).

Jules has a definite style that is concentrated and exact, using short lines and short stanzas (often of ten words or less). An example is 'Ladybird' (Koch 2002):

A ladybird appears
on the lawn
psychedelic orange
(with black spots)
knee pad
for a grasshopper

Imagist poetry is often thought of as being closer to painting than it is to literature (Rice University 2002). This is consistent with Koch's claim that he is 'more interested in the picture than the language or the words … [and] more inspired by art galleries—paintings, drawings, art, than … by literature' (see interview, p. 68).

Quite a bit of the poetry contained in *Each Goldfish Is Hand Painted* could be said to have a cinematic quality. The following lines from 'A Wet Night Along Punt Road' (Koch 2002) are an example in point:

Stars eaten by clouds
on lit streets
daggers of rain
fall
passing trams
a truck driver's fist
is a hammer changing gears
the moon is half
rusted out

This imagery is also used in Koch's haiku poetry, for example 'Kings Cross Haiku' (Koch 2002):

A woman walks late
along the dark inner thighs
of Darlinghurst road

stopped at a red light
a turbo charged Monaro
is heavy breathing

As Ribner and Morris (1962) write, 'poetry may or may not include rhyme or meter. Although historically it has included both, neither is essential'. Because Koch writes predominantly using free verse, his poetry relies heavily on devices such as assonance and alliteration rather than formal metrical schemes to give it structure and rhythm (Carpio 1998). The only formally structured kind of poem Koch published in *Each Goldfish Is Hand Painted* is the haiku (Koch 2002).

Koch makes particular use of alliteration, a term which can be defined as 'the audible repetition of consonant sounds at the beginning of words or within words' (Hirsch 1999). As Reeves (1965) points out, alliteration can become monotonous, but when used correctly, it confers the poem a song-like quality that is characteristic of Koch's poetry in *Each Goldfish Is Hand Painted*. Although Koch uses alliteration often, he avoids monotony by keeping it to short bursts rather than long lines of repeated sounds such as those found in 'Leaving Home' (Koch 2002). The lines contain combinations of words such as 'leaf leaves', 'free fall' and 'perfect as a promise'. Another example of Koch's use of alliteration can be found in 'Wearied Afternoon' (Koch 2002) in the line 'the sun sags on my shoulders'. Koch adeptly uses alliteration to make descriptions more concise whilst at the same time avoiding monotony. Alliteration is used most in the first section of Koch's book.

Koch also makes extensive use of assonance, which can be defined as 'the audible repetition of vowel sounds within words encountered near each other' (Hirsch 1999). Assonance could perhaps be seen as a modern alternative to the traditional rhyme (Reeves 1965). It 'pleases the ear' (Hirsch 1999) and is an effective way of helping to encourage rhythm within free verse (Reeves 1965). Koch uses assonance in a similar way to how he uses alliteration—often, but in short, understated bursts, the theme being only carried out across two or three words. Examples can be seen in 'The Man in the Bookshop' (Koch 2002), 'daily he plays the same'; 'Moonta Bay' (Koch 2002), 'stars have started'; and 'Kirribilli' (Koch 2002), 'mist drifts'. As with alliteration, the use of assonance is most common in 'A Mermaid's Sketchbook', which is the first section of *Each Goldfish Is Hand Painted*.

Keeping with the themes of imagism and free verse, Koch rarely uses rhyme in his poetry, and when it is used on occasion in poems such as 'Logbook Sketches' (Koch 2002), 'Harbour' (Koch 2002), and 'Bio-dynamic Gardener' (Koch 2002), it seems almost accidental. As Fraser (1970) points out, the main function of rhyme in English poetry is much the same as alliteration and several other poetic devices—to link particular lines of poetry and contribute to the creation of rhythm (Fraser 1973). Rhyme has been largely replaced in contemporary poetry by other more flexible poetic devices. Koch follows this trend with 'Each Goldfish Is Hand Painted'.

Koch makes good use of both simile and metaphor in his poetry. These devices have been called the 'chief resources of poetry' (Reeves 1965). Simile is defined as 'the explicit comparison of one thing to another, using the words 'as' or 'like'. Lowell (1917) writes that 'imagist poetry must be original and free of clichés ... it must be original and natural to the poet. Koch's similes and metaphors are original. He claims that he is inspired by metaphor and simile and that his usage of them comes naturally to him (see interview, p. 77).

As Hirsch (1999) writes, 'a good simile depends on a certain heterogeneity between the elements being compared. An example of this would be 'they race each other/ like sheets on a clothesline/ in the wind' (Koch 2002). This is a fresh comparison which creates a pleasant image in the mind.

Metaphor is defined as 'a figure of speech in which one thing is described as another—as when Whitman characterises the grass as 'the beautiful uncut hair of graves' (Hirsch 1999). Much of the English language is built on metaphor (Reeves 1965), and it is therefore a very natural part of poetry. Metaphor, like simile, can create obvious relationships which may not otherwise be visible, and enrich language. Koch frequently uses metaphor in his poetry, for example: 'Moonta Bay' (Koch 2002) with 'The moon/ is a pale feather/ of an extinct bird'; and in 'Outpost' (Koch 2002) with 'Yachts are crayon smudges/ on the horizon'. Koch avoids overuse, which can 'crowd' a poem (Macneice 1968), with careful use of short, original metaphors.

How a poem sounds is not the only important factor when analysing poetry. Aesthetics on the page is also important (except in performance poetry). The organisation of the poem into lines and stanzas, and the use of punctuation are all part of this. Koch's poetry has a 'sharp' look, with short lines and stanzas and little punctuation. According to Martin Johnson in the *The Bunyip* (2002) 'the sparseness of his lines, often two or three words, six at most, coupled into three, two, one and sometimes five lined verses, take the eyes of the reader quickly down the page'.

Koch most often writes using non-rhyming couplets, indeed some poems in *Each Goldfish Is Hand Painted* are written entirely in this format (e.g. 'Jetty', 'Street Performance' and 'A CFS Officer Contemplates the Universe'). Other poems are a combination of single lines and couplets (e.g. 'Outpost' and 'Ladybird'). Koch's poetry is fairly simple poetry that is easy to read and easy to look at, which are attractive features for many readers. As Koch himself points out, his poetry is 'fairly uncomplex, it's precise. It's not elitist' (see interview, p. 69).

Punctuation—or lack thereof—affects both the aesthetics and rhythm of poetry. An abundance of full stops and commas creates an 'interrupted' poetry with short bursts and many different emphases, while a lack of punctuation creates a free flowing poetry. Koch rarely uses punctuation, though he does use capital letters at the beginning of most stanzas in order to emphasise certain lines and to give structure to the poem. Another function of the capital letter is to create a 'sentence-like' structure without interrupting the flow of the poem. Andrews (1991) claims that most poetry still operates in sentences, and these often are the cross rhythms that help create a musical dimension within the poetry. This may also be a contributor to the song-like quality of Koch's poetry.

Jules Leigh Koch is a very talented local poet, who has received excellent (albeit limited) reviews to date (e.g. 'Fragility Is the Poet's Strength' from *The Bunyip*, 28 August 2002). Despite having published just one full-length book titled *Each Goldfish Is Hand Painted* in 2002, Koch is an established poet, having featured in many different publications both in Australia and overseas. These publications include *Social Alternatives, The New England Review,*

Mattoid, Overland, The Weekend Australian, and the *Canberra Times* in Australia, and *Southern Ocean Review* and *Takahe* in New Zealand.

If, as Aristotle claims, the vehicle of expression is language, Jules Leigh Koch drives a Holden. A simple car that is accessible to the majority, good for all ages, and nice to look at, with some fancy extras here and there.

References

Andrews, R. (1991) *The Problem with Poetry*. Philadelphia: Open University Press.

Aristotle *Poetics*,[viewed 1 September 2002], http://libertyonline.hypermall.com/Aristotle/Poetics.html

The Bunyip (28 August 2002), Bunyip Print, Gawler, South Australia.

Carpio, B. (1998) *Form*,[viewed 8 September 2002], http://litera1no4.tripod.com/form_frame.html#imagism

Fraser, G.S. (1970) *Metre, Rhyme and Free Verse*. London: Methuen and Co. Ltd.

Hirsch, E. (1999) *How to Read a Poem and Fall in Love with Poetry*. New York: A Harvest Book, Harcourt Inc., pp. 38, 266-268, 289.

Johnson, M. (2002) 'Fragility Is the Poet's Strength' in *The Bunyip*, 28 August.

Jones, P. (1972) *Imagist Poetry*. Middlesex, England: Penguin Books Ltd.

Koch, J.L. (2002) *Each Goldfish Is Hand Painted*. Adelaide: Wakefield Press.

Lowell, A. (1917) *On Imagism*,[viewed 2 October 2002], http://www.english.uiuc.edu/maps/poets/g_l/amylowell/imagism.htm

Macneice, L. (1968) *Modern Poetry: A Personal Essay*. Oxford University Press.

Monaco, R. and Briggs, J. (1974) *The Logic of Poetry*. New York: McGraw-Hill.

Morris, H. and Ribner, I. (1962) *Poetry: A Critical and Historical Introduction*. Chicago. Scott, Foresman and Company, p. 1.

National University of Singapore (2000) *Imagism*,[viewed 2 October 2002], http://65.107.211.206/post/modernism/imagism.html

Porter, P. (ed.) (1996) *The Oxford Book of Modern Australian Verse*. Melbourne: Oxford University Press.

Reeves, J. (1965) *Understanding Poetry*. London: Heinemann Educational Books Ltd., p. 168.

Rice University (2002) *Generations*,[viewed 27 May 2003], http://www.cs.rice.edu/~ssiyer/minstrels/poems/102.html

Taylor, A. (1987) *Reading Australian Poetry*. Melbourne: The Book Printer, pp. 20–21.

Wright, J. (ed.) (1957) *New Land, New Language, Anthology of Australian Verse*. Oxford University Press.

CATH KENNEALLY

Chapter by Lauren Kourtidis

Published poetry books

Harmers Haven, Little Esther Press, Adelaide 1996
Around Here, Wakefield Press, Adelaide 1999
All Day All Night, Salt Publishing, Cambridge 2003

Biographical note

Cath Kenneally is a familiar name in the Adelaide arts scene. She is an arts journalist, the arts producer at Radio Adelaide, and hosts the weekly Arts Breakfast program. Cath is a critic of visual arts and literature, and has published three books of poetry and a novel, with a second novel manuscript completed in 2004.

She has made a significant imprint on the South Australian arts community, and has been rewarded for her talent numerous times. In 1998, she won the Adelaide Festival Barbara Hanrahan Fellowship, and in 2000 spent six months at the Australia Council Rome studio with partner Ken Bolton. Her second poetry book, *Around Here*, received the John Bray National Poetry Award at the Adelaide Festival in 2002. Cath is currently completing her PhD in Creative Writing.

Interview with Cath Kenneally

Lauren Kourtidis (LK): At what stage in your life did you fully immerse yourself in poetry, and why?

Cath Kenneally (CK): I began to write poetry in about 1990, a time when certain family events unfolded that seemed to require me to write poems. Up until then I had written only criticism. Once I began, I found writing poetry both satisfied an urge and created the urge to write more. I tried to write a poem a fortnight.

LK: In Edward Hirsch's *How to Read a Poem*, he quotes Robert Graves in *The White Goddess*:

> True poetic practice implies a mind so miraculously attuned and illuminated that it can form words, by a chain of more-than coincidences, into a living entity—a poem that goes about on its own (for centuries after the author's death, perhaps) affecting readers with its stored magic.
> (Robert Graves, *The White Goddess*, in Hirsch 1999, p. 6)

Describe what poetry means to you.

CK: Robert Graves is probably spot-on. More-than-coincidence is about right. And 'living entity' is certainly what you want to end up with. Now that I've been writing novels for a few years, I realise more sharply what the different nature of poetry is. It does involve going 'down' into a realm where connections or associations can be formed, without too-conscious direction by the poet. It's a matter of keeping lines open, as on an old-fashioned telephone switchboard, and listening in to other conversations going on elsewhere in one's own brain. The trick is in the non-directive approach, which can't be forced, but either happens or doesn't. You can force a poem into a shape or conclusion that is neat but inauthentic. A real poem goes its own way and surprises you, the poet, with where it ends up.

For me, poems are permanently-resonating sounding-boards, set off by the poet who has managed to plug into a truth or a perception by a mix of channelling, aptitude with words, and luck.

LK: How do you become inspired to write poetry?

CK: Actually, I find all sorts of excuses not to write poems. I write one when it forces itself on me. This may be for any number of reasons—reading someone else's work, finding some old writing of my own that suddenly seems to have potential, finding old notes taken on a trip, being particularly moved to record an event so it doesn't get forgotten; mostly finding scraps of ideas noted down at an earlier date, which time seems to have given me a new perspective on.

LK: What is your favourite poem, or poet—or both?

CK: I think my favourite poet is probably Jenny Bornholt, a New Zealand poet. Another New Zealand poet is a close second,

Janet Charman, and Dinah Hawken, also from New Zealand, third. I vacillate between them for favourite poems at any one time.

LK: When and where do you write?

CK: Usually at home, alone, in the kitchen or bedroom. Sometimes in cafes. Occasionally on public transport.

LK: How did you get your poetry published?

CK: My first poems published were submitted to *Otis Rush* magazine in Adelaide, at that time edited by Ken Bolton. Others later appeared in other Australian literary magazines, until my first collection appeared in 1996 from Little Esther Press, also operated by Ken Bolton.

LK: What do you think of the poetry and arts community in South Australia?

CK: I have quite a bit to do with South Australian poets and artists, as the Arts Producer at 5UV radio station, and presenter of a two-hour arts show each week. The poetry community seems productive, if a little self-satisfied in patches, but you get that anywhere. Poets self-sort into groups, or remain steadfastly independent. I don't have any particular allegiances myself, so this makes me one of the latter. South Australian poets and artists can be afflicted by a cultural cringe in relation to artists elsewhere, in the Eastern states especially. There is an isolation factor here, and a 'cliqueyness'. The same people can seem to be chosen for any public purposes. The Writers' Centre is a helpful institution, but may also contribute to this pigeonholing of certain poets and writers and overlooking of others. Creative Writing courses are bringing many good writers I didn't know about out of the woodwork, and doing the Creative Writing PhD myself at Adelaide has put me in the way of many new connections. It's hard to generalise. There's a lot of good stuff going on, much that's mediocre, a great number of enthusiasts. I think the government funding bodies have overdone the 'emerging artists' thing, and some younger artists have become overexposed and peaked too early.

LK: What advice would you give to budding poets?

CK: Read other poets. Read a great deal of everything, in fact. Write a lot and throw a lot away. Read literary theory as well, and find your way onto a poetry list on the web. Don't be discouraged by early knock-backs. Revise first drafts, having left them to sit in a drawer for a couple of months without looking at them, so you can come to them as a fresh critic. Keep paper and pencil on hand everywhere, in the car glove box, in your backpack or handbag. Write whenever you have the urge, don't put it off. Keep submitting on a regular basis to journals and the like. Take criticism on board, but insist on what seems important to you. Keep a portfolio, and keep good records.

LK: In Hirsch's book, he also quotes Emily Dickinson's reaction to a good poem:

> If I read a book [and] it makes my whole body so cold no fire could ever warm me I know *that* is poetry. If I feel physically as if the top of my head were taken off, I know *that* is poetry. These are the only ways I know. Is there any other way? (E. Dickinson, in Hirsch 1999, p. 7)

What do you think makes a good poem, and how do you react to one?

CK: Emily has it pretty right. A good poem has a rightness about it. It may be long and discursive or brief and punchy. There's a rightness in the tone, in the voice, in the choice of words and in what's not said. There's evidence of the openness, all channels open and antennae out for connections that I tried to describe above. And for all these reasons it makes you shiver, or sigh, or smile, and not forget.

LK: How would you describe your poetry?

CK: I have tried to write a kind of lucid, undecorated poetry that keeps its finger on the pulse of domestic life in particular. It tries to be contemporary, witty, perhaps politically astute, attuned to currents of thought and contemporary issues but filtering them through an everyday lens. It's personal, autobiographical but not exclusively literary in the sense that I've studied a lot of English and continental literature and that finds its way into my thoughts and phrasing, phrasing that often echoes formal poetic structures that have stuck in my brain, but rarely actively emulates them. I hope it's never didactic. I hope it's memorable, and that it says some useful things about women's lives, mothers and children, men and women. I hope it's funny. I try never to be ponderous or self-important. My more recent poetry is perhaps more interested in cultural relativism, less intently focused on the home, much of it arising from travels over recent years.

Talking to Cath Kenneally

I first came across the poetry collection *Around Here* quite by chance. When searching for a South Australian poetry publication in Borders bookshop in Rundle Mall, Adelaide, I was surprised by the number of poets—most of whose names I was not aware. I chose Cath Kenneally's book after looking through and becoming immediately intrigued and captured by the poetry, and because I found it simple to understand. I did not feel I was being 'talked down to' like some other books had left me feeling. I found Cath's poetry straightforward and honest, which is the way I tend to write my own poetry. The actual production of the publication seemed very professional; it was bound nicely so that it would last longer, and the colour on the cover made it appealing to the eye.

I found out that Cath is involved with Radio Adelaide, and the University of Adelaide. I was not aware that Cath was studying until I received her answers. I chose to conduct the interview via email for convenience. I understood that Cath was fairly busy, and this saved a lot of time for us both. Cath was always prompt with her replies, and gave her answers within a week of me sending the questions. She offered to send more information if necessary, but I found her answers gave enough information—and like her poetry, her answers were easily understood. Emailing was a very productive way to obtain information, as it allowed Cath to give succinct, pre-thought answers.

One disadvantage was the lack of interaction in a face-to-face interview, where perhaps more detailed information could have been obtained. Overall, emailing was very effective and I believe it gave a true reflection of Cath and her poetry.

I found the entire process of formulating questions for someone I had only just begun to learn about quite a challenge. I did not want to ask unoriginal or boring questions that Cath would have encountered before. My aim was to find out as much as possible, from her perspective. Asking open-ended questions was the key to gaining more detail, as it precluded 'yes' or 'no' answers.

As a result of this project I gained a substantial amount of knowledge on not only a South Australian poet, but poetry and its analysis in general. I was able to successfully apply critical thinking to an area I hadn't previously worked on, and this gave me confidence for future projects that may involve interviewing skills.

Reading the poems

Contemporary poetry has come to be identified with reality—from its content to its form and style. It lends itself to the reader, it is accessible and concerned with simplicity, elegance and experimentalism, more than a formal guided style.

According to Cath Kenneally, the South Australian poetry community is 'productive, if a little self-satisfied in patches'. Many young poets are keen to have their poetry heard and are open to constructive criticism. Poets in South Australia are active and realise the necessity to create spaces for themselves and others to be heard. 'Written off' is a University of South Australia organised poetry night where mostly Professional Writing students come to enjoy and read poetry in the comfortable environment of the Crown and Sceptre pub on King William Street, Adelaide. Similarly, 'Word is' is a poetry night held on the last Monday of every month at Riffs music lounge on Gouger Street. It offers an 'anything goes' policy for musicians and poets who are willing to reveal some of their creative productions. Friendly Street Poets is an established poetry venue with regular poetry readings from special guests and open-mike opportunities.

Apart from poetry events, South Australian poets contribute to a range of publications. Various selections of poetry are printed in *Vernacular*. The editors of *Vernacular* reiterate the need for an outlet for writers: '…*Vernacular* has been inundated with submissions … while the interest is flattering, it also reaffirms our belief that writers have far too few mediums for expression' (Garnett and Groff 2000). The editors of *Vernacular* and *Sidewalk* work to produce volumes of poetry that is accessible to Australian readers. Other similar outlets include *piping shrike* and *Orrmulum*, both University of South Australia-produced poetry and prose publications.

Today, the Internet also offers a global outlet for poets to get their work released. *Otis Rush*, unfortunately no longer publishing, was a site that started as a magazine in Adelaide, and where Cath Kenneally submitted her first poem.

Kenneally's second poetry book *Around Here,* was published by Wakefield Press in 1999. *Around Here* is described by Ken Bolton as follows: 'What is most valuable in these poems, and what is rare, is Kenneally's avoidance of metaphor and of the conventionally poetic in favour of intelligent and educated plain speak' (Bolton 1999). Bev Braune enlightens further: 'Her words do not strive; it seems to me, for empathy; rather to make themselves heard as statements of analysis, to the point that their form in poetry often seems arbitrary' (Braune 2000).

Kenneally's voice can be heard clearly in her poetry. Her often experimental style may seem arrived to by chance, but it is the intelligence behind this experimentation that cements the actual content. Some poetry contains words and phrases from different languages—usually French and Italian, or cultures that the reader may not be aware of. Yet Kenneally never seems condescending. Any new words only serve as fuel for curiosity. Kenneally always offers something honest and personal in her writing. She lets the reader in on her train of thoughts, and although they may not know where they are being taken, the ride captures them and sends them on a journey. This journey is centred around the city, the family and issues of femininity.

Kenneally's lack of elaborate language effectively creates strong imagery because of her specific choice of words. The way Kenneally structures her phrases says enough without the need for metaphor or lengthy description. An example of this is the poem 'Tonight This Headache'. The description of the headache thudding around the temples and joining hands in the middle of the forehead gives the feeling of a headache clasping and cloaking—a pain that readers could readily identify with. The phrase 'desk lamp is mercifully gentle' personifies and creates strong imagery with little effort. The short, two-line stanzas feel like the 'thuds' of a headache—rhythmic pounding in the head. The structure of the lines also helps portray that 'off' and 'on' feeling that a headache can give—the pain comes in thuds, then there is momentary relief. The break after 'and', gives the impression that the 'thud' came at that point and interrupted the flow of thought:

Tonight this
headache

starts somewhere at the
base of my skull

thuds around to my
temples and

joins hands in the
middle of my forehead

The line 'it has to be awfully deliberate', is a reference to the purposeful, almost forced way that Kenneally had to write in order to manage. The word 'manage' is used with multiple connotations—firstly managing the headache, but there is also a deeper meaning produced when Kenneally later says 'Tonight I can't think how I ever manage except …', alluding to a wider concept of managing, perhaps her life or family.

The second half of the poem drifts onto other subjects (such as the desk and her earrings) that seem to act as a distraction from the headache:

tonight I notice the different
strident black of the pen against it

and how very Ancient-Briton my earrings
roughly-cast silver discs 'depending'

from each other (I've read too much
Iris Murdoch) seem there / they should

be worn with a woollen shift and thronged
leggings not likely

there's a tiny paper-and-matchstick
parasol on the desk here that

opens and closes like a real one
tonight it wouldn't take any more than

a whimsy like that to bring down
the whole house of cards.

The further reference to the headache being only one thing that is bothering Kenneally finally comes full circle with the last three stanzas, with the simple imagery that at this point the poet is feeling so fragile, it wouldn't take much to 'bring down the whole house of cards'.

References

Bolton, K. (1999) blurb of *Around Here* by Cath Kenneally. Adelaide: Wakefield Press.

Braune, B. (2000) 'Musing on Chaos: Two Books of Poetry', *Australian Women's Book Review: Online* volume 12. Available online at http://emsah.uq.edu.au/awsr/recent/7.html

Garnett, M. and Groff, M. (2000) 'Editor's blurb', *Vernacular* volume 2, Adelaide.

Hirsch, E. (1999) *How to Read a Poem and Fall in Love with Poetry*. New York: A Harvest Book, Harcourt Inc., p. 7.

Kenneally, C. (1999) 'Tonight This Headache', *Around Here*, Adelaide: Wakefield Press, p. 55.

MIKE LADD

Chapter by Andre Starr

Published poetry books
The Crack in the Crib, Wakefield Press, Adelaide 1984
Picture's Edge, Wakefield Press, Adelaide 1994
Close to Home, Five Islands Press, Wollongong 2000
Rooms and Sequences, Salt Publishing, Cambridge 2003

Biographical note
Mike Ladd, born in 1959, grew up in Blackwood in the Adelaide Hills. After completing a Bachelor of Arts in English and Philosophy at the University of Adelaide, he began to publish his poetry widely throughout Australia. In 1980, he formed 'The Drum Poets', a group of musicians who performed his poetry using conventional instruments, found objects and pre-recorded sounds. In the early 1980s, Ladd travelled through Europe and Africa. After returning to Adelaide, he began work with ABC Radio and is currently producer and presenter of the Radio National poetry program *PoeticA*.

Interview with Mike Ladd

Andre Starr (AS): How often do you write?
Mike Ladd (ML): How often do I write? Specifically poetry, you mean?
AS: Yes, well, anything really.
ML: As I said a bit earlier, Andre, it depends on the moment. In the *Close to Home* book for example, I wrote many poems about my son. I had not written a word about him in years and then they all came in a hurry. They wanted to be written. I would write one at say, eleven o'clock at night—I do a lot of writing late at night—I'd go to bed and then another poem would be tapping me on the shoulder at midnight, and I'd

have to get up again and write it down. I'd go back to bed and then a 'one o'clock' poem would come along, and it was like 'oh no, not another poem'. So that was unusual in the sense that I was really being driven by something. It was almost beyond my control. Words kept wanting to be written down.

At other times, I'll wait for months. I used to believe in trying to write all the time. When I was seventeen or eighteen, I'd be writing three times a week at least. Now I write one, maybe two, every month. I just wait for it to come. I start getting words in my head, but I don't write them down straight away any more, I just keep them up there, circling around. When I feel that the poem is there, I'll write it.

AS: Do you think you wrote more when you were younger because you had this need to get them out?

ML: Definitely, I was in a hurry to get it all out. Now I'm more patient. I look back on those poems and I think only one in ten was any good. I believe in mental editing these days, that things will actually form themselves better if you wait. It's like wine, you gotta...

AS: Let it mature?

ML: Yes, let it mature a bit.

AS: At what point do you find that you are into a poem that is working?

ML: When do I think it's working?

AS: Yes.

ML: That's an interesting question. I think that when I've got it in my head to the point that I've got a need to get it down and think yes, there's something there. That's when I think it's working. Quite often, I'll put it down—I always write it freehand first. I don't like the sound of a computer, or I don't like the process of typing onto screen. I always write freehand, and then it depends on how it's flowing in that first moment. In my experience, my best poems have always been almost written without the need for re-drafting—a bit of tinkering maybe. Usually for me it's getting rid of things; it's rarely adding things, it's almost always eliminating. Then I'll type it up and I'll look at it again. If I still like it, I'll send it away somewhere and see if others like it [laughs]. It's not always the case.

AS: So what makes you look at a poem after you have written it and say 'no this just doesn't work'?

ML: I can hear myself straining for an effect, otherwise I think it's a cliché. That's another thing, if I think it's a cliché I don't like it. When does it work? When it's got the right form for what it's trying to say. When I think yes, I've got that, I've got the words right. It's actually working as a statement. And it's rich; it's not just a piece of chopped up prose. It actually has a musicality to it. The images are working and it says something. I believe poetry should say something. I'm not one of the school who thinks a subject is a bad thing for a poem to have. And there are people who think that poetry should be just playing around with words rather than trying to say something about the world. I disagree, I think poetry *has* to say something about the world and it has to say it in a very personal and strong way. It has to communicate something from one person to another person.

AS: How long have you been writing poetry?

ML: Since I was a child. I used to muck around with little jingles that I'd picked up from people like Lawson and Patterson. I think I was around eight or nine. I grew up in a suburb that was still virtually bushland—Blackwood, in the Adelaide Hills. It's now a suburb of Adelaide, but when I grew up we had a dirt road in our street, there were no traffic lights and there were paddocks all around us.

AS: It's still called 'Main Road'.

ML: That's right. But I grew up in bushland, and that poetry just seemed to fit the landscape so well. I loved the musicality of the language and the way the rhythms actually seemed to fit the landscape. So I copied that. I don't know … I just started copying it. I must have been around eight or nine. I first started writing poems that were getting published and were serious when I was sixteen. I wrote for the school magazine and then I sent poems in to Rodney Hall, who was the editor at *The Weekend Australian*. Hall wrote me a nice long letter saying that he thought I could be a poet, you know, that I had something and that was really a wonderful sort of reinforcement for me. He then published some poems of mine when I was seventeen.

AS: Hall gave you some confidence.

ML: Absolutely, it is very important. We can all try with words, but somewhere along the line you need to have reassurance that there could be an audience for your work, that someone could value your words enough to call you a poet. The other big step was when I went to university. I studied as much poetry as I could and I went along to Friendly Street, the local poetry reading, which was very dynamic in those days. It was the place to be. That was very influential because I met a whole lot of poets, found an audience for my poems, and could test poems on a live audience. That was very exciting to me. That was the very first year of Friendly Street, which was in 1975, when the Whitlam government was sacked.

AS: Would you say there was a profound moment of inspiration which made you start writing poetry?

ML: Not really, there was always this love of language. There was no blinding moment, no. It was an early love of language. I've always been encouraged in that; my parents had a lot of books. I can't give you an actual age, but I think I always had words playing around in my head, just like a painter always sees the world as a picture, and a composer hears music. I think I always had that, and it's a matter of whether that's encouraged or not. Some people may be born with that, but have it stamped out of them by a family who doesn't want them to do that, or an environment that doesn't encourage it. That's tragic, but I was always lucky enough to have lots of encouragement. So there wasn't a blinding flash of 'you will be a poet', you know.

AS: It grew organically?

ML: It grew organically, and I would say the other thing was discovering key poets that I absolutely love. The first was Robert Frost, when I was sixteen; I memorised whole poems of his. I can still recite Frost. And then, as I started, I discovered lots of different poets I liked; a huge range from right across the world.

AS: Is there anyone that you're really into at the moment?

ML: Yes, my favourite poet at the moment—and this is really saying something, because I love thousands of poets—is Nâzim Hikmet, the Turkish poet. Why do I like him so much?

I don't know, he just somehow accords with how I feel about the whole world I suppose.

AS: There's a connection?

ML: Definitely, I feel a connection to his way of thinking, very much. I love his poetry because it is hopeful; it is offering something without avoiding the darker issues in life. I mean this is a guy who spent thirty years locked up in Turkish prisons for his beliefs, and he never lost his optimism for humanity. He had this rich kind of love in his work, despite really quite dark images at times. He just used a simple language. Obviously, I am reading him in translation, as he wrote in Turkish, but the translation shows a simple language. He wanted to communicate very widely to people, but used very beautifully crafted poetic imagery, and I liked that combination. I think poetry is not a matter of spouting a huge vocabulary at people.

AS: It keeps it sparse.

ML: Yes, you can deal with complex issues and emotions using simple words; I've always liked that. The Eastern European minimalists had an effect on me, definitely, and people like Rózewicz were trying for fairly minimal poems with big impact, big philosophies, big ideas using small lines.

AS: Making the reader work?

ML: Yes, making the reader work as well. That's right, not spelling it out, and not fluffing up lines with dozens of adjectives and things like that. Keeping it pretty concrete. I always liked that—that was an influence on me.

AS: How do you see South Australian poetry heading in the future?

ML: Oh! [laughs]

AS: Have I dropped a bomb?

ML: No, no, no. Where will it go in the future? I think poetry—not only in South Australia, but everywhere—has a future. Some people believe it doesn't have a future.

AS: It's kind of never gone.

ML: No, because even if they're not going to be featuring poets on chat shows on television and on the cover of *Woman's Weekly* or whatever, there will always be enough poetry lovers around to treasure it and keep it going. Is there a particular

South Australian future, as opposed to an Australian future? I don't know.

AS: Well, that was my next question.

ML: The scene here seems to me, given our population, reasonably healthy. If you look at it, Friendly Street is still going, but we could probably do with some alternative readings. Occasionally they happen, but they tend to be little group things, organised as a one-off event. And that's healthy.

AS: We need more *Vernaculars*.

ML: Definitely. We've got a terrific magazine, *Vernacular*, that's a wonderful thing. *SideWaLK* is another South Australian magazine that's publishing poetry; and it's sort of just hanging in there. I hope that's got a future. A lot of these things depend on the finances and energy of the editors who are doing it for the love, not the money, and they have to make a living etcetera, etcetera. So that can be a bit precarious. I would like to see more debate in the poetry community; more opposing groups or something like that.

AS: Do you think that people pat each other on the back too much?

ML: It's a bit of a small town. If you step on someone's toes, it is possible that you will meet them tomorrow in the market. I feel it could be a bit more dynamic.

AS: Do you think it's the same in Australia as a whole?

ML: Possibly. In Sydney, obviously, there are more divided schools. But, whether that's healthy I don't know, because I don't think there's any debate either. They just split off into separate camps and don't talk to each other. It'd be good to see another reading besides Friendly Street. I know they have some little ones around the place, but another big one would be great.

AS: Another regular one.

ML: Yes.

AS: We had some people in our class at university who tried to set some poetry readings up, but they died because people didn't go.

ML: That's the thing, it's hard to get people out of their lounge rooms at night to go to a poetry reading. I don't know why that is. In Melbourne there's eleven readings every week. It's a bigger town, of course, but I think it must be more than population—a critical mass or something, of people who are interested.

AS: Is there such a thing as a South Australian style? Or is there even an Australian style?

ML: I don't think there is, as opposed to seeing it as something that's unique in modernist writing right around the world. Not really, I think it's something that has been influenced by modernism in English in general, from the UK and US. It's not that much different, stylistically. Obviously, there is unique subject matter—the flora and fauna of Australia and the language. Australia's slang and idiom make Australian poems unique. I mean you can look at it and say that's an Australian poem. Look at John Forbes's work—you can say that's definitely written by an Australian. But it would be great if we could invent a new style, wouldn't it? [laughs] What would that be? Who knows? Poetry is going beyond the page now as well, so you are getting all kinds of things. Video poems—I just came back from the Sydney Poetry Festival and we had a video poetry prize.

AS: Is that like a poetry reading and visuals?

ML: Sometimes it's like that, but sometimes you don't see the person reading at all. It's a soundtrack, or sometimes there's no sound at all; it's just the words on the screen. It uses the techniques of film-making and video to create poetry. Similarly, there are sound compositions—things being released on CD. Maybe that is part of the future.

AS: Including the Internet and other technology?

ML: The Internet, there are websites, very interesting websites now that are producing visual poetry. That is a very interesting question. I'd love to see something that was a recognisable Australian style of poetry in the way that a dot painting is uniquely Australian, in that it is created by our Indigenous people. I don't know that we have achieved that with our music or our poetry, but maybe it takes more than a couple of hundred years.

AS: OK, last question. I've been debating this with my colleagues for a while. Are the best poets published?

ML: Oh! Best, who defines 'best'? Interesting question, isn't it? 'Best' in what sense? We all have our aesthetic judgements to define what's best—it's quite personal. In a way, the concept of 'best' is a little out of the poet's hands. The broad poetry community decides what's best. As in 'I love this book, I'm going to buy it'. That's about the best of it, or 'I like this person's CD so much, I'm going to get it'.

I think editors are generally looking for something that they genuinely believe in, and therefore a lot of the best poetry is published. Although, it's quite possible that there are people out there who are not yet published, whose work is just not fashionable, but it's still good and could prove in time to be really good. Emily Dickinson wrote wonderful poetry; however, her work was rarely published in her own lifetime. It's only a century later that she is now seen as the greatest female American poet, certainly in the nineteenth century. I don't know about that; I think it's a tricky question. My guess is that most of the best poetry in Australia is getting into print, but I also think that there is a lot of stuff that's not very good getting into print, because somebody owes somebody something, or there's a poetry club that is pushing it.

AS: Or it may be something that the editor likes personally, and poets are being published that way?

ML: That's possible. Editors are human beings and eventually they have to decide. So my answer is that most of the best poetry is being published, but it's quite possible that some of the best isn't. [laughs] How about that for a cop-out?

Talking to Mike Ladd

It was the lines 'The summer sleeping spell of a million runs, a thousand tumbling wickets,' from the poem 'Domestic Mystery #2' that first drew me toward Mike Ladd's work. I was standing in a busy bookshop flicking forward through his book *Close to Home*, reading as many poems as I could without suffering the retailer's withering glare. I nodded sagely at 'Mythology—A Rough Guide' ('Don't forget that a king may well have the head of a pig'), and chuckled at 'Dream' ('Sometimes in the night I wake to find you sleeping beside me. When did you crawl into our bed?'). I then read 'Shadow Story #2 (Angela)'. I had read work by many poets for the class I was attending (Writing and Reading Poetry) and it was an even race in my mind for the 'best poet' until I read this particular poem. I had to meet this guy.

First contact
I call Mike at his office in the ABC building, speak to his answering machine, and wait for his reply. A week later, I try his e-mail. He responds the next day—we were to have lunch later the next week at the ABC building itself.

The interview
I arrive late. If I am not intimidated by the imposing building, I am a bit rattled by the nonchalant security at the front desk as I am asked to sign myself in. I had never done this before; this is a big building and I'm a young wide-eyed kid from the country. As I stand there waiting, with schoolbag on my back, I realise that I am about to meet Mike Ladd—former worker at the BBC, traveller of Europe, and a man who recorded music in Africa. He is probably too busy with his own radio show to bother with a Bachelor of Arts student with a schoolbag on his back. As I go in, I realise I have become quite nervous.

He greets me at his table in the cafeteria and doesn't appear to be annoyed with my delay (perhaps he remembers studying for his BA). I grab lunch and sit down. We speak about music, poetry and really bad pop music. I discover that we have a lot in common. We both played in bands, we both studied a BA, and both consider ourselves from the country. I suddenly feel amused that I was ever nervous.

I get the impression that Mike is someone who has led a full life and is still actively living it. He answers every question with deliberation and consideration. Yet always present, behind every word, is a passion that drives him to speak at length. We are talking about how bad pop lyrics sound when delivered as a poem, when I consider pulling out my little tape-recorder and getting some of it down. However, Mike finishes his spicy-smelling pasta dish and we head to the elevator.

'That's the newsroom in there', he says pointing to a long room visible through a wall of glass. I try to act like I'm not that impressed as I gaze at the people on phones and hurrying notes between desks. They bring us the news every hour, on the hour. I imagine the background of those Late News shows on television.

The elevator takes us high into the building. Mike's office looks out over the city. The suburbs appear as though they go under the building. I want to gaze a little while longer, but we reach his workplace. Mike offers me a seat and I take a moment to look around. It's a little like my study the day before an assignment is due. Books line a number of shelves and pile up on flat out-of-the-way surfaces. His desk is dominated on one side by a computer. It has the hectic, paper-clad appearance of a person who deals with writing on a daily basis. What strikes me is the lack of pretentiousness. There are no flashy framed certificates, no gaudy gold pen-sets—just enough personal items to keep him company while he works.

After the interview, we walk to the elevator. Mike offers me a string of advice about getting my poetry out there and published. The enthusiasm he has for the industry shines through him. We shake hands at the elevator and I begin the descent back to Earth.

The fear of the interviewer settles into me. I imagine that Mike liked me. I doubt it and then imagine he thought I had wasted his time. The interview had become a conversation, a testament to his easy-going nature, and whatever formal barriers there were had disappeared. Mike probably just thought of me as an inexperienced poet with a long battle ahead. He took on a mentor-like tone and pointed out how important it is to start reading my poetry at readings and sending it off to wherever poetry is published. It was clear, honest and thoughtful advice—much like his poetry.

Reading the poems

> What is poetry?
> It is the street talk of angels and devils.
> It is a lighthouse moving its megaphone over the sea.
>
> Lawrence Felinghetti

For whatever reasons, poetry has earned itself the reputation of being the most unapproachable literary genre. Students, teachers and general readers often feel the subtle complexities and unfamiliar forms of poetry too difficult to simply enjoy (Bizzaro 1993, Spurr 1997). Edward Hirsch believes that

> there are many people who have become so estranged from the devices and techniques of poetry, from poetic thinking, that they no longer recognize what they are reading. (Hirsch 1999)

People have not stopped reading, discussing and criticising poetry. There are still poets writing in the present day and, despite some opinions, there is evidence across the world that interest in poetry will not wane (Carpenter 1997, Hirsch 1999, Spurr 1997).

Poetry in South Australia

In Australia, nation-wide literary journals, such as *Meanjin*, *Quadrant*, *Island* and *Southerly*, have reasonably large sections devoted to poetry. The South Australian poetry scene is lively enough for writers like Mike Ladd, Tom Shapcott and Ken Bolton to be able to publish poetry collections. However, published material of South Australian writers is largely reliant on the enthusiasm of writers and editors, as the editors of *Vernacular* write in the first volume:

> The major motivating factor behind *Vernacular*'s existence is the appalling lack of platforms for writing ... We know the writers are out there; writers of all sorts yearning for a chance to display what they love to do. (Garnett and Groff 1999)

The poetry published in South Australia is mostly new, fresh and varied, like much of the new poetry in the rest of the world. It is also, like the rest of the world, stylistically influenced by modernism and emerging into various experimental post-modernist forms (Abrams 1999).

Mike Ladd's poetry

Mike Ladd writes in free verse and has a particular interest in presenting ideas and meanings in his poems. Ladd is both a 'big picture' and 'detail' poet. He has found a style of expression that can build a complex image from carefully selected visual details and metaphors (Abrams 1999). In the last paragraph of '2,4,6,8', Ladd builds a complex image by describing a moment in his life:

> 2,4,6,8
> He said it suddenly, loudly, one afternoon,
> interrupting himself and stopping the class dead—
> *'The date is the second of April, 1968!*
> *Don't you realise, none of us*
> *will ever see a day like it again.'*

To explore Ladd's poetry properly, it may help to understand two major influences on his work: Modernist writers, such as Robert Frost, and the Eastern European minimalist poets, such as Rózewicz.

Ladd's inspiration: From Rózewicz and minimalism

It will be advantageous to look at the Eastern European movement in relation to Ladd's minimalist observational poems. Post-war Polish poetry was written by Polish people who had witnessed some of the worst human suffering under the Nazi occupation. The style they adopted for their poetry reflected their need to find a way to live and survive after losing six million of their population (Carpenter 1997, Hirsch 1997). As Hirsch writes,

> I admire post-war Polish poetry for its unfashionable clarity … its suspicion of absolutes and rejection of tyranny. I admire its humane values, its eminent sanity, its deep humility before the plenitude of the world. (Hirsch, 1997)

Tadeusz Rózewicz himself wrote in 'The Survivor' (translation by Adam Czerniawski),

> 'I am twenty-four
> led to slaughter
> I survived.'

The experiences of the Polish writers, as well as the Holocaust, affected Ladd deeply, as emphatically established in his poem 'Untitled':

> There is no better condemnation
> of the words of beautiful retreat
> than the diaries of Auschwitz commandant
> Rudolf Höss—
> his love of describing trees in blossom,
> bright flowers in a window box.
> Refreshing moments. They helped him in his work.

'Untitled' has the pared-down language that could be expected of a poet like Rózewicz (Hirsch 1999). The opening two lines present a feeling of contradiction, using the word 'condemnation' for 'words of beautiful retreat'. The reader is then presented with the word 'Auschwitz'. As Ladd writes in 'Reading Primo Levi on a Warm Spring Night',

From Auschwitz
everything recoils just
sounding the name
invites death to the dance.

The name Rudolf Höss, which has been given an entire line to itself, is the name of a commandant who writes about 'pleasant' things like 'flowers in a window box'. The final line is made up of two short sentences that juxtapose the 'pleasantness' of 'refreshing moments' against the grotesque realisation of who the man was—'They helped him in his work'.

Ladd keeps the reader's thoughts occupied with images of 'beautiful retreat', 'trees in blossom', 'bright flowers', even 'Refreshing moments', before the true meaning of the words 'condemnation', 'Auschwitz' and 'his work' is realised. The poem creates an unsettling conflict within the reader, because Rudolf Höss is using symbols of beauty to help with his terrible 'work' at a concentration camp. With simplicity reminiscent of the Eastern European poets, Ladd is able to create strong emotions and powerful ideas.

Mike Ladd and future directions

Ladd has an interest, or a passion, for the human condition. He is honest and has a sense of irony that compliments his style of simplicity, without the 'stripped down ... drastic simplicity' of Rózewicz (Hirsch 1997). The result can be a wonderful human insight, as in 'Power Cut',

When the lights come back,
the computer screens
are locked on 'WAIT',
as if a God logged in,
gently kissed them,
told them how to find peace.

Ladd is also a poet who works with ideas. In 'Power Cut' he plays with the idea that computers—often a source of frustration—have found peace by 'waiting'. Indeed, he does not play much with form or words, but with ideas. Poems such as 'Natural History #6', 'Shadow Story #2 (Angela)', '2,4,6,8' and 'Coda' explore multiple or complex ideas.

In what direction Ladd takes his poetry is still uncertain, but it is hard to imagine he will stop taking an interest in the human experience.

References

Abrams, M.H. (1999) *A Glossary of Literary Terms*, 7th edn, Fort Worth, Texas: Harcourt Brace College Publishers.

Bizzaro, P. (1993) *Responding to Student Poems*. Urbana, Illinois: National Council of Teachers of English.

Brower, R.A. (1963) *The Poetry of Robert Frost: Constellations of Intention*. Oxford: Oxford University Press.

Carpenter, B. (1997) 'Wislawa Szymborska and the importance of the unimportant', *World Literature Today*, vol. 71, no. 1, pp. 9–14 [viewed 2 November 2002] Available: EBSCOhost; Academic Search Elite.

Felinghetti, L. (2000) *What is Poetry?* Berkley, California: Creative Arts Book Company.

Garnett, M. and Groff, M. (eds) (1999) *Vernacular*, vol. 1. Adelaide: Vernacular.

Hirsch, E. (1997) 'After the End of the World', *American Poetry Review*, vol. 26, no. 2, pp. 9–13 [viewed 4 November 2002] Available: EBSCOhost; Academic Search Elite.

Hirsch, E. (1999) *How to Read a Poem and Fall in Love with Poetry*. New York: A Harvest Book, Harcourt Inc.

Ladd, M. (2000) *Close to Home*. Wollongong: Five Islands Press.

Ladd, M. (2001) 'Untitled', in Garnett, M. and Groff, M. (eds), (1999) *Vernacular*, vol. 3, p. 48, Vernacular, Adelaide.

Rózewicz, T. (date unknown) *Selected Poetry*, [viewed 2 November 2002] http://www.geocites.com/Paris/6170/poetfeat2.html

Spurr, B. (1997) *Studying Poetry*. Sydney: University of Sydney.

GEOFF GOODFELLOW

Published poetry books

No Collars No Cuffs, Goodline Press, Adelaide 1986
Bow Tie & Tails, Goodline Press, Adelaide 1989
No Ticket No Start, Wakefield Press, Adelaide 1990
Triggers: Turning Experiences into Poetry, Wakefield Press, Adelaide 1992
The Sex Poems Unleashed, Goodline Press, Adelaide 1998
Semi Madness: Voices from Semaphore, Common Ground, Melbourne 2001
Love is Cruel, Common Ground, Melbourne 2001
Poems for a Dead Father, Vulgar Press, Melbourne 2002

Biographical note

Geoff Goodfellow, born in 1949, grew up in Adelaide's inner-northern suburbs with a family whose stories appear in his poems. With war veteran father John, mother Lois, and siblings Annette, Mark and Brian, he lived in a war-service group housing scheme in a street where all the houses looked the same. He left school at fifteen to work in the construction industry until a severe back injury forced him to retire in the early 1980s. It was then that Geoff began writing poetry and his life changed.

Retired from the building industry and thrust into a world of language and punctuation, Geoff went to university to challenge his preconceptions about Indigenous Australians and prove his intelligence to his children. After a year, he left to write poetry full time. His career as a poet has led him to write and read in many different and exotic locations—Cuba, Toronto and China to name but a few. He chooses to read in extraordinarily different settings, from York University in Toronto to the 'B' division at Yatala Gaol, giving meaning and life to the poetry of the working class.

Geoff continues to write and publish poetry about and for the working classes. *Poems from Semi Madness: Voices from Semaphore* and *Poems for a Dead Father* are being trialled in 2004 by SSABSA in a new unit for Stage 1 English students, 'Understanding Mental Illness'. *Poems for a Dead Father* was short-listed for the *Age* book of the year after it was launched at the 2002 Adelaide Writers' Week. In 2004 Vulgar Press will release *Geoff Goodfellow's Top Forty*, a combined book and DVD of Goodfellow's best forty performance poems from his twenty-year poetry career. Geoff Goodfellow lives in Semaphore with his daughter.

(Compiled by E.L. Benn)

Interview with Geoff Goodfellow

by E.L. Benn

E.L. Benn (ELB): Why do you write poetry?

Geoff Goodfellow (GG): I write as a way of understanding my own life and the lives of those around me. More often than not it's poetry about people that I'm having some interaction with. Often I'm only writing about a moment in time, but I do try to invest the poem with a good deal of detail, including the type of language used in a particular situation, to allow my readers and listeners to gain some broader understanding. I try to tell people's stories too, stories I find unusual, sad, tragic or funny, and I set out to try to tell them in a very compressed way.

ELB: Why poetry instead of prose?

GG: I like the idea of poetry because of its compression. And it is so transportable. A lot can be said in one and a half or two minutes and poetry allows a lot of stories to be told. I like that I can sit down for four or five hours, drafting and re-drafting, and in the end walk away with a finished product. That excites me. I couldn't bear to sit at a desk day after day after day structuring a novel. I like the thrill that comes from writing a good poem and you always know whether you have written something good or half-good.

ELB: What attracted you to poetry?

GG: I ruptured a couple of discs in my lower back in the early 1980s and I spent a lot of time in bed recovering. During that time I started to read. It happened that some of that reading material was poetry and I found it often engaged me. The more poetry I read the more I thought that perhaps writing poetry may be something that I could do myself, and I began to give it a go in about 1982.

ELB: All authors have different experiences with publication—how did publication happen in your case?

GG: I started attending Friendly Street Poets in 1982 and soon became aware that if I wanted to get published I would need to change my style. I was greatly encouraged by Graham Rowlands and began to read widely and experiment with writing free verse. My first free verse published poem was titled 'June in Hurtle Square' and appeared in *Ash Magazine* in the Spring Edition of 1983. Many others followed in various magazines and journals, and in 1986 at Adelaide Writers' Week my first collection *No Collars No Cuffs* (Friendly Street Poets) was launched. This book is now in its ninth printing.

ELB: Do you believe poetry can change the way classes are perceived?

GG: I think in some cases my poetry has been able to inform the middle class in respect to issues and topics and attitudes concerning working class life and the struggles working class people often encounter. I don't think poetry can change the world, but I do think it can be a catalyst for change. Publishing poetry does give me hope.

ELB: What do you want to achieve through your poetry?

GG: I want to be able to communicate ideas, attitudes, scenarios, moods, etc., in a compact style and in a way that allows poetry to be understood by ordinary people. I want to attract general readers as my audience. I think that poetry can educate and inform, and I'd like to think my writing assists people's understanding. I also want to be able to derive an income through my writing and I'd like to live off the proceeds without having to live too close to the poverty line.

ELB: As a poet, who has had the greatest influence on your work?

GG: Reading Charles Bukowski in the mid 80s made me realise the working class, the under-class, the marginalised, drunks, misfits, drug addicts, thieves, bash merchants, etc., in fact so many of the people I'd grown up around and with, were subjects for poetry. He showed me that the language people used, the idioms, slang, the colloquial rhythms of natural speech, were all food for the page. He proved the use of informal language allowed poets to convey particular sub-cultures and was quite valid, indeed necessary, for a certain type of poetry. This gave me some freedom.

ELB: How do you write poetry? Do you sit down at the same time each day to write or do you wait for inspiration to hit you?

GG: I write poetry when it arrives. I'll know when it is knocking on the door ... sometimes it may be mid-morning, sometimes early afternoon. Invariably for me though, it seems to occur in the early hours of the morning, when sleep has evaded me. If I know it is there, I'll get up, go downstairs to where I normally write, and begin with a biro to scratch out a first draft. Usually I'll get onto the electric typewriter by about draft four. By draft seven or eight I'm usually content, although it varies. Sometimes I'll be happy by the sixth draft, yet with others I may have to continue to play around. But they will generally be minor or pedantic changes after six drafts. When I'm happy that the poem is complete, I'll usually then type the finished copy into my computer to store it.

I'm not structured enough to sit down on a daily basis to write ... I know people who do it, but I can't say I've ever been impressed by their end results. That sort of structure may work well for the writing of prose, but poetry, it's a different animal.

ELB: Your anti-war sentiments are a common theme in your latest publication—could you tell us why?

GG: I grew up in the northern suburbs of Adelaide in a War Service Group Scheme house in the 1950s. Everyone's father had fought in the Second World War. I saw firsthand the results of what is commonly referred to now as Post Traumatic Stress Disorder. I lived in a street where adult nightmares were commonplace and bizarre behaviour patterns were the order of the day. This was re-enforced when men who wore RSL badges on their lapels taught me at school. I too was often subjected to their rage reactions and unpredictable tempers, and then their absences for periods of hospitalisation when I would sometimes see them in the Repatriation General Hospital in the Psych Ward when I was visiting my own father.

And we were being told that we won the war. I think there is a paucity of information surrounding this issue and my latest book *Poems for a Dead Father* (Vulgar Press, 2002) sets out to address this and allow a rethink of whether going off to a war is in fact a 'boy's own adventure'.

ELB: You are often invited to read in schools. Does this affect the way you write?

GG: I don't set about writing poems to take them into schools. I write because I have something to say. It happens though that a good many poems I do write will work well in schools. It is equally true though that there are poems that I've written and published that I'd never read in schools.

A lot of year 11 and year 12 students choose to study my work, especially in School Assessed Subjects. One of my old favourite poems 'Don't Call Me Lad' from *Bow Tie & Tails* has often been one of the most highly studied poems for end of year exams, according to the moderators. I think the general reader can grasp the majority of the poems I write and students don't feel excluded from gaining an understanding of my work. A written response from a student at Salisbury High School following a recent performance stated: 'you wouldn't think that an older man like him would know how it feels in this part of someone's life, yet he shows it so well in his poem.' (referring to 'Don't Look So Glum'). Fiona, another Salisbury student said: 'His performance has given me a new point of view on poetry and I am probably going to read one of his books now.' But I don't just appear at northern suburbs schools, you'll find me at St Ignatius College, St Peter's Girls, St Mary's, Concordia College, and a diverse range of other private and state schools and colleges. Most schools that believe in giving students a liberal education wouldn't be too frightened to invite me in.

ELB: How and why is poetry relevant to Australian society?

GG: Quite simply, people want to see themselves reflected. Poetry is obviously not the most popular medium but it is a vehicle whereby we are able to validate and give dignity to people's lives by putting them on the page. Sit at a coffee shop and watch the passing parade of people. Many of them will be looking into the plate glass windows and hoping to see their own reflections. I want to reflect them on the page and poetry allows me to do this.

Talking to Geoff Goodfellow
by Maria Kiland

I went into a second-hand bookshop downtown and asked for South Australian poets. While the man running the shop took time to find his glasses, and the ladder from the corner, I took time to have a look around the shop. If it hadn't been for the bell that rang as I entered the door, I would've thought I was in this man's living room. It was spacious, but very personalised. There was a sofa and a table in the middle of the room and a rug in front of the counter. There were some food leftovers on the table. I had obviously interrupted his lunch but he didn't seem to care. On the contrary, he seemed really excited about this person visiting his living room in the middle of the day, sincerely interested in poetry. He was already on the top of the ladder and was handing me various books. The walls were covered with bookshelves, and as I saw the yellowish, dusty and worn out books, I understood where the funny smell came from. Standing there with a pile of books in my arms, I reminded him that I was looking for a *South* Australian writer. As I suspected, he had forgotten that. 'Ah, yes,' he said and got down from the ladder. He was now on his knees and picked out some books from the bottom shelf. 'Geoff Goodfellow is a name I come across all the time. He's from around here. There's a great circulation in here of his books.' Sounded interesting. A poet with a big audience. The bookseller smiled with a little sneer: 'It's probably because of the ladies who want to be so *poetic* all of a sudden and then get offended by his poetry, and then return them to me and buy some Shakespeare instead.' 'Offended?' I asked, ignoring his condescending tone. 'Yes, he's a very straightforward person. Good poetry, though.' I couldn't get a better recommendation. I bought two of his collections and started to read on the bus home. I liked what I read.

Geoff Goodfellow met us at an Italian café in the Central Market, wearing a lime green t-shirt with 'PERVERT' written across his chest (the trademark brand of the Melbourne based clothing manufacturer who sponsor his clothing needs). Talking about his own poetry career, he quickly distanced himself from the middle and upper class poets writing for the educated. Goodfellow sees himself as a 'working class poet' writing *from* the working class, *for* the working class, but is aware that his writing is also read and understood by the 'more sophisticated' class, which he thinks is good. His goal is to reach out to everybody, not only to one group of people. 'What is the point of that,' he laughs, 'when you have the chance to meet the whole field?'

I enjoyed talking to Goodfellow as I understood that he is a very open and honest man. He doesn't give himself any bounds on revealing his own life. As he told us with a grin: 'I have only had *one* lawsuit against me from one of my family members.' At the same time he seemed a little reserved, humble even. I was a bit disappointed, as I didn't quite recognise the man behind the poems that I had read over the last few weeks. Where were all the 'beatings', the 'slashed lips', the 'drugs' etc.? Maybe he wasn't sure if we were really interested in his work, or if it was 'just another assignment' due after the weekend. A little blasé maybe? As the conversation developed though, his body language got more and more vibrant, and it seemed like he didn't care about who we were anymore. He just loves to talk about his life and poetry anyhow, hoping to reach out. He even gave us a little performance reading one of his latest poems. He stood up from his chair and bent over the table looking us firmly in the eyes. I discreetly took a firmer grip around the tea and coffee pots on the table, not quite knowing if I was a bit scared of this man spitting out words, or if my jaw dropped at the astonishing performance. I decided to let the poet speak, and I listened. He reached out.

Reading the poems

by E.L. Benn and Maria Kiland

Geoff Goodfellow's poems pack such a punch that the effect lasts for days. He is by various opinions, including his own, a working class poet. With deceptively simple words and yet sophisticated and down-to-earth language, Goodfellow focuses on the daily issues faced by Australia's working classes. He once said 'the sort of power that I give people is the verbal power, the power to use language'. This language, together with his working class themes is exemplified in this paper.

The analysis focuses on five poems, taken from two separate collections. These poems are representative of his poetic style and draw on his experiences and beliefs as well as working class themes.

The first poem, 'Just a Twist', is from *Bow Tie & Tails*, his second collection, which was published in 1989. The poem is about a man's sexual thoughts and reflections when he meets a woman who nurses him while he is sick. The poem is written in the first person. There is not much hidden meaning in the poem—it is a description of a man's perception of meeting an attractive woman. Throughout the poem the male character compares lemons in the fruit bowl with the nurse's breasts. Goodfellow is straightforward as he writes about the woman's breasts saying: 'I want to squeeze them' and he continues by writing that the end protrusion of the actual lemons in the fruit bowl resembles her nipples, and again he wants to 'squeeze and suck them'.

At the same time, Goodfellow plays with words in 'Just a Twist' to hide the sexual undertone. The main character in the poem has a cold and the female character 'recommends i [sic] squeeze a lemon and have it hot—in bed'.

'Just a Twist' is written in a free form. There is no consistent rhyme, but there are examples of alliteration, such as: 'she suggests my cold sounds worse', and 'when we whisper …' There is also rhythm in the way the poet breaks his poem with his short lines in between: 'but so close', 'of her breasts', and 'hot and sweet' are a few of many examples. These lines all consist of three syllables and confer a specific rhythm to the poem. While the poem is written in free verse, certain stylistic features ensure its success.

The very beginning of the poem explains what Goodfellow wants to describe. 'We're miles apart when she comes to me but so close …' The narrator is obviously attracted to the woman who takes care of him. He may even be in love with her, but as the first line says, they are 'miles apart'. The last stanza reads:

> i settle for black coffee
> hot & sweet
> with a twist of lemon
> discard the two portions
> & wait for sweetness
> tomorrow.

The use of the word 'settle' shows how he leans back and is not pushy anymore. The word 'discard' is formal, and chosen with the intent to hide the disappointment and bitterness having to let go, and also makes it seem like his decision. The last two lines, though, are positive and reveal a sense of humour: '...& wait for sweetness/ tomorrow'. Even though the male character has realised that his thoughts are not reciprocated by his nursing female friend, he looks forward to her care the next day.

'Poem for Annie', published in *Bow Tie & Tails*, describes a woman who has been badly treated by several of her partners but still exposes herself to the same danger repeatedly. This is a taboo theme in some circles, similar to the sex theme in 'Just a Twist', and Goodfellow is not afraid to write about it.

Once again, Goodfellow uses straightforward language: 'they beat her badly', 'he jammed a glass into her face, smashed two teeth & slashed her lower lip', and 'he blackened y' eye six months ago'. The way Goodfellow describes the female character stereotypes working class women. She is a single mother working as a secretary with many 'poor, poor misunderstood...' relationships in her past. Goodfellow is not afraid to say what he feels about this by saying 'it isn't just her hair that's fair'.

Another poem exemplifying Goodfellow's working class themes is 'Epitaph for Robbie'. Robbie is a young boy addicted to drugs. The poem starts with: 'Robbie lost his head inside a plastic bag of glue & couldn't find it'. As the poem continues, he experiments with marijuana, runs out of money and his health deteriorates. Robbie tries speed, and after a life spent using drugs, he ends up 'stretched out on his back ... his body's cold he won't be back'.

What makes this poem special is that the serious theme is hidden behind the fixed form genre as Goodfellow uses rhyme to tell Robbie's story. This might be to protect the reader, or himself, from the sad content. It may also be, as modern poetry often looks upon rhyming as a cliché, that Goodfellow tries to create a nonchalant mood as a contrast to the story about Robbie. This drives home the theme, leaving the reader with a poem about substance abuse and the effect it had on a young boy's life.

Poems for a Dead Father was launched in 2002, quite some time after *Bow Tie & Tails* was published in 1989, but Goodfellow's working class themes are just as strong. In his latest book, he looks at workers from a different perspective—from that of his childhood and his father. *Poems for a Dead Father* is a journey of pain, discovery and the effects of alcohol and war.

'A Mirror to My Childhood' is one such poem. It starts by defining the Vietnam War and how it affected people's lives afterwards, particularly children. Goodfellow uses words like 'violence', 'terror' and 'hopelessness' to evoke a powerful picture of his childhood and its similarities to the one described in Bill Bennett's docodrama *A Street to Die*. Throughout the poem Goodfellow uses repetition to paint a picture of the long-lasting effects of war. In particular the words 'only happened' are used to convey his disbelief as well as to move from one point to the next. Throughout the poem Goodfellow uses the word 'and' ('&') as a thread linking ideas and decades in the poem. It is also used to rhythmically tell a violent and sad story.

To ensure the poem remains realistic, Goodfellow also incorporates direct speech and slang. The direct speech serves to ensure his father's voice is heard, and also to add authenticity to the poem. The slang gives the poem a distinctly Australian flavour and distances his father's experiences from those of other servicemen such as the British or Germans. Evocative slang includes 'smash'n'grab' and 'buckling for a heartstarter'. Not only is this Australian slang, but unique to the 1950s era too. Goodfellow combines these elements to produce a poem about his father's experiences with war as well as his own beliefs.

'Miles Away' is another of Goodfellow's many poems dealing with war and violence. This poem is written from the detached view of a teenage Goodfellow, who is aware of the conflict in Vietnam but ignorant of many other international aspects including geography. However, there is one aspect of life the adolescent Goodfellow is not ignorant of: the effect of a war not only on his father but also on all the men he knows. Goodfellow goes on to construct the poem as a detailed list of the ruined lives of these men. He tells these stories using the effective technique of repetition. The repetition at the start of each stanza '& I thought about the madness' places war and its destructiveness on a par, and also contributes to the poem stylistically as a rhythmic pattern.

Many of Goodfellow's poems deal with his life and the people around him. He often places their lives in a broader context, making reference to Australia's social and political climate. He also focuses on working class issues and uses humour, slang and alliteration to ensure his poems have an impact on readers. With his poetry Goodfellow continues to shock and amaze his critics and fans alike.

References

Aristotle *Aristotle's Poetics*. Translated by S H Butcher.

Bogen, N. (1994) *How to Write Poetry*. New York: Macmillan.

Goodfellow, G. (1989) *Bow Tie & Tails*. Adelaide: Wakefield Press.

Goodfellow, G. (2001) *Poems for a Dead Father*. Adelaide: Vulgar Press.

Hirsch, E. (1999) *How to Read a Poem and Fall in Love with Poetry*. New York: A Harvest Book, Harcourt Inc.

James, B. (2002) *Poems for a Dead Father: Study Guide*. Adelaide: Vulgar Press.

Jones, R. (1986) *Studying Poetry: An Introduction*. London: Edward Arnold Ltd.

Morisson, M. (1997) *Poetry and the Public Sphere*, from the Conference on Contemporary Poetry April 24–27, 1997, http://english.rutgers.edu/morisson.htm,[viewed 2 September 2003].

Parrott, E. (1990) *How to Be Well-versed in Poetry*. UK: Viking Press.

Strachan, J. and Terry, R. (2001) *Poetry: An Introduction*. New York: New York University Press.

Warburton, A. (2003) 'Geoff Goodfellow: poet for hire' in *ABC Tasmania*, 8 May 2003.

GRAHAM ROWLANDS

Published poetry books

Stares and Statues, Makar Press, Brisbane 1972
Replacing Mirrors, Saturday Centre, Sydney 1975
Poems Political, Makar Press, Brisbane 1976 (with G. Pitt and L. Walker)
Adam Scolds, Cochon International, Townsville 1976
Dial-a-Poem, Friendly Street Poets, Adelaide 1982
On the Menu, Friendly Street Poets, Adelaide 1988
Selected Poems, Wakefield Press, Adelaide 1992

Biographical note

Graham Rowlands was born in Brisbane in 1947 and moved to Adelaide in 1971. He was educated at the University of Queensland and Flinders University. He has worked as a lecturer in literature, a freelance journalist and an educational editor, and is now teaching creative writing part-time at Flinders University. As well as editing two anthologies of South Australian poetry, he has published seven poetry collections and several hundred uncollected poems. For many years he reviewed poetry for *Overland*. Rowlands was awarded the Barbara Hanrahan Fellowship in 2002, and in 2003 he won the Satura Prize for his poem 'Down on the Ground'.

(Compiled by Liam Monkhouse)

Interview with Graham Rowlands

by Iain Spalding and Liam Monkhouse

Iain Spalding (IS): How did you get started in writing poetry? Do you have any advice for budding poets?

Graham Rowlands (GR): I got interested in poetry when I was at secondary school. There was really no poetry taken seriously in the home, there weren't many books there at all. My interest in poetry was a product of education, so three cheers for education. There are some good things to be said for education, a lot of bad things, but some good things too. The main advice for poets, or any writers, is that there are always a hell of a lot of poets and writers who don't actually write poetry or write anything, and I've met quite a few of these people. You have to get down to write. You have to write your work and then you have to get it published. With poetry it's comparatively easy because you can get published in magazines and newspapers. I mean, you can have an individual poem published in a magazine, so you've got a publication up. I feel sorry for novelists because you can toil away for five years and then you can get the thing rejected by about twelve people, after you've been through agencies, *if* you can get any agents to accept you. That must be extremely disillusioning. From the point of view of poetry it's easy because you can get into magazines and newspapers. I have listed in *Southern Write*, the South Australian Writers' Centre newsletter, what I have published over the past month. The big difficulty with poetry is that hardly anybody wants to read it, of course. And in Australia the main publishers are no longer publishing collections of poetry.

Liam Monkhouse (LM): What is your creative process for your writing? Do you have any particular conditions that you find produce good writing?

GR: I don't write anything unless I've got an idea. Some people start in the morning it's 9 am, they sit down at the table and they start doodling, or they write letters to people, whatever, and hope that a poem will come out of it. Well fine, if that works for them it's terrific. But if I don't get an idea for a poem for two months, I just don't write a poem in two months. When I get an idea for a poem I want to write it as soon as possible, preferably I'd write it straightaway. And if I can't do that, then in a few hours, certainly no more than a day or two.

IS: Where do your ideas come from?

GR: I think the answer to that is as diverse as the poems that I've written. I'm very interested in history and politics, and, increasingly, I've written about politics and history because I'm able to do it. I have worked out ways of doing it. I didn't have that ability when I first started writing. So I keep up with my current affairs—I listen to AM and PM. I always invent something to do around the place. While those programs are always quite informative, I like informing myself on as much history as possible, so I'm interested in these things anyway, and I know that they're going to be a source of poetry. But I also like writing poems about daffodils [Graham points to a daffodil on his mantle]. I'm crazy about daffodils. I like the colour yellow. I come from Brisbane and the only daffodils you can get there are very high up in the Great Dividing Range, and the stuff that's imported. Bulb flowers are just absolutely wonderful as far as I'm concerned. Halfway through every winter in Adelaide you get all these bulb flowers coming up. I've written about a dozen poems about daffodils. They're not just totally descriptive poems. Some of them are, but I work daffodils into saying other things and expressing other emotions quite often. So if I can handle politics and history, and if I can handle daffodils, I'm reasonably happy with the diversity of what I do.

LM: Can you tell us about your poem 'Down on the ground'—how were you inspired to write that poem?

GR: I simply heard a report. I don't remember whether it was AM or PM, it was one of those two, and the guy was explaining his own experience. He said himself that he was down on the ground after hearing the first of the twenty-one-gun salute. In fact, every time he'd heard guns like that going off, he knew he'd be down on the ground again. He sort of half thought that he might not be, but always is because of shell shock. The poem came through to me in the media. Then I had to work out how to actually do it. And so the character in the poem could be me because I heard it and could have just written a poem about what I heard. But I gave the speaker a personality. The personality is a little less informed probably than I would be on the subject, and he's working out what happened, and he's trying to remember things. He doesn't really understand the implications of what he's saying, he uses double meanings all the way through the poem. It's a dramatic monologue in that sense.

IS: In relation to your poem 'Down on the ground', which won the Satura Prize in 2003, I would like to ask what it was like meeting Mike Rann, the Premier, who presented you with the award.

GR: I didn't actually meet him. I mean he gave me the award. He shook my hand. There was a cheque in the envelope and I don't quite know what he was expecting me to do. But I think the convener and I had agreed that I would not be giving a speech because the Premier had given a reasonably lengthy speech about New Zealand poetry, which he knows quite a bit about, and he got some information from his department about South Australian poetry. So he had already spoken for a while and quite effectively. There really was no need for the poet who won the Satura Prize to give a talk. I asked the convener about this when he told me a couple of days in advance that I had won the prize—I said, well, but I'd like to do something, otherwise I just get the envelope, shake hands with the Premier, and sit down in my seat again. What's wrong with reading my poem? And the convener said that'd be OK. It's not a particularly long poem. So I did that.

IS: Had the Premier read your poem or was he just the award giver?

GR: Oh no, he chose it. It was quite obvious he had chosen it. He talked about a number of other poems in that particular Friendly Street Reader and he talked about some very impressive poems, but he thought that in that particular Reader my poem was the best.

IS: Would having met him change your vote in the next election?

GR: Oh well, it wouldn't change because I vote Labor anyway. But he picked up on something that I had said when I won the Barbara Hanrahan Fellowship. The two Premiers were there, Rob Kerin and Mike Rann, and I did my usual assault on the *Advertiser* because the *Advertiser* doesn't publish a poem a week, unlike the *Weekend Australian*, the *Canberra Times, The Age*, and sometimes the *Sydney Morning Herald*. The *Advertiser* just won't come at it at all. Mike Rann knew that I had very strong thoughts on the issue of getting a quality poem a week into the *Advertiser*. He mentioned that in his talk, and of course the whole audience would have agreed that that should be the case, and he knew they would agree. He was electioneering, but also he was saying what the case is as well.

LM: What makes good poetry, from your perspective?

GR: It varies, I think. I do quite a lot of poetry editing and I don't try to impose my particular interests in poetry on anyone I edit. If I'm editing someone who writes political poetry, like Erica Jolly whose book was launched last night, I am quite keen to select her best poems—we wouldn't want her to turn around and write comic verse or just descriptions of shells on the beach, or something like that. On the other hand, I edit for some people who do that sort of thing. So what I'm looking for in descriptions of shells on a beach, I'm looking for vivid, visual images. If the poet wants to write a descriptive poem, it's my job to make sure that it's a well-written descriptive poem. In terms of my own poetry, when I write a poem about daffodils I'm aiming to produce vivid, visual imagery, written in suitable line lengths, so there's a good rhythm in the poem but also something that is certainly visually impressive. But when I'm writing a political poem, I use the techniques of Shakespearean rhetoric. You can find all the techniques for rhetoric that you ever need to know in Shakespeare's plays. I've developed political poetry now through the influence of performing poetry a fair bit, going back a lot of years at Friendly Street, but also watching the videos of Shakespeare. I claim to do this regularly—it's fairly time-consuming to watch a three hour video, but I do it from time to time.

IS: How does the word 'fame' sit with you?

GR: [Graham shakes his head vigorously] Oh, it used to be what I wanted to achieve and obviously that's a preposterous thing to be aiming for, it's farcical. If you're aiming for that at the age of twenty, I think it's OK. If you want fame at my age, you're a fool. I mean you should just concentrate on writing the best poems you possibly can, and publish them as widely as possible. I said some rather embarrassing things about fame when I was younger. Yes, well, it's all there, you know. You can't retract it, it's in print, but I don't feel like that anymore.

IS: How do you feel about being one of South Australia's favourite, if I can say, poetic sons? How does that sit with you?

GR: I've written most of my poems in Adelaide. I come from Queensland and I wrote for several years in Brisbane, before I came here. So there have been two locations. Sometimes I look at my Queensland poems and wonder how different they are from my South Australian poems. But I think the only difference is that I've developed new techniques in my writing. I may have done so in Brisbane, I don't know. You can't really know something like that. Now as for the states' rivalry sort of thing, Rick Hosking was quite appalled at the talk I gave to students at Flinders University. The general topic was South Australian writing, and I was brought in to talk about South Australian poetry. I insisted that most of my poems weren't South Australian, and he was astonished because I have been here since 1971, and I was standing up in front of his students and saying that my poems weren't South Australian. He asked me to defend what I was saying. I said well look, if I write a poem about my wife, it's a poem about relationships, as far as I'm concerned. It's not a poem about South Australia. I can tell where she was born and went to school, and what she's been doing with her life—that's South Australian. But surely, if you write about your wife the key thing you're doing is some sort of psychological coverage of a relationship. A South Australian poem to me is one that's got a place name in it. I've got a poem, 'Stingray, Whyalla'. That's a South Australian poem. I wouldn't have written a poem about the stingray if I hadn't been in Whyalla at that particular time and seen a boy catch a stingray on the jetty. It's a descriptive poem and a sort of semi-lyrical type of poem. To me that's what South Australian poetry is. It's something that is identifiable with South Australia. I don't just mean identifiable in a country town context. If you wrote a poem about Hindley Street, that would be quite definitely a South Australian poem.

LM: Considering you've had a lot of work published over the years, what's your current ambition?

GR: I haven't published a collection of poems since 1992. The reason is that I am not all that keen on the publication of collections of poetry anymore. The situation has changed enormously since I started writing. I think you need to publish poems in magazines and newspapers, then you need to bring out your first collection of poetry, and then I think you should make that your only collection of poetry. You should continue publishing in magazines and newspapers because there is an audience there, otherwise the newspapers wouldn't run them and the magazines wouldn't exist. After quite a number of years you should bring out your collected poems, so that you have two books. Your first collection, well really, your only collection, and then your collected poems, which would be selected or collected, the best of the poems that you have put in the magazines and newspapers. The major publishers in Australia no longer publish poetry collections. There isn't sufficient audience for them, and I'm not at all sure that it's worth bringing out a collection of poems if you're going to have three hundred readers. You're going to have more readers in magazines and newspapers, and so that's where I put most of my efforts and that's where I have chalked up this sort of massive number of publications. I have had nearly nine hundred individual poems in magazines and newspapers since I started writing poetry. I get a lot of satisfaction out of doing that. The disadvantage is that nobody is really seeing a group of your poems or your poems overall. So the answer to that is to bring out a collected poems, which is what I intend to do, seeing that I have already done a selected. It would be about three hundred pages and, in my view, the most representative poems, and I'll sit on that. After that comes out I'll continue to publish in magazines and newspapers, but the collected poems is the thing that's of importance. I mean, no one wants to read nine hundred poems of mine. It's just absurd to think that anyone would, and how would you market such a thing anyway? Posthumously somebody might want them all together or something, but I really couldn't care less. I want to produce the best poems that I've written across the widest range, and I think that is marketable. But it's marketable in different contexts. I would want to send it to all the people, the major publishers that still publish anthologies of poetry. This collected poems of mine is intended to be a book that lasts for quite a long time. And it would be, even ten years after it was published, the same that I'd been handing to people, either selling or giving away or whatever. I think there's a fair amount of vanity in bringing out collections of poetry. I'm not sure that too many of us really need poetry collections.

IS: How does performing live make you feel?

GR: Nervous before I do it, but once I start I'm OK.

IS: How do you prepare for performing live?

GR: First of all, I try to choose poems that work in public. I very rarely read a descriptive poem or a lyric poem, or even an elegy for that matter, although elegies can work quite well. I try to read either comic poems or satires. And I want to get the audience laughing or gasping, if possible.

IS: Do you find that's the best way to get the audience involved in the poem?

GR: Yes. In live performance, if you read a poem that's packed with intricate visual imagery, the audience is not going to be able to visualise that very well because the audience will be looking at the performer, and this is not assisting in any way with the visual imagery in the poem. It's better to read such poems from the page because when you read on the page, you can unpack the imagery and think about the visual side of it—which is not the same thing as the black and white page. It's what you imagine from the descriptions on the page.

LS: In regards to poetry and education, what's your opinion on the emphasis on classical poetry, particularly at the high school level where it's still very prominent? There's not much modern poetry, or contemporary poetry studied. What do the classics have to offer modern poets?

GR: You're more in touch with that than I am, but I used to do poetry performances in schools, and certainly in some cases the students were very familiar with contemporary poetry. I mean Bruce Daw was one of the most well-known poets for most of the students. Wilfred Owen obviously isn't contemporary, but students did so much Wilfred Owen, I've heard stories about it, that they just didn't want another Wilfred Owen poem. If the emphasis on classical poetry has returned, or was always there, I think it's better to start with what people know. I think contemporary poetry is a very good way to get people interested in poetry. I'm all in favour of the historical study of poetry, but I wouldn't start with way back poetry initially, because it is likely to turn people off.

LM: Do you have any reflections on your role in the creative workshop that you do at Flinders University?

GR: The students are extremely demanding these days and it's very hard work. I took three classes this year. That was the first time I had taken three. I had taken two and had taken one before and I was hourly paid. Another lecturer (who was also taking three classes) and I, both maintained that we were working full time. And I was stacking up the newspapers. I wasn't reading my magazines that were coming in, and I wrote two poems in four months. That's the four working months of first semester. I wrote two poems in four months and I was really getting quite concerned about it. That's a shocking performance rate as far as I'm concerned. Fortunately, I have now started to write quite a lot of poetry, but I had to be about six weeks out from the marks meeting to really start a burst of poetry. That's not an answer in terms of how the students find it, but I just find contemporary students incredibly full on. They want to get the highest grade imaginable and they're willing to work hard to achieve that, they're prepared to contribute in the session, and they're prepared to meet the deadline requirements. Students tend to perform well in 'Craft and Culture', which is the subject I take, to get the grades. In order to do that they do a lot of very good writing. What bothers me is that not enough of the best work, the best work in the opinion of their peers and in my opinion, is being submitted for publication. It doesn't happen very much during the semester. I know it's only a short time, but it should be happening more during the semester, and it should also happen after the semester. I just fear that it isn't happening after the semester once the subject is finished and the student has got the grade. In the cases where the students have gotten high grades there must have been good writing done. The next step would be to send off the best writing, and I would like to see a lot of the names of former students cropping up in newspapers and magazines. I don't see that, and I do read quite a lot of magazines. I just wonder what happens to these people. I know we've all got to earn a living, but I wonder if they just stop writing or whether they come back to it after ten years. I really don't know, but there is this idea around that people in creative writing classes can't write, you know, they don't write anything worth reading. That's absolute rubbish. I've seen excellent work across a fairly big range of students. But for students who are oriented to universities it tends to be a closed world. So many things are laid on at university and so many achievements can be attained there, it's almost a world that's closed off. At Friendly Street I am constantly in touch with people who are submitting for publication all the time. They are performing their poems because they want an audience, and they're submitting because they are surrounded by people who keep submitting. There are references made to 'somebody's got a poem in such and such last week'; 'did you see that one by somebody?' The university students tend not to be moving in that kind of circle. A lot of people at Friendly Street have got university degrees, and a lot of people have only a little education. But it's an environment where the writing and the performing is the key thing. There are no grades, there is no qualification, there is no degree at the end of your visits to Friendly Street. And it does appear to make a difference to the behaviour of writers. At university they just tend to be happy with the grade, but at Friendly Street there is no grade, and you can't be happy with anything but a good audience response and an acceptance by an editor.

You know, I'm a bit alarmed to hear about that emphasis on classical poetry.

LM: Oh, I don't think it's an over-emphasis. It's just the fact that much classical poetry is still being taught. There's less contemporary poetry than there perhaps could be.

GR: I don't know what actually happens in schools, but the feedback I get is quite mixed. And certainly some teachers seem to put quite an emphasis on contemporary poetry and they have contemporary poets out performing for them.

LM: I remember that in year 12 my teacher was quite good because there was a lot of contemporary poetry studied, but I know perhaps in different circumstances that there would be more of an emphasis on classical and more traditional forms.

IS: For me it was a lot of Shakespeare to be honest. That's what the main focus was on. Just Shakespeare.

LM: And things like *Beowulf*. But there was a balance. There was some really good contemporary poetry. I can't recall the names, just some free verse and more contemporary sort of styles, forms. But definitely the Shakespeare elements were there.

GR: That's fine as far as I'm concerned, because I think that Shakespeare is completely contemporary.

LM: That's one of the questions I had. What can they offer from a contemporary perspective? What can you take from the classics?

GR: If it's Shakespeare, it's completely contemporary because I use quite a lot of the rhetorical side of the language in my performance poetry, my political poetry, my satires and my dramatic monologues. I quote often—nothing will come of nothing. Never, never, never, never, never! To be or not to be. Tomorrow and tomorrow and tomorrow. I am always tinkering with word structures like that, sometimes actually using the Shakespeare, and sometimes just imitating the same kind of sound pattern. And that absolutely exquisite line—*Richard III* hasn't got very good visual imagery in it and the language isn't terribly distinguished either in a rhetorical sense—but there's that just astonishing line and a half, 'I myself find in myself no pity to myself'. The whole play is worth having for that one and a half lines. Just think of it. 'I myself find in myself no pity to myself'. Three 'myselfs' in one sentence. I use a lot of repetition in my poetry, and that's influenced by Shakespeare and by the fact that when you're reading to an audience, you have to have the audience understand what you're saying. There is absolutely no point in reading a totally obscure poem if nobody can follow it. Repetition, obviously the original reason for rhyme, was so that people could remember it, get a grasp of it, and have no difficulty understanding what the poet means. But I didn't do that kind of stuff for about the first ten years that I was writing poetry. It was more using visual imagery, and there was a lot more lyrical stuff because I really didn't know how to write political poetry. I didn't know how to write dramatic monologues or satires, but over the past fifteen years I've been doing more and more of that. And that's the stuff that works in performance and I very much enjoy performing it.

Talking to Graham Rowlands

by Liam Monkhouse

Hurrying from the hectic pace of Unley Road I was glad to enter the relative calm of Graham Rowlands's leafy suburban street. He has chosen an ideal location for writing poetry, and recalling writing in a similar environment I remembered the drifting travelling mindspace it tends to produce.

Iain and I made our way through Graham's impressive garden and we were greeted by the man himself at the door. He was very welcoming and polite. Settling into our seats I was struck by one of the most comprehensive collections of classical and contemporary literature I've seen in recent years. Iain set up the camera while we all chatted informally, and eventually the interview got under way.

Graham seemed to be an interesting and sincere person and poet, and was enthusiastic in answering all of our questions. I had made a note to discuss the role of classical literature in school curriculum. This was a question that interested Graham greatly considering his teaching role at Flinders University and, personally, I agreed with his point that a balance between contemporary works and the classics is necessary to maintain student interest. It quickly became apparent that Graham is a poet's poet who values the human exchanges poetry ideally generates. His modesty is reflected in the way he dismissed 'fame', preferring instead to emphasise the creative nature of poetry.

Considering myself a poet too, I enjoyed talking to Graham and feel that his thoughts have added to my own perception of contemporary poetry. It was interesting to be able to put a face to the writer of the words I had read previously, and the extensive number of works he has published encouraged me to pursue my poetry writing further, with the hope that one day I'll be able to produce a piece of collected works such as Graham has done recently.

Reading the poems

by Clay Hunter

There was a review written after the publication of Graham Rowlands's *Selected Poems* which suggested that his work had reached a plateau, that the work he was producing was neither better nor worse than the work he had produced in the past. Invariably, however, nobody produces a collection of selected poems that represent the scope of good and bad—people select their best poems, so all would, within reason, be similarly good works. It should be taken into consideration that a poet cannot produce over 800 published works without constantly evolving within their art. There are reasons why Rowlands is a premier poet of South Australia—such as his political poetry, his dramatic monologues, his vivid visual imagery, and his ability to 'grab' a concept that most people struggle to put to mouth, and explain it in verse. This paper will explore Rowlands's work with the dramatic monologue, and the way it has evolved over a number of years, by discussing three of his dramatic monologues from different writing periods.

Hirsch (1999) describes a monologue as a single person speaking alone, with or without an audience. A dramatic monologue involves an imaginary or historical figure speaking to another imaginary or historical figure. The speaker in a dramatic monologue is therefore not going to be the author of the piece, because they are neither imaginary nor yet historical. Robert Browning's 'My Last Duchess' and Alfred Lord Tennyson's 'Ulysses' are excellent examples of dramatic monologue. Dramatic monologue is a first person fiction in verse. The poet is not the speaker, therefore it is fiction, the speaker speaks in the 'I' therefore it is first person, and whether free verse, sonnet, rhyming couplets or lyrical, it is most certainly poetic. In this form the poet assumes the mantle of his subject, and through imitation, shows the reader how that subject thinks, feels and works.

'Bulldozer Driver' was featured in an older collection that Rowlands published in 1988, called *On the Menu*. This was Rowlands's sixth collection of seven he has produced to this date. His eighth will be his *Collected Poems*, which is due for publication in the very near future. The poem sees Rowlands taking on the voice of the bulldozer driver as he speaks to a professor, presumably of an earth science or archaeological background, given the subject matter.

Rowlands shows the audience that he is talking as the bulldozer driver in the opening line, and immediately after that he creates the sensation of the one-sided conversation—the reader knows there are two sides, but only hears one:

> Look, I only drive the bloody dozer.
> It's 4,500 years old. So what, Prof?

It would not be enough in a dramatic monologue to just assume the voice of another, without assuming their characteristics also. In this instance those characteristics include the colloquial language of the bulldozer driver, who is outwardly rude to the professor because he is trying to stop him doing his job. The poem itself is written in free verse—no rhyme or meter to stand by. However, the length of each line and the way the poem flows are indications of the rhythm and speed of the action—it is fast paced, an argument, with short sharp bursts from the character that is heard:

> What's 4,500 bloody years? That rock
> over there's as old as the earth—
> it is the bloody earth & yer not

The pause suggests that the bulldozer driver has realised he has presented a good argument and should back up the previous statement. The speed of the language and thought that transpires within the poem makes the dramatic monologue realistic. The reader learns more about the driver as the poem progresses; he is rude, he doesn't think much of those with an education, he doesn't see reason in preservation, and everything relates back to sport. He is not so much arguing with the professor, as he is responding to a stereotype:

> Tell ya what I'll do when she goes down.
> Find yer mate Buddha in the top branches
> & I'll turn bloody Buddhist. Fair dinkum.
> It'll only take a few more beers. Yeah.

The driver has stereotyped the professor because he is obviously an educated conservationist, and therefore a greenie, hippie etc. The monologue finishes with a final reference to sport through the well-known cricketing call, 'Howzzzat?'

'Benjamin Guggenheim on the Titanic' appears in *Fluorescent Voices: Friendly Street Poetry Reader 21*, which came out in 1997. In this poem the lines are longer and the timing is deliberate—it is a slow wound-out time, not the fast paced one-sided argument from the previous piece. The poem presents the musings of one man as he is about to go down with a sinking ship. In a slow and deliberate format Rowlands spells out what is happening to his character. As with the heated interaction in 'Bulldozer Driver', the reader can feel the pace of this piece—it is a slow prolonged effect, the syllabic pattern of the poetry is almost like the slow rocking of the waves beneath a boat, and this may or may not be by design. Throughout the poem there are scattered references to 'up and down', the motion of the water, but also a heightened sense of the downward motion the subject is feeling, a gradual sinking. This is the thought process the reader is supposed to go through, albeit more subconsciously than spelled out, because the poet wants the reader to visualise what the subject is experiencing—it is the major tenet of all creative writing, 'Show, don't tell'.

The final line is different from the rest of the poem because it consists of three very short, fragmented sentences:

> The cuff links. The last button. Now the bow tie.

The final thing always done before presenting oneself is to straighten up the bow tie, so it is fitting as the final action of the poem. The fragmentation is more interesting, because it closely follows the action of gasping for breath as the water rushes into the ship. Looking at the subject, one can get a sense of the time and the character in question—by his own admittance he was not always a good man. Tugging on the heartstrings of the audience however is the slow deliberate way in which the character is accepting his fate—he is resigned to it, not struggling, his own metaphoric downward descent similar to the one the ship is going through. A thought that constantly runs through his mind is what other people think. The reader can infer that he is a socialite, a man from a well-to-do family, a man on the up and up. His final realisation is that all his money has bought him nought, all he can do is act like a gentleman to the end, and accept how he is judged. The reader is left with the feeling that in his life he did what he wanted, because he wanted, and that it was his choice to sink, rather than the 'decision' being thrust upon him.

The dramatic monologue 'Hemingway's Last Sentence' was

published recently in 2003, and appears in *Blue: Friendly Street Poetry Reader 27*, and also in *Five Bells*. This dramatic monologue, when compared with the two previous poems, shows an even greater shift into prose poetry, but with a difference. This poem is, like 'Benjamin Guggenheim on the Titanic', a musing of the subject to himself—it is not the single-sided interplay that we saw in 'Bulldozer Driver' or in Browning's 'My Last Duchess'. The pace is entirely different, neither slow nor deliberate, but erratic; the shift in speed from one line to the next, and then to the following, creates dramatic tension.

> Women. I don't trust them. Never have. Not since
> my mother did my father in & sent me his revolver.
> She didn't squeeze the trigger. **He** had to do that.

The second line has a metrical foot not unlike an anapest—the action speeds up, and then when it hits the next line, slows down again. The statement that he doesn't trust women begs the question 'why?'—was it the fact that he believed his mother drove his father to kill himself, or that she sent him the revolver, as a hint maybe? The man is untrusting and believes that women are manipulative and sly. Throughout the poem there is the resounding use of 'me', which hints at the self-centeredness of the man in question. Unlike 'Guggenheim' this is not about a realisation, this is more of a fight, there is a distinct lack of acceptance about what is happening that comes through, and as with all the movement in this monologue, it is erratic.

> They blew me to bits. There's no long term. Never was.
> Not that it's their fault. There's nothing wrong with me
> that a new collection of short stories wouldn't fix.

The last three lines flow very fast, once more with that anapest-like accentuation, a sort of final motion of slipping away. The final line is slow and deliberate, like in 'Guggenheim'; there is an allusion to peace and war, symbolic of the peace and calm of death as opposed to the war and struggle of life. Throughout the work there is this interior struggle, and this is a mimicry of the denial and struggle that the man is facing because he is going to die, which is a compaction of an entire life's worth of struggle and hardship, self-inflicted or otherwise. This dramatic monologue is possibly more emotionally involving than the previous two, because it describes a state people watch loved ones go through often—a denial of death and a bitter fight to the end.

Most poets do not write for themselves alone, but for sharing, therefore poetry is open to interpretation, and interpretation may very well be different for each person. The opinions stated in this paper may be completely different to the view of Rowlands himself, and perhaps to those of his reviewers and critics, but poetry as a creative art allows for audience interpretation, otherwise there would be no surprise and enjoyment.

References

Catt, G. and Mann, K. (2003) *Blue. Friendly Street 27*. Adelaide: Friendly Street with Wakefield Press.

Hirsch, E. (1999) *How to Read a Poem and Fall in Love with Poetry*. New York: A Harvest Book, Harcourt Inc.

Murdoch, G. and Sexton, R. (1997) *Fluorescent Voices. Friendly Street Poets No 21*. Adelaide: Friendly Street with Wakefield Press.

Rowlands, G. (1988) *On the Menu*. Adelaide: Friendly Street Poets.

Rowlands, G. (1992) *Selected Poems*. Adelaide: Wakefield Press.

PETER LLOYD

Published poetry books
Black Swans, Wakefield Press, Adelaide 1997
Collage, Wakefield Press, Adelaide 2001
A Fingerpost for Rembrandt, Wakefield Press, Adelaide forthcoming

Biographical note
Peter Lloyd was born in the English Midlands and emigrated to Australia in the late 1970s. Most of his working life has been dedicated to providing housing for the under-privileged. He lives in the Adelaide Hills and is married with two children. Peter has had work published in Australia, Canada, the United States, the United Kingdom and France.

(Compiled by Ben Taylor)

Interview with Peter Lloyd

by Ben Taylor, Rebecca Oakey and Brad Cameron

Brad Cameron (BC): For how long have you been writing?

Peter Lloyd (PL): I have been writing seriously for about six to seven years. By that I mean writing daily—part of a day given over exclusively to writing and reading as opposed to working by inclination or on a hit and miss basis. I would like to make the point here that in answering your questions, I shall be referring to two further books, one to be published early next year and another that's two thirds finished.

Rebecca Oakey (RO): What made you begin?

PL: Politics. I've lived through a time that promised so much: free education for all, a good health system, decent state housing for the not-so-well-off, a measure of dignity. It was there, we had it, then we let it all slip through our fingers. I share the general disgust at the juggernaut politics of 'Market Forces' and what Harold McMillan called 'the unacceptable face of capitalism', especially the government's behaviour towards people just barely balanced on the edge of existence—the homeless and the mentally ill.

In short, what made me start writing was fury at the whole mess the world was getting into. Reaganomics, Thatcherism, trickle-down economics, deregulation, globalisation, war. You name it, we've got it. For me, writing about it became compulsive.

Ben Taylor (BT): How did you first get published?

PL: I really had no idea that it would happen at all. Years ago I accumulated about forty pieces, which took me an inordinately long time, then sent off a few of the better ones. After waiting around for a couple of months and hearing nothing, I sent the lot to a certain professor, now retired, who slated me unmercifully, even brutally. I was about to junk my typewriter when, suddenly, *Meanjin* accepted one, and *Poetry Australia* three. I was able to write back to the professor and say ten per cent of my little collection was about to be published and I would build on that. As for the first book, again, many years later, I phoned Michael Bollen of Wakefield Press and told him that I had about fifty pieces, most of which had made it to the magazines. He was doubtful but agreed to consider them. Graham Rowlands was the reader, and after two or three deletions and additions he approved publication. This went on to become first choice of the Poetry Book Club of Australia. But it did take a long time and I was lucky.

BC: Does the fact that you have been published change your subject matter in any way?

PL: No. My choice of subject matter has always been eclectic. I don't think that applies.

RO: What poetic themes or thoughts are most appealing to you?

PL: Those that involve people and social conditions: the dump as the ultimate destination of hopes, lives, cities, symbols of planetary hell. The wasteland, symbolic of urban ugliness, isolation and poverty. Religion in its irrelevance and its failure to revise old doctrines. War, as I put in one piece, 'the unpasteurised anima of poison minds while people watch ouchless TV'. The police, internationally, as corrupt enforcers of amoral government policies and the front line robot storm troops wherever there's protest against injustice, unemployment or green issues. Then there's big business, poverty and the juxtaposition of beauty and ugliness, which I'm quite fond of. I hope that my poetry reflects in part some of the hopelessness that many people feel in the face of the multi-nationals and the sort of divisive politics that are leading to a two-tiered society in Australia.

BT: From where do you draw inspiration?

PL: The streets. From my earlier experiences in England and the slums, the ugliness and dirt. From what I sometimes see in the faces of the homeless and immigrants, the body-language of dossers, grassers, old men, old women. At the same time, all the colour of streets. The courage of the unemployed. Then there's the Stock Market with its fear/greed drive. And music, of course, which always opens a door into some other dimension. And religion, we mustn't forget religion, with all its morality and immorality. This is a giant source of inspiration, even as a born-again agnostic, I can't entirely escape the past.

BC: When and why did you move to Australia?

PL: I grew up in England and came here about thirty years ago. I've got two children who were not thriving in the English Midlands—a lot of smoke and dirt, and it all started because I took a holiday in the south of France for a month and I thought there's got to be some place on earth where we can settle where there is sunshine, and so here we are.

RO: What are your methods for writing poetry?

PL: Usually I make a lot of notes so that the subject matter is clear; that's the important thing, the subject matter, so it has a beginning, a middle and an end, very much like an essay. Then I knock it around in my mind and clothe it with whatever, you see I use a lot of surrealism so it's easier to make up these nice phrases and see how it all fits. It's all in the mind, I try and compose the whole thing in my mind and get it down in one go. I keep corrections, if possible. I have twenty or so pieces in note-form. A number of these are looked at every day. Fresh notes are made. New topics often arise at this point, they are offshoots but a piece of what's already going on. I aim at writing a poem each week. From notes I work the lines through in my head, then write it. This seems to give my work immediacy. I don't like a long drawn-out wrestle with words or subject matter. Slosh the imagery around and go for the jugular—that's what I mean about the excitement and the rush of poetry writing.

BT: What is it about poetry as opposed to other forms of writing that appeals to you?

PL: The excitement, the rush, the violence of words, whatever you want to call it. Surrealism is like having enormous buckets of paint to slosh around and the world's one great big blank wall. In comparatively few lines it's possible to encapsulate a condition or situation, present it forcefully, then bring it to a close, hopefully with an appeal to whatever remains of our humanity that hasn't been lobotomised by tacky journalism and TV. I can't do that with prose. At least it doesn't seem to work for me. Wordwise, prose is footslogging, poetry is doing one hundred and fifty down the straight and sliding into a corner.

BC: Whom do you write poetry for?

PL: Anyone who'll read it. I've tried to make its appeal as wide as possible. Moving up through *Quadrant*, the *Sydney Morning Herald*, *The Australian*, *The Age*, up the gradient to some of the glossies: *Southern Review*, *Poetry Wales*, *Literature and Aesthetics*, and a raft of magazines that are still publishing or, sadly, gone under. As to who reads it, that's another thing. Precious few. Forty per cent of people admit to reading difficulties, the tabloids and the funnies are about as far up the literature ladder as most of the others aspire, and I can sympathise with the remainder. A great deal of poetry is solipsistic, dull and without many redeeming features. The general perception is, I feel, that real writers write books and modern poetry is written by arty-fartys who chop their lines up like spaghetti. The bookshops don't help, they say there's no demand—but if there's no stock on the shelves beyond Browning, Shakespeare and the safe old classics how can there be? But that's another matter.

RO: What styles or other poets do you enjoy reading?

PL: It's got to be modern, anything with bite. Style is immaterial,

I don't care for structure at all. A number of European poets: Zbigniew Herbert, Miroslav Holub, Tomas Transtromer, Sorescu. English poets: Harrison, R.S. Thomas, Plath, Peter Reading, Ken Smith. The Beat poets of course: Kerouac, Ginsberg, Frank O'Hara. Of Australian writers I enjoy Dransfield, Allen Afterman and a few early pieces by Murray. But I always return to Eliot. It's not particularly for the form or anything, he's a superb poet—'Preludes', 'Rhapsody on a Windy Night', 'Ash Wednesday' and 'The Hollow Men'. Great atmosphere, great poetry.

BT: What advice or encouragement do you have for budding or struggling poets?

PL: Poetry is very exciting, it really is, once you get over the initial hump and feel that you are in control. The other thing, of course, is that it's not like writing a book, you can go from one subject to another very quickly, you never get bored. I can't imagine anything worse than sitting down writing a thousand words a day following on from what you've already, remorselessly, written—no excitement. You can never look forward to making money out of poetry but it looks good on your CV.

Talking to Peter Lloyd

by Ben Taylor

Browsing the bottom shelf of poetry in Wakefield Press I was hard put to find a South Australian poet that I really enjoyed. Out of the few volumes that were there I spied the covers of *Collage* and *Black Swans*, both bound in dark and mysterious pictures, swathed in melancholy. For some reason the darker side of things appeal to me although I'm quite a cheery guy. So I went ahead and judged these books by their covers and was surprisingly rewarded. Within these pages I found a poet whom I not only liked but one that got right inside me and twisted things about.

Peter Lloyd is somewhat of a mystery, a South Australian cipher and it looks as though he wants it to remain this way. However, my interview with him revealed a little about the poet who began his career late in life and shot to top ranks of Adelaide's most respected wordsmiths. Three phone calls with Peter's wife and I was beginning to suspect that he didn't really exist and maybe Mrs Lloyd had been moonlighting as the recognised SA poet. This situation fed my fantasies and my curiosity grew. Eventually an appointment was arranged with Mrs Lloyd and I was expectant of the strange things I would discover. Unfortunately I was greeted with a far more mundane reality—Peter did exist.

Well-spoken and nicely dressed, he sat in the formal dining room of the family home and submitted himself to our interview. He, the poet, at the far end of the table, three poetry students huddled at the other end. He spoke quietly and politely, occasionally his voice revealing a sadness that can be seen far clearer in his poetry. He struck me as a melancholic poet trying to caution others through his poetry. During the three phone calls, I gave his wife the list of questions that we were going to ask and consequently the interview was all pre-prepared and little spontaneity arose during the exchange. Mr Lloyd came across as a little diffident but quite confident in what he had to say. Peter is not all doom and gloom and misery, and after the interview we were able to see that indeed he does like to smile and can appreciate the good things in life. Peter Lloyd is simply another person saddened and disillusioned by what seems to be the human condition and the divisions all too apparent in society. Riding home from the interview I was happy with all that I had found out and far more satisfied with this truth than any of my imaginings. I am very pleased to have met such a respectable South Australian poet and seen past some of the mystique—Peter just doesn't like being bothered.

Reading the poems

by Brad Cameron

Peter Lloyd's 2002 poetry collection, *Collage*, is a collection that fits together as a whole like segments of an orange, but like an orange segment, the poems are just as tasty when separated from the other segments, though some may contain seeds or a grub.

When reading Peter's poetry, I finish a poem often not fully understanding what I have just read. Sometimes the feeling I was left with was unsettling, as with 'One Foot':

Ghastly mould-ladies, mutants,
The ratpacks of the world.

Midnight strikes. Its clock-skin glows like a Nazi
Shrine,
the giant white legs of landlords stride effortlessly
beside the bus,
terraced clouds leave scorchmarks at the terminus,

and a hag-bird wails.

This unsettling nature pervading some of Lloyd's poetry comes from his tendency toward surrealism—as he said in the interview (p. 134), 'Surrealism is like having enormous buckets of paint to slosh around and the world's one great big blank wall'. According to Andre Breton (website: What is surrealism), founder and theorist of the surrealist movement, the purpose of surrealism was 'to resolve the previously contradictory condition of dream and reality into an absolute reality, a super-reality'. This style is at its strongest when it challenges the pre-conceived notions and expectations of its audience, and thus has the power to unsettle or unnerve those who come into contact with it. It is in this capacity that Peter Lloyd succeeds triumphantly—drawing on dreamlike-seemingly-impossible images to piece together an overall picture.

Among other poets, Lloyd reads 'The Beat poets: Kerouac, Ginsberg, Frank O'Hara' (see interview p. 135), who were also fond of surrealist imagery and felt life to be both real and dream (Ginsberg 2000, p. 246). Lloyd's own poetry throughout *Collage* thrives under the unrestrictive conditions that surrealism affords his writing through his freedom from set form. Allen Ginsberg (2000, p. 247) said of poetry form:

> [The] Trouble with conventional form (fixed line count and stanza form) is, it's too symmetrical, geometrical, numbered and pre-fixed—unlike to my own mind which has no beginning and end, nor fixed measure of thought ... other than its own cornerless mystery.

Alternatively, 'Ballast' is less surrealistic than many of the other poems and less threatening in its presence. Lloyd's subject matters are eclectic, just as he draws on different feelings in different poems and translates them to the page once they are arranged in his mind (see interview p. 134). 'Ballast' has a very different tone to 'One Foot', and far from being unsettled, it made me feel like I was sitting on a veranda on a summer night:

> drop the moon over the mountains
> into the mist so that its planetary string or tie
>
> becomes entangled in the swaying branches, of a white apple-blossom tree.

The final line is:

> 'but without thinking about the second moon in the pond.'

This last line strikes me as funny because the rest of the poem goes into detail about the surroundings, while this line recognises a further part of the surroundings but makes a point of doing so *without thinking about it.* It is almost like Lloyd was acknowledging being aware of something on a subconscious level but not on a conscious level, which is why it seemed to me a bizarre yet brilliant line—because were it only a subconscious thought then how did it make its way onto the page?

Poetics by Aristotle (The Internet Classics Archive) describes how plot does not have to mean that a poem is story-based, but that it can still be a narrative description of action within a scene with the poet acting as a spectator:

> In constructing the plot and working it out with the proper diction, the poet should place the scene, as far as possible, before his eyes. In this way, seeing everything with the utmost vividness, as if he were a spectator of the action, he will discover what is in keeping with it, and be most unlikely to overlook inconsistencies.

In 'A Whiff from the Dumps', Lloyd seems to place the dump(s) before his eyes and sees vividly a garbage-land scene where 'Old men's hands go dipping for treasure in the mist' and 'A ten-year-old cherry pit, rooted by the dump gates, flowers again for the Emperor'. It is a surrealistic scene where anything is possible, and Lloyd is 'a spectator of the action'.

This suggests that even if the lines may concoct seemingly unconnected sequences, Peter is working cohesively and towards a goal. No matter how disorganised the progressions may seem, the poems have a rhythm and the ability to 'leave a taste in the mouth' since they are part of the same action that makes up the scene. This ability to have an overall effect regardless of seeming unconnectedness impressed a feeling upon me, such as with 'Pink':

> As you rush into the garden in a pair of
> soiled pyjamas
> To the Yes! Yes!
> Glow irridissimus and pure splendissimus of
> wallpaper
>
> That's never been touched or sucked before: to
> watch, gaping,
> that fantastic oofy-doofy sky-canvas, that
> nursery of smoking French

This is a prime example of abstract poetry that may appear at first to be nothing more than an unconnected series of dots, yet with regards to abstract poetry, Allen Ginsberg (2000, p. 243) says of Gregory Corso's poetry that it is

> built on some kind of later explainable ellipse—the mind instinctively attracted to images coming from opposite ends of itself which, juxtaposed, present consciousness in all its irrational, unfigureoutable-in-advance completeness.

The last line of 'Pink' suggests that 'Hitler was a Magic Chocolate gobbled by Hysterectomies'. Taken out of context this kind of line is weird, but as part of an abstract, surreal poem such an incredible line does not seem out of place.

Peter Lloyd has a book ready to be published, and another that's two thirds finished. It will be interesting to see how he follows up *Collage*.

References

Breton, A. (1936) *What is Surrealism?* http://www.shaviro.com/Classes/Surrealism.html
Ginsberg, A. (2000) *Deliberate Prose*. London: Penguin Books Ltd.
Lloyd, P. (2002) *Collage*. Adelaide: Wakefield Press.
The Internet Classics Archive *Poetics* by Aristotle http://c1assics.mit.edu/Aristotle/poetics.html

SHEN

Chapter by Hilde Haraldseid

Published poetry books
City of My Skin, Five Islands Press, Wollongong 2001

Biographical note
Chinese-Australian Shen was born in Malaysia, and immigrated to Australia when he was thirteen years old. He has travelled through Europe and has lived in Western Australia. He now lives in Adelaide where he works as a general practitioner.

In 2001 Shen's poetry collection was chosen to be part of the new poets program published by Five Island Press. *City of My Skin* is his first and only book so far. He has also been published in various literary magazines, and the *Friendly Street Poetry Readers* in which he debuted in 1995.

In September 2002 Shen travelled to Vietnam to research, write, and speak to literary groups. The trip was granted by Asialink, an Australian arts body which sends artists and writers on overseas residencies, and was funded by Arts SA and the Australia Council.

Interview with Shen

Hilde Haraldseid (HH): How do you write? Do you write when you are in a certain mood? What inspires you?

Shen: I keep a sort of journal, scribble on scrap paper and write down lines that linger in my head. Every three to four weeks or so, I collect the notes and form them into poetry. I am inspired by images in my daily life and stories I am told, but my themes have changed slightly over the last few years. I don't write about immigration anymore, this is 'old stuff', at least in respect to my poetry. My job as a GP lets me see situations which move me, and which many of my poems are based on.

HH: How long have you been writing for?

Shen: I have been a writer my whole life, but only in the last eight years have I worked constructively with my writing and tried to get published. I was first published in the 1995 *Friendly Street Poetry Reader*; it was a great feeling. Not only to see my poems in the reader, but to read at the Friendly Street gathering. Despite being very nervous, I felt that the audience appreciated my poetry. I only write poetry.

HH: Have you undertaken any writing courses?

Shen: I started off writing without any formal creative writing education, but have since done three writing courses. The first course was with John Malone at the Workers' Educational Association, the second with Jeff Guess at the Technical and Further Education facility Adelaide, and the last was a masterclass with Jan Owen at the SA Writers' Centre. The first two classes dealt with writers who had not had their poetry criticised before, and thus focused on giving positive feedback. The masterclass on the other hand was more harsh and direct, but I did not find this intimidating; I was ready to handle direct constructive criticism at that point. What I appreciated about all the courses was the useful technical polishing, and the absence of avant-garde poetry attitudes.

HH: Do you write poetry in Chinese as well as English?

Shen: I am not at all bilingual. I came to Australia when I was thirteen and have not kept my Chinese language. Also, the two Chinese dialects I would be using, Hokkien and Teochiu, are practical dialects. This means they are useful for practical everyday communication but not creative writing; there is simply not the necessary word choice. But considering that the written Chinese language is the same despite the differing oral dialects, I could potentially create poetry in the standard written form.

HH: Do you write for a certain audience?

Shen: I do not write with a certain audience in mind, but I know the effect I want my poetry to have on my readers, how I want them to react. What I'm trying to achieve in the reader is that delicate balance of intellectual exploration, but with enough of an emotional 'hook' for them to keep reading. I believe that to create a poem which makes the reader wonder what comes next is important. Writing about an object, or nature alone, is not enough. Stuff that I've heard read this weekend at the Australian poetry festival reinforces that—some clever, witty, intellectual stuff but the only poems that made me sit up and listen bolt upright were the emotional things—the darkness in the tone of Jordie Albiston and Ian McBryde from Melbourne.

I want people who read my poems to be able to say that 'this is real'. I feel less enthused and comfortable about people adopting others' voices and writing about them, as when people who haven't even witnessed war write about their World War II experiences.

HH: Do you read poetry? If so, what styles and authors do you appreciate?

Shen: I read and buy a lot of poetry, and in general I like free verse American poetry, while I find English poetry 'strict'. There are many poets I have found immensely influential and still go back to quite often. Mary Oliver (United States) writes lyrical nature poems, with that 'feel' that I love so much in poetry.

Other American poets I have read multiple collections of are William Carlos Williams who has a sparse and, above all, subtle style, and Li-Young Lee who immigrated to the United States from Indonesia at about the same age that I moved to Australia. Although roughly ten years older, I identify with many of his experiences. I also appreciate Denise Levertov and A. R. Ammons for their intellectual vigour, and Louise Gluck and Galway Kinnell for the sensual quality of their poetry.

I loved the confessional quality of Sharon Olds and Anne Sexton when I was younger, they opened me up to this world of—I hate to use these words but see no way around it—female quality of seeing the world. This quality is more emotive and often more irrational than men's view of life, and perhaps better and richer. But I find their work less interesting as I have grown older. There's a kind of histrionic tone to it which I find after reading three poems at a time. But I loved them very much when I first discovered them.

HH: How were you introduced to poetry at school?

Shen: At school I was introduced to 18th century poetry which involved lots of English people in tights poncing around the

English countryside, admiring Greek vases or 'freedom' or the like—nothing I found connected with colloquial Australian life. It irritated me immensely when someone this weekend at the Australian poetry festival described Shakespeare as the world's greatest poet. Let's just start refutations by rediscovering that up until the end of the 19th century English was spoken by what—a sixth, at best, of the world's population? Hmm ...

I remember also reading the Polish poet Csezlaw Milosz, and really enjoying the experience. Another international poet who influenced me earlier in life is Bei Dao, a Chinese poet in exile, who uses lots of symbolism and allusions because of communist writing restrictions, and thus is odd and stark and different from much of American, British and Australian poetry.

HH: How do you compare yourself to Melbourne poet Ouyang Yu?

Shen: I haven't connected so much with his style of writing, but very much with his content and his emotional honesty. He writes about his experiences as a Chinese poet in exile in Australia, about the racism that he finds, and disconnections and homesickness and attraction to assimilate—all things that I too wrestle with on a daily basis.

HH: Please tell me about the process of getting your first book published, and how it felt when it was accepted.

Shen: I submitted sixty or seventy poems to Five Islands Press to be considered for the annual New Poets publication. The editors receive work from all over Australia. Through Five Islands Press I attended a one-week residential workshop in Wollongong with seventy other writers and about seven tutors. It was an intense experience where, among other things, I worked on editing the poetry intended for what was to become *City of My Skin*. I had to reduce forty to fifty pages down to thirty-two. There is a mixture of poems in my book. Some of them I have put behind me, but others are more recent work.

HH: Do you introduce yourself as a poet or a general practitioner? How do you feel about the title 'poet'?

Shen: Depending on the context it would vary which title I used about myself, it does not feel right to define myself as a poet because I do not make a living from writing poetry, nor do I formally set aside time to write. But I do agree that this is the case for most poets. The title 'poet' doesn't encompass a 'role in society' for most people. Maybe there's a stereotype of a doctor and a stereotype of a writer and I'm more comfortable with chatting to people on a superficial basis by saying I'm a doctor than vice versa.

HH: *The Australian*'s poetry editor Barry Hill said that (27–28 July 2002, pp. 2–3) 'the thing with a lot of poetry [is] there are words on the page, many of them the right words in the right order, but still the poem does not emerge.' What makes a poem emerge for you?

Shen: There's a lot of technically clever poetry, but I believe that poetry can also be of an almost spiritual or mystical quality, that lifts it up out of the page. So yes, he (Barry Hill) is right, but I think he's trying to avoid saying there's something immeasurable about poetry. I have just spent a couple of hours this weekend (just prior to the Vietnam residency) trying to write my talk that I am giving in Vietnam about it. So it's not an easy question to answer. A good poem takes over and goes to places that you would not have expected it to.

Talking to Shen

I first learned about Shen when I attended the Friendly Street Poets' meeting in August 2002. His poems stood out to me as clear and fragile, but still very strong, although afterwards I could not remember what they were about. My friend who came with me to the meeting lent me her copy of *City of My Skin*, and I then decided to do my project on him.

I emailed him because I thought it less intrusive than phoning. Shen replied immediately and we arranged to meet for an interview at Café Frappe in the city. We chose this place because it is rather quiet. When working with authors in my editing classes at university I have been advised by my professors not to do interviews in the homes of either the interviewer or the interviewee, as this might create an atmosphere of intrusion and power. A neutral place gives the interview an unbiased base. I was ten minutes early and ordered hot chocolate while I was waiting, something I regretted when Shen ordered red wine—wine is just so much more poetic.

As Shen had appeared to me both at Friendly Street and via emails as a gentle and helpful person I was not worried about the social part of the interview. But I was nervous before the meeting because I felt like an amateur moving around in real life. Students are often not taken seriously because they act on behalf of projects and assignments, and thus are often expected to only contribute half-heartedly and with less knowledge and experience than a 'professional' person. Knowing this I came well prepared, with knowledge of his poetry style and his life, but most importantly an honest interest in his writing.

I knew clearly which questions I wanted to ask Shen, but I added more to my list as we spoke because the conversation brought up issues I had not considered. For example, I realised during the interview that he might write in Chinese as well, but it turned out he does not. I was a bit worried if he might be bothered with questions about his Malay Chinese background, but hoped that his openness about this theme in his poetry would also reflect in him as a person. Shen spoke openly about his background, but at the same time it was not a major part of this interview to question him about his past, so I left it at a few basic questions.

The discussion in class about what makes a good poem inspired me to ask him about his views on this issue. I decided to base my question on a statement by poetry editor Barry Hill in *The Australian* (27–28 July, 2002), as I found this conclusion very technical. It was interesting to discuss this with Shen, and he put words to my thoughts—I too have felt that poetry is not measurable.

I did not use a dictaphone during the one and a half hour long interview, which left me with a few holes in my notes. After the interview I emailed Shen to clarify a few matters, and I also used the opportunity to ask him some extra questions, which I felt, were missing from our previous conversation.

The most interesting outcome of the interview for me was to realise that even published poets with a promising future can come across as unsure about their own work and talent. I have believed that there is a huge gap between published and unpublished writers, that writers who don't have any published material to refer to are not really writers, they are only pretending, living a dream. Unpublished writers may be unsure of what others may think of their work, and are thus afraid to send their poems out there. My conversation with Shen made me realise that whether or not their poetry exists in a publication, the poet may still feel unsure about the quality of their work. There is a genuine opinion, even among writers, that writing is not a 'real job' and my talk with Shen confirmed this. But as long as your self-criticism does not keep you from trying to reach your goals, a little insecurity is not so bad.

Reading the poems

Since the mid 1960s Australia has become more open to a diversity of poetic influences, which was initially encouraged by post-war immigration and developed communication systems. In the 1960s a rhythmic pattern was developed by poets such as David Campbell, Judith Wright, James McAuley, Rosemary Dobson, A.D. Hope and Gwen Harwood. These and other poets of the time wrote as an opposition to the then current anti-intellectualism.

By the 1970s freer forms were established, and the range of topics in poetry opened up encouraged by the technical change towards free verse. The free verse line is a combination of everyday language, and a wide vocabulary and reference (ed. Leonard 1990). As poetry writing was undergoing change, Rodney Hall, Tom Shapcott and Kevin Gilbert challenged the conventional writing in the late 1960s and early 1970s (Tranter and Mead 1991).

South Australian writers are privileged to have a very active Writers' Centre that organises such events as National Poetry Week, and the monthly Writers' Caf at the SA Writers' Centre, which features established and emerging authors alike. The centre also runs several workshops and seminars such as Publish It Yourself, run by representatives from Open Book Publishers, Seaview Press and *Vernacular*. Such Writers' Centres can be found in most major cities in Australia. Writers' Week is run every second year as part of the Adelaide Festival, and provides the city with a social outdoor event that includes both Australian and overseas writers as guest speakers. The Adelaide poetry scene also has various regular poetry readings, such as *Written off*, which is organised by the University of South Australia's professional writing students, and Friendly Street Poets who meet on the first Tuesday of each month.

All the above-mentioned literary events help poets develop their poetry writing and their interest for language. Shen believes that writing courses based on constructive criticism help writers get their work out there. Whether this is due to inspiration and the creation of a common ground, or professional editing—it is successful. Christopher Smart said that 'the poem refreshes language, it estranges and makes it new' (Hirsch 1999). Shen's poetry is simply worded, however, this does not detract from the strength of his message.

Shen's main and recurring themes are immigration, interhuman relationships, displacement, and nature. His poem 'Today' compares Scottish highlands to the nature of Indonesia and leads into a comparison of the third and western world, the normality in the huge difference. Peter Pierce (the *Canberra Times*, March/April 2002) says in the article 'Robust and Varied', that the title of Shen's book *City of My Skin* is 'suggestive' because of Shen's background; he 'is always alert to the racial politics that his physical appearance can randomly incite'. Thus, Pierce writes, the title and some of Shen's poems are responses to 'the often-posed, offensive, but perhaps well-meant question, "Where d'ya come from?"'. Pierce gives credit to Shen's lack of preaching, and his way of presenting situations and issues to the reader to judge for themselves. Shen's poetry has 'a voice that we read to attune ourselves how to hear'.

O'Flynn (2001) suggests that the title *City of My Skin*, makes it quite clear what the subject matter in the book is, although 'the location of this city remains deliberately ambiguous'. O'Flynn believes the poetry collection to a degree debates migration issues, and that Shen's exploration of 'writing as an act of conjuring' is just as much in the message of the poetry. 'From Ancestral Shadows' tells a story that could belong to Shen and shows how, although Shen often writes in different length stanzas, they are just right, he invents his own perfect rhythm. O'Flynn (2001) says that this poem (among others) is

> politicised as well as deeply personal, exploring familial relationships through generations past and future. They are also concerned with issues of translation and migration where ideas of otherness and alienation are examined in a fresh and lively voice. Coupled with this are notions of exile, banishment and belonging; the true nature of home.

In 'The Way I Like It', Shen portrays the careful interaction between two flatmates on a weekend morning:

> I know how
> she'll pick it up later, dribble hot water in,
> rub her fingers around the rim.

The absorption in regular tasks, and the watchful attention to habits lingers in this poem. Also, the fact that the details of any lust and interest are so slight, creates a secretly calm picture of the male in this poem. Shen stated that he only writes about what is real (see interview, p. 142)

Although Shen often writes about wildlife and scenery, this is always more than just a description of nature. It is a background on which he describes social and political issues. In 'A Revelation', the story about killing crabs is telling us not only of the fascination of life and death, but of not being able to follow a process from start until finish. Shen also uses more comparative images, such as the straightforward but strong simile in 'Certifying the Dead', which tells us of the doctor's handling of the dead:

> But when their eyelids are opened,
> there is no sparkle, only the
> dull reflection of a torch,
> shone in a painted glass eye.

Another more direct and powerful simile is present in 'Rooms without Doors':

> Everything in our lives revolves over and over
> like a clock's interior exposed …

In the poem 'Today' the reader is struck by the power of metaphors:

> … hot chips from an unfolded newspaper
> have smeared an inky oil over
> stories of rape in Indonesia.

The oil has greased the newspaper, not the actual events of the rapes, but the clever metaphor suggests this, and also that the western world ignores the issue completely, by using the newspaper that covers this event to wrap around greasy food. The metre, or rhythmic pattern, in Shen's poetry flows perfectly. The sequence of feet in the accentual-syllabic metre he uses is iambic, the most favoured metre in the English language.

Hirsch (1999) says that a major part of post-romantic lyric poetry is about 'connections and disconnections'. Relationships, or lack thereof, and the communication to establish this status, are often debated in poetry towards an imagined reader, a 'you'. Shen's poetry about inter-human relationships rarely addresses a 'you', and hardly ever in a traditional 'to my lover' style. In 'Inside Stories', he speaks to a foetus about the safety of its world, and is unexpectedly touched by its expected movement. In 'An Abstraction, My Daughter', Shen sees his future daughter in women he meets, planning her life, acknowledging that he is not ready to have her yet, longing for when he will be.

It will be interesting to see what other styles Shen will choose to experiment with in the future, as the quality of the structure and his natural but original images could prove successful in other styles. Currently, his themes may be compared to that of Melbourne poet Ouyang Yu who also writes about assimilation problems, but Shen is hesitant to suggestions that their styles compare (see interview, p. 143).

The fact that his volume was chosen for publication by Five Islands Press, and that he has been published in top shelf magazines indicates that Shen's voice is acknowledged in the Australian writing scene. Hirsch (1999) says that poetry might exist because the human information told through poetry cannot be informed as well in other ways. When reading Shen, this observation seems to be confirmed because his poetry writing comes through as careful, strong and clear.

References

Hill, B. (2002) *The Australian*, 27–28 July, pp. 2–3.

Leonard, J. (ed.) (1990) *Contemporary Australian Poetry*. Victoria: Houghton Mifflin Australia Pty Ltd.

Shen, 'Certifying the Dead', in J. Dally and G. Kemp (eds) (1996) *Friendly Street Reader No. 20*. Adelaide: Friendly Street Poets with Wakefield Press.

Shen (2001) *City of My Skin*. Wollongong: Five Islands Press.

The University of Melbourne, n.d., Asialink,[viewed 12 September 2002], http://www.asialink.unimelb.edu.au/arts/residencies/Litrescurrent.htm

Tranter, J. and Mead, P. (eds) (1991) *The Penguin Book of Modern Australian Poetry*. Victoria: Penguin Books Australia Ltd.

MARTIN JOHNSON

Chapter by Nathan Gogoll

Published poetry books

After the Axe-Men, Penguin Books, Australia 1995
The Clothes-prop Man, Wakefield Press, Adelaide 2002
Home Town Burial, Cornford Press, Launceston 2002

Biographical note

Martin R. Johnson was born in Gawler, northeast of Adelaide, in 1950. Martin has been publishing poetry regularly in a wide variety of literary magazines since 1988 when he had a poem aired on Radio 5UV. The first 12 years of his life were spent growing up at the married workmen's camp at nearby Humbug Scrub, during the building of the South Para Reservoir. Born into a working class family, who lived poorly, Martin joined the RAN as a 15-year-old 'boy recruit' in 1966. Discharged for medical reasons, he got a job as a factory worker in 1971.

The next 15 years were fraught with emotional and physical hardship, yet throughout this time his sense of humour and optimism has prevailed.

Interview with Martin Johnson

Nathan Gogoll (NG): What is your favourite poem? Can you recite any of it?

Martin Johnson (MJ): My first answer is I don't have any particular favourites (there could be 100!) but then I think of the lines such as 'a four foot box, a foot for every year.' ('Mid-term Break' by Seamus Heaney). And 'a savage servility/slides by on grease' ('For the Union Dead' by Robert Lowell). The most constructive 'lines' from a poet I recall and attempt to relate are from French poet Arthur Rimbaud (1854–1891):

> The first task of the man who wants to be a poet is to study his own awareness of himself, in its entirety; he seeks out his soul, he inspects it, he tests it. As soon as he knows it, he must cultivate it.

NG: What poetry have you read recently?

MJ: I read as much poetry as I can. Poems sent to me when I was arts editor at *The Bunyip* (1997–2003), current magazines, books sent to me for review, and those that I buy. But not only contemporary Australian poetry. I own a fairly substantial collection of poetry from around the world, plus anthologies (Russian, Irish, etc.), which includes poetry found on broken earthenware from 4,000 years ago.

NG: What poetry can you relate to, and what poetry inspires you?

MJ: Apart from the simplistic ballad rhyming style of poetry (which is not poetry at all, or even literature), I can relate to and be inspired by most poetry that is published in a wide range of literary magazines and books. But what bothers me is the 'types' of poems that are almost unintelligible. Writing which rejects logical thinking. Imagery inconsistent with the theme, if one can fathom out just what the theme is. Or poems that simply state facts. Good poems come from somewhere inside the writer's feelings and those inspire others to express themselves willingly.

NG: When did you begin writing poetry?

MJ: I began writing terrible imitations of Henry Lawson's verse while cutting timber in the Mt Crawford Forrest, 1 August 1984. It took me four years, and my partner Cathy Young's urging for me to change my style (she introduced me to the *50 Modern European Poets* book, from where, incidentally, I got the quote from Arthur Rimbaud) to get my first poem published. It was aired on Adelaide University Radio 5UV on 1 August 1988. So the 1st of August has continued to show up.

NG: When do you believe your poetry matured? (I am interested in when you recognised your poetry reaching a level that you were pleased with, and when you began to think about submitting work to be published.)

MJ: As I stated above, it took me four years to get my first poem published. During this time I got a famous rejection letter/note from the editor of the *Adelaide Review*. 'Martin,' it read 'why don't you save your stamps.' I have always worked hard at my writing (every day) and at getting published. But even so, after over 200 poems in around 150 magazines, it doesn't get any easier. A tip here is (a) you must practise every day, (b) try to experiment with different styles, and (c) say something new or make what has gone before new. (Ezra Pound liked to say 'make it new'.)

NG: Please describe one of your publishing experiences that stands out in your mind.

MJ: When the then poetry editor for Penguin Books Australia, Judith Rodriguez, handed me an envelope in a room crowded with poets at a seminar held at the SA Writers' Centre in 1995. Inside was her decision to publish *After the Axe-Men*. I can tell you that when I read her badly hand-written acceptance, it was like I could fly. It had taken me seven years to get this manuscript accepted.

NG: Do you enjoy reading/performing your poetry? Why/why not?

MJ: Doing a public performance depends on a few things. Timeframe is the most important. A ten minute slot barely gives you the chance to warm to the audience (I always like to include the audience, whereas some poets stand here/audience there), so poem selection is critical. I like a longer time. Forty minutes is good because it gives me time to cover the themes in a book. In any case, it is good to see live people and read to them. Let me emphasise the word **read**. I find performance a bit ugly. Poems can end up as comic sketches. This distracts from the poetry. I have always written for the page and for the quiet reader.

NG: Do you change your poetry if it is read aloud, or do you find that your poetry lends itself to being read?

MJ: I'm not sure if my poetry lends itself to being read aloud. It is, mostly, fairly serious. And I have certainly read very serious poems out loud. Poetry is serious, in my mind. I don't know anyone who writes poetry who goes to their writing desk only to burst out laughing. So, no, I don't change my poetry when I read aloud.

NG: I've noticed that your poetry is often based on locations and people. Has this always been a feature of your poetry?

MJ: When I think of writing a poem, I always think of a

collection. In fact, my forest poems and South Para poems, I think of the collection first then draw on experiences, etc., for individual poems to fit. It is important for me to present working life/history in my poetry. Even my very personal poetry has an essence of history and location about it. I guess that this is instinctive, a natural trait.

NG: Are you a deep/emotive writer or do everyday experiences inspire you to pick up a pen?

MJ: Everyday experiences do inspire me, but I believe the poem would be shallow without deeply felt, or at least felt impressions. I'm not sure about emotive though. I like to present the poem and leave the emotive reactions to the reader/listener. In my mind a poem should contain the following three elements:

1. Personal Experience, including events that, in the first place, have permanently shaped the poet's way of thinking.

2. External Influence, inspired by the poet's observation and contact with other people.

3. Philosophical Reckoning, the poet's moral understanding of self, and of life.

NG: What advice do you have for young, or aspiring poets?

MJ: 1. Never let rejection stop you from writing your poetry. All poets go through periods of self-doubt which, I believe, ultimately shapes their character as a successful poet.

2. Read widely, but don't try to deliberately imitate the writing styles of other poets. Write *your* way. It really is unique and valuable to our understanding of life and the world.

3. Use a three-stanza method as an exercise:

(a) first stanza, set the scene

(b) second stanza, what the poem is about

(c) third stanza, logical conclusion to title of poem, first and second stanzas. (About five lines each stanza.)

This is a successful beginning-middle-end concept.

4. Find out about current markets (SA Writers' Centre) and submit up to three poems for selection. It is the relationship that you establish between editor and yourself that is important to the development of your poetry.

5. Avoid writers' groups if you are serious about having a career as a poet. You will end up writing for the group. Leave

it to editors and reviewers for criticism and constructive comment.

6. Be true to yourself. The long-range ambition of having your own book of poems published by a reputable publisher (avoid self-publication; especially vanity publication) will be achieved by persistence and self-belief.

Talking to Martin Johnson

Martin Johnson has a beard as big as I have ever seen, he is seldom found without his black hat, and is adorned with several tattoos. However, these characteristics are not the reason why I chose to find out more about him. The reason why I got to know Martin was to study his poetry. There probably aren't many people who know Martin that don't know the story of his now famous rejection letter. I was talking to Martin at his house one late summer afternoon and we were discussing poetry, and Martin was providing me with books and pieces of poetry. Whilst I read at his kitchen table he was searching for things to show me, and at one point he emerged with a chuckle and I got to read *the* letter, the letter that asked Martin to 'save his stamps' … luckily he hasn't.

Choosing to study Martin's poetry wasn't a momentary decision, more of a progression of events. The first of these events was when I received a copy of the October 2001 *Southern Write* (newsletter of the SA Writers' Centre). This issue had a photograph of Martin on the front (with hat and beard); it was promoting the launch of his book, *The Clothes-prop Man*. My interest was further spurred through discovering the title of one of his poetry collections, *Poems from the South Para Reservoir*. Even before seeing the cover or reading a page I was interested, as my grandfather and great uncle had worked on this engineering project between Lyndoch and Gawler on the edge of the Barossa Valley. I borrowed a copy of this book via the Flinders University Library, and found that I enjoyed reading Martin's poems.

My first contact with Martin Johnson was through phone calls and then through a written conversation/interview via postal mail. Since receiving his interview responses I have met Martin in person a couple of times, both at his house and at the *poets in the pub* reading that he runs monthly at the Railway Family Hotel in Gawler. Martin suggested that we send each other questions and answers via the post, and this scheme worked well. An interview run in this manner allows for insightful and clear answers. Martin has since provided me with lots of material that reinforces what he said in the interview. The whole experience was thoroughly enjoyable.

What appealed to me about Martin's poetry was the way in which he writes about a particular area of South Australia near where I grew up. I have some idea what it might have been like growing up in the area (post WWII) from the stories I have heard from my father who is of a similar age to Martin.

Martin's answers were thorough and interesting. Even though my direct contact with the poet came after the interview was completed, I felt that he was speaking from years of experience, in both his reading and writing. It was great to be exposed to that sort of knowledge from such a down-to-earth and modest man. He provided a wealth of knowledge that might have taken me years to find by myself. I always felt comfortable talking to Martin and I was blown away with the interest he took and the time that he offered to help me.

Martin has a new book just released, *Home Town Burial*, which I have been inspired to find and read.

Martin's interest in poetry began with the classics and he showed me a book that he used to read in his breaks in the Mt Crawford forest, when he was a woodcutter. It contained the likes of Chaucer and Milton. Some of his earliest poetry, neatly handwritten in a small notebook, reflected these classical poets. Whilst looking through this notebook he stroked his beard and chuckled to himself, but did not share his thoughts. He sweated out (sometimes literally) his development mostly by himself, in a caravan in his driveway, encouraged by his partner Cathy Young. The caravan is no longer, but it's clear that the work has paid off. He reassured me that rejection, when it comes, is not always easy to understand but is a step in the progression of writing poetry.

Through this assignment I have come to realise that my university degree is helping to broaden the horizons for my own poetry. An essential part of this realisation has been the interaction with the South Australian poetry scene. Getting acquainted with the work of poets/authors such as Martin Johnson, Peter McFarlane, Ken Bolton and Peter Goldsworthy, to name a few, has been a pleasure as well as a huge resource. Discovering publishing opportunities within

Australia and Adelaide was like discovering the tip of an iceberg. But I have also now begun to see some of the work that needs to go on under this tip, something I needed to see to recognise that my poetry needs lots of development if I ever want to be published. I have come to see that I need to find my own 'voice' and shape it to make it a valuable and unique one. My interview with Martin Johnson has sped up and focussed this understanding. Hearing of his early attempts at publishing has given me evidence that often you have to 'do it tough' before becoming successful, I now know that my first 50–60 poems may not be publishable material, but are an important step in the right direction of finding a voice.

My line of questioning had two purposes. The first was to discover Martin's inspiration and to find out about his development. The second purpose was to reassure myself that my development is somehow similar to a successful South Australian poet. Elements of Martin Johnson's poems that I enjoyed were: the realness, the feelings that are on offer for the reader, his talent of describing people and places and the relationship of the two, his Australianness and indeed his South Australianness. Reading about places that I have seen and been to was refreshing, rather than reading about events and places that exist only in my imagination. It is special for me to know that a South Australian experience or reflection can be as valid as any other.

Martin put the writing experience almost into the language of his poetry in his answers—simple but not basic, intelligent but not bragging. Martin Johnson is only one example of the talented poets in South Australia; I take him as inspiration, not only in the way he shapes images with words on a page, but also for the steps and struggles he has taken in his craft, in order to succeed.

Reading the poems

Martin Johnson creates images through words on a page. He is a South Australian poet writing in a contemporary, free flowing style, who began his career drawing on the poetry of the past for ideas and inspiration. The language he uses is simple and his writing has a distinct voice. In his book *The Clothes-prop Man* this voice captures the working class environment of the period following the Second

World War. Johnson's poetry is shaped by life experience and has been crafted over the last eighteen years. His poetry fits into the current stylistic preference of free verse and demonstrates a wide variety of poetical tools.

Nowottny (1962) explains one way that poetry may be analysed. The author shows us that poetry may be looked at on two levels, firstly; 'what is—*there,* in a sense that it can be described and referred to' yet at the same time considering 'the symbolic meaning, overtones and subconscious elements which are so important in poetry'. This method allows us to see the literary elements (words and patterns) of a poem at the same time as we study the images that it begins to suggest and any meaning that is created.

Hirsch (1999) provides an excellent description of poetic imagery, explaining that images occur where 'the literal literally bubbles over into the symbolic'. He clarifies this, saying that 'the poetic image is always delivered to us through words'. The creation of images in poetry may conjure up many variations of feelings and pictures in our mind and has the ability to bring back memories.

Poetry is a form of reflective art that has been around for centuries. Aristotle's description of poetry as an artistic 'means of imitation' (Roberts 1954) is still valid. He explains that the poet serves as an 'imitator' and 'the objects (that) the imitator represents are actions, with agents'. Aristotle describes these 'agents' as 'diversities of human character', referring to the nature of a developing story in a poem. The poet reveals this plot to the reader through suspense, emotion etc. However, another interpretation of these 'agents' could be the poetic devices used by the poet, such as alliteration, metaphor or onomatopoeia.

To understand poetry at present requires an understanding of free verse. Contemporary poetry, like all poetry, provides strong imagery, but it does so with a fresh use of language and a less structured interpretation of metre. The use of poetic techniques within free verse poetry is not all that different to the use within the classic ballad or epic.

> Epic: A long narrative poem, exalted in style, heroic in theme … the Anglo-Saxon epic *Beowulf* … they seem to be written versions of texts long sung and retold, composed … over time, all telling the tale of a tribe. (Hirsch 1999)
>
> Ballad: narrative song preserved and transmitted orally. It unfolds in

> 4-line stanzas (quatrains) and customarily alternates four- and three-stress lines, the second and the fourth lines rhyming ... It often opens abruptly, focuses on a single, crucial episode, and moves decisively—dramatically—toward a tragic conclusion. (Hirsch 1999)

The difference lies in the overall structure, and in many cases the removal of it. Martin Johnson's poetry uses free verse and many of the tools (or 'agents') of poetry.

Martin Johnson's poetry does not require a metrical sequence or rhyme to have a flowing nature. Johnson produces a natural rhythm very, similar to that found in spoken word to create a poetic rhythm. This is the use of patterns of language that reflect more closely the patterns of modern speech and develop a natural rhythm, a trait of 'free verse'. This style allows for the use of as many or as few poetical devices as decided by the poet.

Martin Johnson's poetry falls in line with a popular, contemporary style of poetry which has moved away from the classical standards of metre, rhyme and rhythm. It is a movement of poetry that embraces the poet's own voice. Campbell (1991) provides 'three independent approaches to interpretation: the poem as a moral fable ('sacrifice to universal love'), as enigma ('the prince of superstitious poets'), and as melody and music ('master of the language of poetry')'. This description was offered in debating the interpretations of Wordsworth's *Lyrical Ballads* but could be applied to poetry in general and certainly to Martin Johnson's poems.

Johnson's poems fall mainly into the third described category, for example the last stanza of his poem 'Friday October 17, 1958':

> Decorated with blue velvet curtain, the tablets
> with their reservoir information were opened
> at the tug of a gold cord, the Premier's fingers,
> pink at the end of his suit's grey sleeve, a salute
> to the workers and what they'd achieved.

But he does not fit into this category in the same way as Wordsworth and Coleridge may have, as he is writing free verse. Johnson also offers some 'moral fables' but again in a contemporary manner; he uses images of love but does so in the environment of working class families. An example of this is found in the poem 'Girl in a Photograph', in the final stanza:

> But it's her face that captures
> the viewer's eye. Plain as a bucket
> there's a vitality in her smile
> you can't describe. Reaches
> inside and touches your heart.

Martin Johnson's poetry is self-described as developing, but has clearly already achieved a very high standard. He quotes from a rejection letter/note early in his writing career that read 'Martin, why don't you save your stamps.' (see interview, p. 151) But after the launch of his third book it is obvious he has found his own voice and begun to create imagery that is enjoyed.

Martin Johnson's poetry is a reflection of places and people, related (in *The Clothes-prop Man*) to the events of working class men and their families. It is clearly Australian as shown by language use, with references to 'blokes', 'pubs', and '44-gallon drums', to name just a few. Martin Johnson's poetry relates to and is inspired by 'the simplistic ballad rhyming style'. His view is that poetry should 'come from somewhere inside the writer's feelings … inspiring others to express themselves'. (see interview, p. 151) But he does not follow the strictness of form as described earlier. The balance of emotion within everyday experience is a technique used by Martin, in fact he describes this as his 'natural trait' or his instinctive way of writing. The phrase 'opened my mind like that gate' in Martin Johnson's poem 'Crossing the Line' shows successful use of metaphor. The patterns in Martin Johnson's poetry often represent a form of conversation on the page. The voice that runs through *The Clothes-prop Man* is a working class voice. It is an everyday voice but not one that is seen on the page everyday.

Alliteration, assonance and consonance are three elements of language use that in modern poetry are a means to develop a natural rhythm, and indeed free verse. Martin Johnson's poetry contains these elements, and he tends to quote or use spoken language. One example of his use of alliteration is in his poem 'Girl in a Photograph' in the line 'she is dancing in the dirt, dressed'. His use of assonance is shown in 'New Australian': 'nothing but his own disposition to dispel'.

Martin Johnson uses a variety of line and stanza lengths, with a voice that often reflects conversation but is also his individual recognisable poetic voice.

References

Aristotle, translated by I. Bywater (1954) *Poetics*. New York: Random House.

Campbell, P. (1991) *Wordsworth and Coleridge Lyrical Ballads*. London: Macmillan.

Hirsch, E. (1999) *How to Read a Poem and Fall in Love with Poetry*. New York: A Harvest Book, Harcourt Inc.

Nowottny, W. (1962) *The Language Poets Use*. London: Athlone Press.

DAVID ADÈS

Biographical note
David Adès was born in Adelaide of Egyptian Jewish parents. He is a lawyer who has worked in both the public and private sectors. He has travelled widely and lived in Israel, India and Greece. In 1979 a housemate took him to his first Friendly Street meeting. He attended for several years before having the nerve to read his own work. He has since become a Friendly Street regular. David's first published poem appeared in 1986 in the *Friendly Street Poetry Reader No. 12.* His poems have appeared in many subsequent Friendly Street readers and in a variety of Australian literary magazines, they are featured on the poetry CD *Adelaide 9—The Poetry of the City*, and have been broadcast on radio. He has read his work at many venues around South Australia and in Austin, Texas. Together with Ioana Petrescu, he edited the *Friendly Street Poetry Reader 26*. He is the current Convenor of Friendly Street Poets, and is working on a collection provisionally titled *The Work of My Face.*

(Adapted from the *Friendly Street* website
http://www.friendlystreetpoets.org.au/ades.htm)

Interview with David Adès

by Christy Van Stralen and Caryn Rogers

Caryn Rogers (CR): David, when did you first start writing poetry and what was it that started you?

David Adès (DA): When I was in my twenties, I moved out of home and into the back half of an antique shop with a friend of mine and we didn't have a TV set. We both had typewriters and he was writing poetry at the time. In fact, he introduced me to Friendly Street, I hadn't heard of it. That was in about 1979 and I started writing then. I'd finished my degree at university and I was doing a graduate diploma that wasn't very taxing, which meant that I had some intellectual energy left at the end of the day and I could spend it writing poetry.

Christy Van Stralen (CVS): Are any of those earlier poems in any of your published works?

DA: No, the early stuff is pretty awful.

CVS: That's encouraging.

DA: It took me about seven or eight years from there before I even had the courage to read any of my poetry, and about ten years before I got any published. People are doing it a lot better these days.

CVS: So that was a bit of journey?

DA: Yes ... well, it was a very intermittent journey, I didn't write throughout that period constantly, I'd write every now and then but it wasn't with any great purpose and it was really only in the late eighties that I started writing a bit more.

CVS: You're the convenor of Friendly Street Poets ...

DA: Yes.

CVS: What does that involve? What do you do?

DA: Well ... how long have you got? Friendly Street's a poetry group that started in 1977 having monthly readings of poetry in Adelaide and has been going ever since. We have about a hundred members or so and we have meetings every month. We publish books, we have a publishing program, a website, guest speakers, guest readers from interstate, overseas, we're involved in Writers' Week, we're involved in poetry events during the year, so it's pretty full-on.

CR: Is it exciting helping people to publish their work?

DA: Oh look ... I love it, particularly now. I think there's a lot happening, there's a lot of small publishers that are publishing poetry out now. It used to be a lot harder to get published, even though there isn't much funding for it. People seem to be willing to risk publishing poetry, even though there isn't much of a market for it, but still there are some people who want to, and there are more opportunities now. There's a lot of acceptance of poetry readings in bookshops, in pubs, festivals, so I think it's a very vibrant and dynamic scene.

CR: Is that a worldwide scene or is it more around Adelaide? Or Australia-wide?

DA: It's certainly Australia-wide. There's a lot of very fine poetry being written in the country and being published, and probably a lot that's not being published as well. There's just a stack of talent, poetic talent, in this country. What's happening elsewhere I don't know.

CR: Do you think that poetry is just for poets?

DA: We'd like to think that it has universal appeal. I know that most of the poetry books are sold by poets or are sold to poets or to friends and family of poets. There doesn't seem to be a large wider market out there. I understand that after pornography, poetry sites are the most visited sites on the web so I think that there is some kind of hidden ...

CVS: Interest?

DA: Interest ... global interest, and since we've had our website, which is about a year now, we've had emails from all over the place, and it's been really interesting to get emails from overseas, and from organisations around Australia who are looking to contact poets so that they can actually get permission to publish their work—individual poems for various purposes. We didn't know there was that interest so we're finding that we're tapping into an interest, and we're also finding that, partly because of the website and more publicity, a lot more new faces are turning up at Friendly Street. We're having record numbers every month, so ... yes, it's good.

CVS: Do you think a lot has to do with people's awareness—because a lot of people wouldn't even know ... the only reason I know about Friendly Street Poets and that places like that exist was from going to uni and hearing about it there.

DA: It used to be word of mouth. For many years it was word of mouth. That's how I first heard about it and then of course people would see the books we published. The Friendly Street committee has made a concerted effort in the last two years to have publicity brochures, handouts, fliers and mail-outs to various places, and we've been putting information in cafes, bookshops, libraries and universities, and we've been on radio. I'm surprised by how many people in their forties and fifties have heard of Friendly Street—I'm always running into people who say, 'Oh yes, I went to a Friendly Street reading twenty years ago'. It's one of the beauties of that continuity, but I think there is a lot more publicity now. There are prizes being offered, there are incentives for people. We've got, for example, a poem of the month on our website, which gives people exposure they wouldn't get otherwise. I think there are more opportunities and word is getting round. Maybe more people are writing these days—I don't know.

CR: So, with your own personal writing, do you find that you write poems quickly, or do you often have to rework them two or three times?

DA: Twenty or thirty times.

CR: Twenty or thirty times?

DA: Writing for me is not so quick. There are the occasional poems that are just one-offs, they're usually very short. Anything that needs to focus on structure and perhaps an intellectual idea or the way that language is used takes a lot of working and reworking, and more reworking. Sometimes, though I've struggled with them, I'm still struggling with them after ten years, I'm still not happy with them, so many do have a long gestation.

CVS: That's interesting because I always look at poems and think that people just write them, and it's once off and that's it. That's how I am with my writing—I write something then just leave it.

DA: I think a lot of people do write like that, but I don't necessarily think their poetry is good quality poetry. Good poetry requires crafting, which is a skill. You can't just pick up a pen after a year of not doing it and hope that it will come. It requires discipline, and it also requires a great deal of attention to detail. It's very, very easy to make mistakes. So I don't write very quickly, and I don't write very prolifically.

CR: We've noticed that you've used a lot of quite sophisticated language in your poetry ... is the thesaurus a good friend to you in that? Or is it all from within?

DA: Actually, I think I struggle a bit with language. I don't have a thesaurus, it's one of those things on my 'to get' list—it's been on my list for a long time. I do have a dictionary, which I use, but I don't aim for sophisticated language in my poetry, and sometimes I think it detracts from it. I don't consider myself a poet, particularly of ideas, or ...

CR: Philosophy?

DA: No, it really derives more from feelings. Some people say that my writing 'is not very male'. I don't know what that means, because men do have feelings too … very often the poems are inspired by someone and are written for someone, so there is that sort of connection between the idea, the person behind it, and the language that's used—it's not … no ... I wouldn't call it sophisticated.

CVS: But it's just a description of things …

CR: I think sophisticated is probably the wrong word, but quite a lot of the words really flow together and create powerful imagery. One poem we were particularly struck by was 'Nightfall, Dalat, Vietnam'. Was that based on feelings and personal experience?

DA: It was a personal experience—I did have that experience, and quite a bit of my poetry does involve a place. I travel a lot, so different places get into my poems. Before I wrote that poem I spent three or four weeks in Vietnam and I probably only got two or three poems out of it. I don't think that at the time I would have necessarily thought that that image would have been the one that would have produced a good poem. That poem ... it's been a while since I've even thought about it, to be honest. I find in a way that description is easy, but description in poetry isn't usually enough so there has to be something to make the description contain an idea or contain a sense of something going on, something perhaps underneath the description. I think that's what I was trying to do in that poem; convey a sense of 'here is this beautiful place' and 'here are these beautiful images' but underneath it there's something else lurking that's not visible to everyone.

CVS: Did you spend a lot of time reworking that poem?

DA: Yes, that would have gone through a number of manifestations. I think it's about a page and a half long. I have many problems with the structure of my poems. I have noticed that a lot of good poets have their own voice, their own poetic structure. My poems tend to tell me that they want their own structure and I can't necessarily put them into a consistent structure, so you'll find that my poetry does change a lot in its structure, the way it's laid out, and some people get really irritated by that. The poetry workshop group that I'm in haven't liked some of the things I've been doing with my poetry. They keep telling me to change the form but I don't want to change the form. That's the form that it eventually takes, so because of the way it's structured across the page that poem probably did have a fair bit of fiddling.

CR: We understand that you are a lawyer. Is that correct?

DA: Yes ... don't hold it against me!

CR: No ... no, we're not. We're just interested because it seems that the world of law is more analytical than the creative world. How does that balance with the creative side of poetry? They seem to be very different elements.

CVS: Do those two worlds cross over?

CR: Or contrast really strongly?

DA: There is some commonality because both involve the use of language. I don't express myself creatively as a lawyer, but it is quite astonishing how many lawyers are poets, and how many poets even in South Australia are lawyers. For example the late John Bray, who was the Chief Justice of South Australia, was a pillar of Friendly Street, one of the founding forces of Friendly Street, and a very, very fine poet, one of the best poets that this State's produced. There are a number of other people who are lawyers who are published in Friendly Street. There's no incompatibility between the law and poetry or between the law and creativity. I guess legal language is very dry and if you want to use language as a creative outlet then you generally have the skills to be able to do it—it's there for you if that's what you want to do.

CVS: You've said that a lot of your poetry's inspired by your travels and experiences. Have you been inspired at all by other poets that you've known or read?

DA: Very much. Yes.

CVS: What are some of your main sources of inspiration?

DA: One of the things that I like to do when I've travelled in different parts of the world is try to find translations of local poets and read them in the country I'm travelling in. It's not always possible. Quite often there are no translations, but I have a great affinity for very lyrical poets, poets who do use language. I can be completely captivated by the language and actually sometimes just forget about the content especially with people like Pablo Neruda, Yevgeny Yevtushenko, Odysseus Elytis. I read a lot of Elytis when I was in Greece, and it was just wonderful hiking through Crete reading poems about Greece by someone who had spent eighty years of his life there and had a great passion for the country.

CR: Were they written in Greek?

DA: Originally they were. I can't read Greek. I did have a very wonderful experience on one occasion. I'd memorised four or five pages of a poem of his called 'The Axion Esti'. It's an eighty-page poem that takes on different forms—an absolutely wonderful piece—I'd memorised the first four or five pages in English, and I had been traipsing round Crete reciting them at the top of my voice, enjoying myself. I happened to catch a train through Yugoslavia and I wanted to get off the train before it hit the Greek border, because it was a lot cheaper than taking the train all the way through Greece. So I got off the train five kilometres before the border of Yugoslavia, and the other person that got off the train was a Greek Cypriot and we started talking as we were walking to the border. It was a five-kilometre walk, about midnight, and I'd told him of my love for Elytis and that I'd learned a poem, and I started reciting it in English and he started reciting back to me in Greek. It was just a very special connection.

CR: Would you say you have a main purpose in your writing?

DA: I don't know. Sometimes, probably less so now, but in the past, it's been a compulsion. I've felt that I've really needed to write, and I think a lot of people who do indulge in what can sometimes be a pretty unrewarding activity, a lot of hours scratching away, trying to make something happen, to perhaps a non-existent audience, have to feel some sort of compulsion, and I have felt that in the past. Purpose? I think, at the end of any exercise in writing there is a desire to connect. I'm a poet who has to have an audience. I can't write something for myself. I want to connect, I want someone to read a poem and walk away with it and say 'It's moved me' or 'affected me', 'I like what was said in that poem'. If I change or affect one person I'm happy, and as time goes on you get more exposure and you get more feedback about your work, both positive and negative. Some of that gloss does wear off and then you realise it's not just about reaching people, it is about doing something with your own creative talent to the best of your ability, for yourself as well—you do get a lot of rewards from it.

CVS: I really liked the poem I heard on a CD about faces.

DA: 'The Work of My Face'?

CVS: I really liked that one, it was really fascinating, thought-provoking. Can you remember where that came from?

DA: That's a fairly recent poem. I've always been interested in people's faces. I think people's faces tell remarkable stories, particularly older people's faces. There is so much wisdom, knowledge, and if you look in a face, you basically see everything, you see a person's history. At Writers' Week two years ago, Dimitris Tsaloumas, a Greek Australian poet, in his early eighties now, was invited to Friendly Street to launch one of our books. I was absolutely captivated by his face. Here's this man, he's mischievous, he's cheeky, his face tells so many different stories, his poetry does as well. And I just started thinking about faces and I started thinking about how, in a way, you are your face and your face is you, but it's always changing. I had an idea of wanting to say something about the need to be inclusive of all people and the need to be open to ideas. This is in the context of what's been going on with the refugees, with Woomera and Australian Policy, the need to explore my own family position that has its own richness, which probably hasn't found its way into much of my poetry, and all of those things got tangled up. That poem was the outcome of it.

CVS: You start talking about your face, and then it branches out into this huge world, and then kind of comes back in at the end …

DA: I guess there is an idea that the world begins and ends with each individual, that if you were not conscious of the world, it would not exist. When you die, the world will not exist. Before you're born, the world does not exist. So you contain the whole world within yourself, and you're a part of it, you belong to it, and it belongs to you, those two things do interact and it's a very fertile subject to explore with poetry.

CVS: Where and when do you usually write your poetry? Is there a specific time, or do you force yourself into a particular pattern?

DA: No. I'm very undisciplined. One of the difficulties I have had for many years is to try and juggle a very busy life—professional life and busy life in other ways—with poetry, and poetry's something for me that requires a space. It has to be a physical space, but it also has to be a mental and intellectual space, and you have to create that space, and there are times when I can't do it. I haven't been doing it for much of this year for example, because I'm over-committed. I took a year off work two years ago and filled that space with a number of different things and that gave me a chance to write, which was wonderful, but if I don't constantly do that then it's extraordinarily difficult for me. I find that I only come to writing when I've done everything else. There's so much 'everything else' to do that I never come to writing. I'm hoping actually to go from full-time work to part-time work next year and then get back to some more writing. Probably in August next year I'll relinquish being Convenor of Friendly Street, which occupies a lot of my time, and that will open up a bit more space for writing. It's a constant battle to actually make the space.

CVS: Would you say that in your life poetry is something that is a big priority for you or something you want to be a priority in the scale of things?

DA: It's a passion, and I've been ambivalent about it at times because, for example, I don't have this huge compulsion to publish a book. I'd like to. I've always liked to. I've never done it. My poetry you'll find all over the place but you won't find it collected anywhere, which probably makes your job a bit more difficult. If I had it as a huge priority I would be, I think, concentrating on getting a book out, and getting another book out, following that path It's very important to me, it is a passion, but I don't want it to alienate me from other things in my life, people in my life. I'm a very gregarious person so I spend a lot of time with people, which doesn't give me the isolation, the solitude that I need to write constantly. That's why I can't seem to be able to write when I'm working full-time. I actually have to set aside part of the working day to be able to write, otherwise it doesn't seem to happen. So it's important, but in the scheme of things, it is not the highest priority. As Convenor of Friendly Street my highest priority now is to make sure that the organisation is exciting, dynamic, that people are getting opportunities, and that people are getting published. I see myself at the moment, just in this little phase, as a kind of nurturer of other poets and other poetic talent, and making a lot of things happen for other people. I quite like that. That is actually, at the moment, more rewarding than my own writing.

Talking to David Adès

by Caryn Rogers

David Adès, the Convenor of Friendly Street Poets, sounded like quite an interesting person, being a lawyer and a poet, and my colleague, Christy, began some initial study on him and his background. She printed off the information published about him on the Friendly Street website. In the corner was a photograph of a very cheerful looking man, flanked by information that demonstrated an interesting and rich cultural heritage. In a sense, it was that grin that put me at ease when thinking about interviewing a complete stranger.

When I spoke to David on the telephone I found him to be warm, humorous and succinct. I was beginning to feel more excited about the poetry project at hand. David told us he would wear a red beanie so we would recognise him, and it was a little distressing waking up to a very sunny and warm day. Christy and I walked into Café Bravo, searching faces for someone vaguely resembling the man from the website photo. I was expecting a broadly built man to appear (this was what I'd gathered from the photo of just his face), when a small, wiry man clutching a red beanie came up to me. And then I saw that beaming smile. We shook hands, found a table, and the interview began.

From start to finish, David chatted easily with us about poetry, work, travel, hopes, passions and the future. He struck me as a highly intelligent man, one with a considerable amount of influence over the face of poetry in South Australia. One looking for arrogance will not find it in David Adès. He was honest about his own shortcomings, and somewhat beautifully child-like in his excitement of connecting with people when he discussed one of his experiences in Greece, where he and another poet really connected over a piece and wandered around reciting it as they walked to their destination. We especially appreciated the interest that he took in Christy's and my poetry, and his encouragement to come out to Friendly Street and participate at the readings.

Out of his slight stature came an enormous persona full of enthusiasm, understanding and humility. It was a pleasure to work with him, and his poems are worthy of recognition.

Reading the poems—'The Work of My Face'

by Christy Van Stralen

> Reading poetry is a way of connecting—through the medium of language—more deeply with yourself even as you connect more deeply with another. (Hirsch, pp. 4–5)

In 'The Work of My Face' Adès explores the idea of a face being a *work*, that is far more than a physical construct, but something emotional, spiritual, historical and universal. Through this exploration, Adès utilises poetry's ability to connect with the reader to its fullness. While all poems are messages in bottles seeking a readership, seeking a connection, Adès takes this a step further by writing about the very connection itself.

This lyric poem comes tumbling out in what appears an almost haphazard manner. 'No one entirely understands the relationship in poetry between trance and craft' (Hirsch 1999). In 'The Work of My Face', one is swept up into the whirlwind exploration jumping from stone to stone all the while discovering more. The repetition here is trance-like but there is also a sense of thought running away with itself. What starts calmly and ponderously soon erupts into an overflowing soliloquy. There is a sense that Adès breaks free of a wood and rushes out into an open plain where suddenly a huge expanse of sky can be seen, in all its limitless possibilities. Adès moves away from himself and begins to lift his gaze to take in all of humanity. He confesses that this poem came surprisingly quickly and with less crafting and reworking than many of his others, which are deliberately structured (e.g. 'Music on My Tongue'). This poem seems to come overflowing and bursting at the seams. The free flowing structure suits the content and idea as Adès opens up his face to all others, and in so doing opens up the poem itself to a broader and more free-flowing structure. Though the structure is unrestrained, harmony and rhythm are retained, and the repetition of phrases creates a steady pace.

'The Work of My Face' reads as a soliloquy and though it speaks on Adès's own behalf, it also speaks on behalf of all the *faces* of the world. Hirsch (1999) says that 'The lyric poem uses words to convey deep feeling and perhaps something deeper than feeling'. I think that 'The Work of My Face' as a lyric poem does convey something deeper than feeling; it conveys a frame of mind, an understanding, a new way of looking at the world, of looking at oneself.

> A poet may speak in his own person, unchanged—or he may present all his characters as living and moving before us. (Aristotle)

In 'The Work of My Face,' Adès does both, speaking on his own behalf and presenting characters as living and moving within himself and before us.

The poem starts with Adès's own face. It is the first set that the reader is presented with. Adès uses metaphors such as 'changing tableau of lines' and 'artist's brush' to create the sense that outside forces are creating this work. The result is not merely in the hands of the person behind the face, but a canvas that many 'artisans' are busy adding to. The concept of time also having its influence ('expressions of every emotion/ of each age') is also presented in the first few lines.

The foundation is being set, there are forces at work—time is an important player in 'The Work of My Face', there is a sense of time personified, time as an artist. But it is more than just time that makes a face. The idea of other faces taking their place within this face is the key theme that now carries on and takes over from time. 'Faces have gathered/ within my face/ like actors for an audition.'—so begins what is to become a steady stream of faces that Adès discovers one by one in a flurry of exploration. Through this poem and the exploration of these faces Adès enjoys, as Baudelaire states it, 'the poet's incomparable privilege of being a will, both himself and other people. Like a wondering soul.' (cited in Hirsch 1999, p. 138)

The faces that are presented are at first generalised and much mystery surrounds them—'that ratbag miscellany of tenants', as he describes them. These first faces described are perhaps the faces of Adès himself, representing the different facets of an individual character that 'peer out from time to time'. Not all these faces are desirable. Many could be 'elbowed' aside. But, 'Let them come!' Adès exuberantly exclaims, rejoicing in the diversity and depth such faces bring to his existence.

From this point on Adès delves into his own face searching for more, looking to see all that he can find beneath its surface, the stories it tells and the people he meets, from his own history and the history of the world. The reader is now presented with a great array of people. Adès continues his search with the faces of his family and relatives, which leads him to the generations that preceded them. This in turn brings him to the history of the world and all its people. Their influence is embraced. Adès takes the reader from general to specifics. He begins with the faces of schoolyard bullies and heroes (generic faces), to the face of Hitler and Mother Teresa (specific).

The comparison or co-habitation of both good and evil is a strong theme throughout this poem. The faces that are found within his own, suggest that Adès's own face is inhabited by both good and evil. The most obvious example is Adès's discovering the face of Hitler, and soon after, the face of Mother Teresa—polar opposites. This same contrast is made in a more general sense with schoolyard bullies and heroes, executioner and the man to be executed etc. Adès incorporates all these faces into his own, creating a universal face—one with the power and potential for great good and for great evil, representing all of humanity.

Adès welcomes all. The invitational 'Let them come' is given a number of times during the poem. Adès invites all, the good and the bad that the world has to offer. The desire to connect with all, to find a sense of common ground is a theme that appears consistently. Adès ends the flow of faces with a final thought of hope:

and when it is finished
I would like
the face in my coffin
to be a face
where every face

has vied for position
a graveyard
for the faces of evil
a face
where love has triumphed.
I would like
the completed work of my face
to be a universal face
to be my one true
momentary
epitaph.

Though every face is welcome and has tried ('vied') for position or 'auditioned', as it is stated in the early lines of the poem, who has succeeded? Who will play the main character? Will evil or good prevail? Adès is hopeful for good to triumph and that his face will be a 'graveyard/ for the faces of evil', yet still a universal face because evil was present, but was overcome.

Like all of Adès's poems, this one seeks to make a connection, but in a far more tangible way than many of his other poems. Each reader sees their own face reflected in Adès's face and sees their own struggle and complexity. The reader feels a connection through this poem, not only with Adès but with all the other faces too. They are the faces we have all seen and done battle with. They are the faces within ourselves and of those around us.

References

Adès, D. (2002) 'The Work of My Face' in *SideWaLK*, issue 9, pp. 7–11.

Aristotle *Poetics* (Translated by S.H. Butcher) [viewed 14 October 2003] http://classics.mit.edwAristotle/poetics.html

Hirsch, E. (1999) *How to Read a Poem and Fall in Love with Poetry*. New York: A Harvest Book, Harcourt Inc.

AMELIA WALKER

Published poetry books

Fat Streets and Lots of Squares—Poems for Adelaide, Bookends Books, Adelaide 2003

Biographical note

Amelia Walker is a young South Australian poet and playwright who recently completed her nursing degree at the University of South Australia. Her first poetry collection, *Fat Streets and Lots of Squares—Poems for Adelaide* was published first using the Independent Arts Foundation Scholarship for Literature awarded through the South Australian Youth Arts Board (SAYAB) and Carclew; a second print run is currently being published through Bookends Books.

(Compiled by Carly Gange)

Interview with Amelia Walker

by Carly Gange and Linda Uphill

Carly Gange (CG): Can you tell us about how you came to be interested in or write poetry?

Amelia Walker (AW): I think I always just liked writing from the time I was a child. It just felt really natural. I suppose I started going into poetry specifically through high school. I think it was a bit because of the teenage angst everyone goes through. But these poems make me cringe cringe cringe!!!

CG: What kind of influence have your parents had on your writing? How do you find parents/people close to you reading personal poems?

AW: My parents found the whole writing thing a little hard to take at first. I mean, seriously, what parent wants their child to be a writer? You make zero money, wear way too much black, hang around with other penniless black-wearing so-called writers, and invariably die young from alcohol poisoning … But seriously, I know this isn't what my parents wanted me to do. However, they've realised how much I love it, and they have been very supportive, which I appreciate more for that reason. With people reading personal poems … um … it's difficult.

CG: What writers have influenced your work?

AW: Too many to say. I think when I first started writing poetry I was really heavily influenced by the Beat Generation. They were a group of writers who lived mainly around San Francisco in the forties and fifties. And I was reading a lot of Allen Ginsberg and Lawrence Ferlinghetti. They were the first poets I read who weren't writing about nature in iambic pentameter and rhyming couplets, and the first poets to make me realise how powerful poetry can be. More recently I have been influenced by Grace Nicholls, an English poet whose collection *The Fat Black Women's Poems* challenges conventional notions of beauty. Her poems are inspirational because reading them makes me feel good. They are simultaneously sad, funny and empowering. I also admire the way that she writes in natural speech patterns. This is something she has in common with the Beats—a writing style that sounds real to everyday people, not pretentious and removed. So she's been a big influence, although my style's very different. I've also been strongly influenced by people I've seen and met at readings in Adelaide.

CG: Being so young have you found the Adelaide poetry scene receptive and encouraging to you?

AW: Yes, very. We've got a great community, it's very supportive.

CG: When and where do you write?

AW: Anywhere, and when I have something to say. I don't really believe in forcing myself to write if I don't have the emotion. If I get writer's block I won't write, I'll read instead and when I feel like writing something I will.

CG: Please tell us about your collection *Fat Streets and Lots of Squares*. Was the localised poetry an intentional or incidental theme?

AW: I wanted to write a collection about Adelaide, I'm not really sure why. I think it stemmed from when I made a poetry video. I applied for a grant from SAYAB and Carclew Youth Arts Centre to make a video with a group of other poets: Finn Kruckemeyer, Fleur Green, James Shepherd, and a young filmmaker, Bec Cordingley. Basically the idea was to make poetry film clips like music videos. So we got the grant and received $400 (I think) to assist us in this youth arts project (so yes, this was a very low budget video!). The finished product was screened at *Off the Couch* and at the *Burning Lines* festival in New South Wales. We filmed a lot of it around Adelaide, and while I was doing that I realised what a cool city it is. A lot of people think it's a dead town, so I wanted to bring out the more interesting side of Adelaide.

CG: Did you actually write the poems *for* the book?

AW: Yes, I did. I applied for the Independent Arts Foundation Scholarship through SAYAB and I had to put in a proposal. I said I wanted to do a collection of poems about Adelaide and they gave me the money and then I went 'oh, now I've actually got to write them'! It was good fun.

CG: Tell us about the editing process.

AW: That was really good. It was the best part of the whole thing. Basically it was really simple. I just gave the poems to Graham Rowlands and he'd edit them and give them back to me. I didn't have to take his advice but most of the time it made sense to. I think it's really hard to judge your own work and sometimes you just need someone to tell you 'look, that's crap'—not that he ever did that, that wouldn't be very professional. He would put it much more diplomatically. Sometimes it was like him reading my journal; it's a bit weird people knowing so much about you. I'd give him about five poems at a time, and then I could apply what he said to the next batch of poems. It was a really intensive learning process, almost like a mentorship at times … I've become a better poet because of that project.

CG: Can you explain a bit about selecting which poems would be used in the collection?

AW: I wrote over a hundred poems over that year and from that we chose as many as you find in the book. So there was a lot that were crap. I basically just let Graham choose and he pretty much chose the poems that I would have chosen. I was happy with the balance of covering different aspects of the city, not too many silly or serious poems. Probably my favourite poem was the generic one about Adelaide.

CG: When I bought my copy there was only one left in the shop. The salesman told me that you've been very popular—were you aware of that?

AW: Serious? That's just weird.

CG: What are you writing at the moment?

AW: I'm working on a novel, which is a pretty big change. It's based on a true story about a woman who became addicted to speed when it was sold legally as a diet pill.

CG: Where do you want to go from here?

AW: I just hope to keep writing.

Talking to Amelia Walker

by Linda Uphill

After much deliberation I had a settled interest in interviewing Geoff Goodfellow, if only because I remembered him as a great character when he read at my high school years ago. However, when Carly told me she had found a poet who was just nineteen and had already published her first collection I was more than a little interested and excited. After reading Amelia Walker's *Fat Streets and Lots of Squares* that excitement bloomed into a colourful blend of inspiration and envy. Not only was she younger than me and published, but she was good. And not just good, she was *good*.

I loved her voice. It wasn't just that it was obviously the voice of a young person that helped me identify with her, it was her keenness for observation and the beautiful and original way she crafted her thoughts. I felt like I had a slice of her life in my hands and her character had been completely made known to me. Through her poetry she came across as very mature, highly social and very confident, also gentle and sensitive. I was not going to like her.

Be that as it may, I was incredibly curious. We contacted her and she suggested we meet her at the City East University Library. Despite my original intentions, the difficulties of city parking brought me undone, and I barely had time to greet my colleagues before we noticed a tall figure eyeing us uncertainly. The three of us swiftly pounced on the poor girl, and as we entered the building together, two things became apparent to me. The first was that she was more nervous than we were. The second, which is not wholly unrelated to the first, was that despite my expectations, I was not going to dislike Amelia Walker. I had anticipated that keeping my envy at bay during a professional interview might prove a strain. Needless to say it was not, although that is no slight to Amelia, far from it.

I was struck powerfully by the maturity and confidence of Amelia's poetry. In meeting her I was struck equally powerfully by the realisation that she was really only nineteen. Although the blurb divulged this information it is not at all evident in her writing. Yet, in person, she betrayed her age in her body language, her self-consciousness, and in some of her verbal responses. It was bewildering to equate this girl who was all quiet friendliness and humility to the strong, confident voice of *Fat Streets*. She was thinner than I expected and had a dark coat wrapped tightly round herself, over a pale nurse's uniform. A pencil was pushed through her tangled blonde ponytail, although she never acknowledged it, and for all I saw, she never even knew it was there.

The interview was foreign turf for all of us. We bounced around her like a hyperactive army. She answered our questions quickly and simply, and even as she grew more at ease this had little effect in raising the volume of her voice. She is one of the most unobtrusive people I have ever met. And yet, if I have been impressed by many people, I have never been so completely inspired as I was by Amelia.

She is incredibly humble, almost embarrassed by her successes. She is happier talking about her collection more as a process and learning experience than an achievement. She repeatedly stated that a lot of her work was 'crap', and despite having had monologues and short plays performed in Sydney, the Adelaide Fringe Festival and by year twelve students, she laughed when we suggested she was a playwright. 'I try,' she said, 'I've never written a full length play.' When I expressed any admiration for her achievement in writing plays she was uncomfortable and repeatedly stated that 'they're not full length plays'.

She spoke with her hands and said very little about her poetry in reference to what she was thinking or feeling or intending in them. Perhaps things will change, but at this stage, Amelia Walker is much more comfortable with letting her poems speak for themselves. She shrank away from personal questions such as how she handles people knowing what she writes about them. While she has the confidence to write and publish poems with detailed aspects of her private life, there is incredible reluctance to talk about those poems and how she handles those close to her reading work that is as intimate at times, as her own journal.

Finding out anything that she has achieved is a ticklish business. She will answer anything you ask her, but she won't volunteer to tell you anything. During our discussion she mentioned that she organised a Spoken Word night once a month, that she began reading her poems at Friendly Street when she was seventeen, that she filmed a Spoken Word poem in Adelaide with a grant that she received. She's good, she must know she's good, but you really can not tell. She is a genuinely likeable person, but when I examined her face and her mildly spoken manner she was different to the person that spoke to me in her poems.

Nothing in her manner indicated to me that here was a person with the self-assurance to read her work in front of large crowds that included well-known and well-established poets. Nothing indicated that here was a person with so much sheer initiative that she had achieved so much in a field outside her degree. Nothing indicated the courage and fearlessness that is evident in everything that she has done. And I found this the most wonderful thing about her. When her age and achievements are underscored by her humility it becomes incredibly challenging and incredibly impressive. I walked away from the interview with Amelia Walker with a whole lot more admiration and faith in her. I walked away with a real sense of hope and optimism that I can succeed at making my own dreams reality. The question 'why haven't I chased my dreams more actively?' has been running through my head ever since. That might sound overstated, but the similarities of her age and ambitions to mine made such a sensation inescapable. I will always be grateful that I had the opportunity to interview Amelia Walker, and grateful to her that through this experience, she gave me something so very substantial.

Reading the poems

by Elizabeth Kidd

Amelia Walker's first book *Fat Streets and Lots of Squares—Poems for Adelaide*, published in 2003, is a collection of poems written about Adelaide. It was inspired during the production of a poetry video made around and about Adelaide, when Walker decided that she wanted to write about and share the 'more interesting side of Adelaide' (see interview p. 177). The major themes of her poems are the places and people that make Adelaide the city it is today.

The popularity and success of *Fat Streets and Lots of Squares* is undoubtedly due to the originality, imagination, insight, and honesty displayed by Walker. Her poetry not only depicts her own personal experiences, but also reveals her youth, energy, enthusiasm, and wicked sense of humour. In addition, Walker displays great creativity in her ability to write about common, everyday things in an exciting, humorous manner. She writes with passion and expresses thoughts that most other people would not dare say aloud. An example of this is 'if you take the other [stance] you're a disrespectful coward', in her poem 'Political poetry'. All of these elements combine to make highly interesting and entertaining poetry that is suitable and appealing to a wide audience.

Seven poems from *Fat Streets and Lots of Squares* have been selected for discussion.

A delightful four-stanza poem which encapsulates the diversity of the people of Adelaide is the poem 'Buskers'. The stanzas, separated by numbers, are littered with alliteration such as 'beneath his battered' and 'ribbon roses'. This, together with deliberate pauses at the end of every first line of the stanzas, creates a sense of rhythm that is maintained throughout the poem. Walker's imagination and creativity are evident in her use of analogy and simile: legs are 'like Cuban cigars' and floating bubbles are 'like dandelion seeds'. According to Tunnicliffe (1984, p. 65), imagery has 'a part to play in the totality of the poetry experience' and the overall appeal of 'Buskers' is mostly due to the language used, which creates great imagery.

In the short free verse poem 'Goth Chick', Walker explicitly reveals the perspective of an outsider and an intentional judgemental, somewhat cynical viewpoint of the subject. The alliterative p's in 'paste; pale cheeks, eyes pinned' and b's in 'big black boots' create a heightened sense of rhythm, as does the repetition of the word 'black'. The poem consists of eleven lines and this has great appeal to the eye. It is enjoyable because it is simple, succinct and sharp: the poet's mood and emotions are directly made known to the reader.

The appeal and effect of the poem 'Rundle Mall' is mainly due to the persona adopted by Walker, that is, of a five-year-old child. Analogy such as being lost is like the feeling of being 'caught in the ocean', and similes such as 'like a melon on a spring box' are used to capture the innocence and creativity of a child. The use of metaphor ('this whole place looks hungry') is creative and effective, and the word 'hungry' is well chosen because it illustrates the fear in the child. The rhythm is constant, yet varied. Overall, Walker's language is creative, with good imagery, and accurately and vividly depicts child-like interpretations and emotions of being lost in Rundle Mall.

According to Kazemek and Rigg (1995), lyrical poetry is typically a very personal form of poetry and is an expression of the poet's emotions and insights. It is these elements that make the panegyric poem 'Political Poetry' so appealing. Walker subtly praises the heroes of the World Wars and her appreciation and sorrow is particularly evident in the first and third stanzas. Alliteration and simile are again effectively used, such as 'like mercury through my veins', which creates impressive imagery. Anaphora, such as 'If you' and 'I like' at the beginning of each line in the first and second stanzas, is effectively used to create rhythm, as is the repetition of the word 'kisses'.

'Pancake Kitchen, Gilbert Place' is a free verse poem that reveals a very personal perspective of Walker. It is fun, humorous, and easily related to one's own personal experiences. The sense of rhythm, which according to Reeves (1970, p. 112) is 'the most important of a poet's technical resources', is again increased by the alliterative 'p's in 'pancakes and pictures', 'g's in 'gossiping about the girl' and 'guided by glimpses'.

Walker uses simple analogy, and her descriptive language and personifications, such as 'doors might be mouths', are effective in creating vivid imagery for the reader.

'They Came Out of the Carpet ...' is an interesting poem. Walker has chosen an unusual topic, one that university students can relate to. The persona adopted by Walker is very natural and honest and the topic is obviously something that she is passionate about. The poem develops as a story and the short first line of each stanza assists in breaking the 'story' into sections. It also creates a pulse. The simile/metaphor in the first stanza is clever and vividly describes the condition of the carpet in the bar. Great, clear imagery is created in this poem, and although the final stanza is incomplete, it finishes the poem beautifully by leaving the reader with a sudden, final realisation.

The most successful poem in the collection is undoubtedly 'Where is Adelaide'. It is honest, fresh, creative, and depicts Walker's appreciation for the small yet significant characteristics of Adelaide. Anaphora, such as 'Are you' and 'Do you', is used effectively throughout the poem, not only in creating and maintaining rhythm, but also allowing Walker to adopt a questioning, inquisitive voice. Additionally, the city of Adelaide is personified by the metaphors, 'Are you a man?' or 'Are you an artist?' Walker uses places, events, landmarks, symbols, and, in particular, people to create the journey through Adelaide. The last three lines in the fourth stanza are of particular interest:

> Are you sixteen years old
> pashing your boyfriend on the bank of the Torrens
> when you ought to be at school?

This is a subtle indication of Walker's youth, yet also her energy and wit. I very much enjoyed reading this poem.

Walker's poetry is a delight to read and is successful for a number of reasons. According to Hirsch (1999, p. 9) 'the sound of the words is the first primitive pleasure in poetry'. Walker's words are descriptive and create a voice, rhythm, and mood. Her use of alliteration in particular is effective and appealing. She is unafraid to be honest in her poetry. This enables her to capture the atmosphere or feeling of a place or person accurately and with feeling, and her reader is able to get a sense of who she is as a person. Finally, in Powell's (1967) discussion of the evaluation of poetry he asserts that 'any genuine piece should ring true even to the reader who has not actually experienced the situation described in the poem' (p. 96). Walker's poetry is indeed consistent with what any person, familiar or unfamiliar with Adelaide, would expect to find there. She has brought out the interesting side of Adelaide and hence has much to be proud of in her writing.

References

Hirsch, E. (1999) *How to Read a Poem and Fall in Love with Poetry*. New York: A Harvest Book, Harcourt Inc.

Kazemek, F.E. and Rigg, P. (1995) *Enriching Our Lives: Poetry Lessons for Adult Literacy Teachers and Tutors*. USA: International Reading Association Inc.

Powell, B. (1967) *English Through Poetry Writing*. Sydney: Ian Novak Publishing Co.

Reeves, J. (1970) *Understanding Poetry*. London: Heinemann.

Tunnicliffe, S. (1984) *Poetry Experience: Teaching and Writing Poetry in Secondary Schools*. USA: Methuen & Co.

RORY HARRIS

Published poetry books

over the outrow, Friendly Street Poets, Adelaide 1982
from the residence, Teachers' Publishing Company, Adelaide 1984
snapshots from a moving train, Friendly Street Poets, Adelaide 1988
16 poems, Studio, NSW 1995
Uncle Jack & Other Poems, Studio, NSW 1998
waterline, Five Islands Press, Wollongong 1999
breeze, Studio 2001
songs, The South Australian English Teachers Association, Adelaide 2003

Biographical note

Rory Harris is a poet and teacher, with the two roles inextricably intertwined. A baby-boomer, he was born in the 1950s in Adelaide's western suburbs. He lives near the sea on the Le Fevre Peninsula, with his wife and daughters.

Rory Harris is a curriculum coordinator at St Paul's College in Gilles Plains. He has published a variety of works, ranging from volumes of poetry, textbooks on teaching poetry and anthologies.

(Compiled by Dorothy Shorne)

Interview with Rory Harris

by Megan Boyd

Megan Boyd (MB): Why did you start writing poetry?

Rory Harris (RH): Love ... love ... I was in love with a girl in Year 12. I was one of those wonderful students that didn't read a book voluntarily until I was seventeen. I went to a boys' school and it wasn't until I went to a co-ed school in Year 12 that I had the opportunity to meet 'like-minded' people (girls) to talk to. If you are lonely and you discover reading late, then you need to find a space where you can go out there and do your business. I would write journals, take pieces out and create poetry from them. This girl gave me a book titled *Good Times Bad Times* by James Kirkwood and it was fantastic. We would drink warm Coopers Stout, smoke cigarettes, and write. It was great having an audience, someone to share that stuff with; it was wonderful.

MB: What did you want to be in those days?

RH: I always wanted to be a teacher though I didn't go to university to do my Bachelor of Education until I was in my thirties. I did however start working 'unpaid' in schools as a writer in 1978. I wasn't doing much back then except writing, drinking beer and getting out of bed late; it was the time when my first poems were being published. I would go to the school, read the poems and take the poetry classes.

MB: What are your main sources of inspiration?

RH: All over … I think that you know there is something to write about when you get that thing under your tongue, you get that shimmer. Lately that has been family or school stuff, but you know it is something when you get that itch, that sense of 'I can't nail that down'. You know that you can generate something when you get that shimmer.

MB: Your poetry is very intimate. Do you find this difficult to express publicly?

RH: No … not really, I'm used to it. I did a book in 1984 called *from the residence*, which is based on the kids at school, and it was really great to 'purge' all that stuff … also the madness and the joy of fatherhood. I get a few criticisms like 'Harris is churning out baby poems', and I do write along those lines. I'm doing it like you are living and breathing it. I guess you make that pitch publicly. A big poem for me is called 'Indonesia September, 1999', which merges the stuff of parents nurturing a child, and trying to get a country like Indonesia to remember those instincts.

MB: You focus on writing poetry rather than other literary areas—was this a conscious decision?

RH: There is something lovely about writing poetry. It's nice to be

'Rory Harris—poet', whereas others will be writer/poet etc. I wrote some articles years ago and that was fun, but I like poetry. It is the short hand—either you get it, or you don't. Right now my poems are getting smaller ... I don't have the stamina for the other stuff. I don't have the stamina to write a large article, then realise that you have to go back and do it again, and again, polishing your work. I would rather polish forty words than forty paragraphs.

MB: How do you work?

RH: I have a little bit of a room. I write by hand to get the idea down, and then work by hand one more time. I still use the typewriter. My kids have shown me how to put the poems on the computer. They are so small that by the time I set the computer up I could have had the poem finished: one copy for filing, one for sending away, and one for the archive—I like the neatness of that. Some other writers spend ages mucking around with fonts or filing the poems away.

MB: Do you have a particular style that you favour?

RH: You put your poem on the page and it is going to reflect the content. For the last few years I have been almost exclusively mucking around with two-line stanzas. I love the neatness; it looks really lovely on the page. 'waterline' is almost exclusively two-line stanzas—it looks pretty and it's easy to read. I'm now mainly working with this style. When you have been writing for a long time, it's nice to concentrate on smaller things with significance, be more minimal.

MB: What do you think makes good poetry?

RH: A poem has to be crisp enough to hold you—if anyone can write something crisp enough to hold in their hand then you have written a good poem. By 'crisp' I mean as long as you are moved by it. I'm not into that high and mighty stuff, you know, 'what makes a good poet'. You need to judge the quality of the poem, not the poet, and that is very brave editing. It's a bit like editing a Friendly Street Reader—you must look at the work and pick a piece that you think is the best. It doesn't matter if say, you hate her guts, or she owes you money, or he seduced my ex-wife's girlfriend, sister-in-law, etc.

MB: How has your involvement in Friendly Street affected your career as a poet?

RH: I have been involved with Friendly Street since the grand old days, about twenty something years. It was the 'jugular anarchists' that they were into back then … it was mad! Though a lot of that stuff was great in performance, but not good on the page. It was from there that we got the culture and the instant feedback; it's very important. We had brilliant times in Friendly Street. If it didn't exist, I wouldn't have a career as a poet. Most likely I would still be writing my stuff in the Bush or in the Suburbs—I wouldn't have had that sort of 'grand coming out'. It's great to be around other poets doing their business, seeing each other face-to-face and experiencing that sort of collectiveness.

MB: How do you feel about Friendly Street now?

RH: Friendly Street has calmed down a lot now, the people are a lot older, and it's a different gig. There are more people and it has changed over the years, but I would say it is still very successful. I think that over the years Friendly Street has launched quite a few characters—it's a lot quicker than just hanging around 'waiting' for something to happen.

MB: Who are your favorite writers, either within Australia or overseas?

RH: The American poet Adrienne Rich is brilliant. I always buy the latest John Irving novel and an old hippie fellow called Tom Robins, though you have to go through a lot of his stuff before you find the good bits. Another one is Peter Corris—I have all of his 'Cliff Hardy' novels. I read all over the place.

MB: How do you feel about the next generation of poets and what advice would you give them?

RH: They don't need my advice. They are organised. I think they are incredibly well-equipped for publication because of the Internet; the price of printing of books has also gone down. The CD thing is also good. I see many new poets through Friendly Street, and the young 'Turks' and 'Turkettes' are really making some noise. The new poets have venues and they are publishing. Someone in the Writers' Centre did a look at poetry readings held regularly in Adelaide—there are probably about five or six of them. They are in the East End, the west, the south and the north. They are up to speed electronically and technologically to get the stuff down, they have got it organised, and they have venues for publication. I guess the intention for them, if there is a pecking order of publications, is to get into more perceived status journals—that's tough. But then, they can just turn around and do it on their own, and that is exactly what they are doing. They are doing the journals, the books and the magazines—they are running the show.

MB: If you had three wishes, what would they be?

RH: World Peace … I nearly didn't come in today because my daughter has the flu. One of the Year 12s, who's a lovely lad, handed me a plastic bag full of chewing gum—all sorts of 'chewies'. His mum is a rep for Wrigley's and he gave me a shitload of chewing gum, which I thought was really funny because if I hadn't come in today to teach and to see you for the interview I wouldn't have got that … so … World Peace. I have the chewing gum already.

MB: What makes you happy?

RH: The kids are sweet, washing on the line, half a bottle of red wine and a full packet of cigarettes—out in the backyard, thinking about the day. That makes me happy.

Talking to Rory Harris

by Megan Boyd

The journey began in books, cross-legged on the carpet at the university library, sifting through Friendly Street publications dating back to 1982. The poem titled 'the Americans don't monopolise passion' runs obscurely down the page, words darting left then right, stepping down onto themselves. The words each have a stage in which to express the poet's ideas. Only a few lines down I noticed the words 'famous fucker' and in my mind I automatically labelled Rory Harris left wing, erratic. Who is this man, this poet?

This initial response was soon discarded, and a picture of a sensitive artist emerged amidst delicate works such as 'Breath' (*Friendly Street No. 13* 1989), a poem about Rory's then baby daughter, which literally took my breath away.

This lovely piece touched something in me, my own maternal instincts maybe. It is only one of many moving poems that created an insight into the emotional life of Rory Harris. Whilst researching his work I was taken on a journey. Touching the nightmare of losing a child ('Breath for Kerrie Armstrong') and the joy of raising them, Rory gains inspiration through his family, watching his offspring thrive and explore. Many of his works demonstrate the unique ability to see beyond the ordinary, using everyday things to open up whole new realms of thought and introspect. I particularly like the last three stanzas of a poem Rory published in *Friendly Street No. 16* (1992), titled 'the walk':

> the tide pulled back
> like a shirt sleeve
>
> pools of water left behind
> needing children
>
> to make them more
> than what they are

After studying many of Rory's works and researching his background, I felt prepared to launch into the interview process. Interview questions in hand, my colleague and I were to 'meet the poet' at St Paul's College, where Rory works teaching English and Poetry.

My immediate impression of Rory was that he was kind, with the charismatic aura of a 'thinking man'. His green eyes were full with the life of a man interested in living, exploring, creating and expressing new ideas, nurturing his family, his students and his audience.

Reading the poems

by Dorothy Shorne

By his own admission, Rory Harris is a minimalist poet. He loves the neatness of two-line stanzas and finds a minimalist, pared down style of writing to be more enjoyable and more concise than a descriptive or more verbose style. He searches for the simplest elements, and places them carefully on white spaces, letting each word tell the story. The aim is to create a composition that is 'crisp enough to hold in your hand' (see interview, p. 187), in the belief that shorter is better. He also varies the layout across the page because he feels that structure influences readability.

Harris is an advocate of reading poetry aloud. There has been the opportunity for plenty of practice in this with his long involvement with the Friendly Street Poets, occasional stints as a performance poet, and also in his role as an English teacher. There is a power in his poetry that sometimes only has half the impact if left on the page. By reading and sharing it with others, the poem will have greater resonance and impact.

Harris came to poetry in his late teens, having not voluntarily read a book before that. His writing started with a journal but rapidly progressed to poetry. Other forms of writing have never appealed to him, although he has occasionally written articles for journals, and has contributed to various publications with the purpose of teaching poetry and poetry writing. The young Rory Harris seems to have discovered a lifestyle along with the poetry, for he talks of the early 'mad' days of the Friendly Street Poets with some nostalgia for the unreserved performances. Times change, and so do the poets, but Harris credits that environment for contributing towards his evolution as a poet.

His environment and the people in it tend to be the sources of inspiration for Harris's writing. Lately, school and his family have been the topical issues, although it can be anything that gives him the 'shimmer' in the course of his day. Harris is aware that there is the perception that he is always writing about his daughters, but that was not a deliberate approach. Rather, he writes about the people or circumstances that have impact and meaning in his life, and as a dedicated family man, his wife and daughters feature strongly.

One poem that has been printed in a variety of publications is '& when', describing the birth of his daughter Molly Carlisle. With economy of word, he describes eloquently her birth, the process of delivery, and the way she first looked upon the world. The reader is able to 'see' the image of the new baby, slick and wet, freshly settled on her mother's belly:

& when
my girl child

Molly Carlisle
was born

her head
was turned

to one side
as if to view

the world
discreetly, & she

almost forgave
us [...]

Harris's poem 'breath' was published in *Friendly Street Reader No. 13* (1989), and the baby, now six months old, is cradled by her father as she dozes gently on his chest. In the same volume, Harris pays tribute to his wife, acknowledging the mundane tasks they share, but which are indicative of the depth of his feelings for her. Each of these three poems is written in a similar style—always with economy of word, short and concise. Each poem is characterised by two-line stanzas, except for a final single line, and there is no punctuation delineating sentence structure. There are no capital letters and no full stops. The word 'and' is replaced with '&' as if, where possible, the words should be depicted even more concisely.

Hirsch (1999), in *How to Read a Poem*, describes many modern and contemporary poets as being terrified of deep feeling or of seeming undefended and sentimental. Harris's writing does not indicate emotional excesses, but he does use poetry to open his heart, depicting the depth of his feelings and emotions without apology.

Harris's relationship with Friendly Street since its beginning allows us to read works spanning at least a twenty-year period. An examination of two pieces published in *Friendly Street Poetry Reader No. 6* (1982) indicates a subtle change in style over the two decades. 'For Paul to start crying' is written in verse paragraph form, with stanzas of uneven length and pattern. Some are up to seven lines long—much more than the short two-liners he prefers today. Each stanza contains a distinct concept or issue, though not necessarily complete, with the common thread spilling from one into the next. The poem scales down towards the end, with the third last stanza comprising three lines, the second last comprising two lines, and, predictably, the last stanza of just one line. The language used is more conversational, though the writing is still sparse. The adjoining poem, 'The student' is more indicative of his later style, with shorter stanzas and tighter line structure. However, even the shorter stanzas contain a distinct piece of information each. Once again, the poem ends with a one-liner.

A stark contrast in point of structure is the breath-length poem 'the father', published in the *Friendly Street Poetry Reader No. 26* (2002). Still characterised by an absence of sentence structure and punctuation, the poem comprises one long stanza of thirty-eight lines. It is a poem in which Harris speaks to his father saying things that have accumulated over many years:

> in your first house
> & most probably your last
> you have changed the locks
> in the age it takes to get old
> for a garden to turn
> rose bushes thin & angry

The words spill out, with the issues running into and over and through each other, so that although there are several topics that he wants to raise with his father, they are all inter-related and merge into one long verse. It is an emotional poem that is delivered with a torrent of passion, and there is no final one-line stanza.

A reading of other recent poems, however, indicates that his poems tend to be shorter—less words and shorter lines, so that each poem is a micro study, a poetic morsel that can be viewed as a distinct observation within a bigger picture. Rory Harris writes about things he knows and loves, and turns them into poetry that he throws 'out there' to be read and enjoyed.

References

Brewster, A and Johnson, R. (eds) (1982) *Friendly Street Poetry Reader No. 6*. Adelaide: Friendly Street with Wakefield Press.

Frazer, C. and Westburg, B. (eds) (1989) *Friendly Street Poetry Reader No. 13*. Adelaide: Friendly Street with Wakefield Press.

Hirsch, E. (1999) *How to Read a Poem and Fall in Love with Poetry*. New York: A Harvest Book, Harcourt Inc.

McFarlane, P. and Harris R. (1997) *Doing Bombers off the Jetty*. Melbourne: Macmillan Education Australia Ltd.

McFarlane, P. and Mansutti, E. (eds) (1992) *Friendly Street Poetry Reader No. 16*. Adelaide: Friendly Street with Wakfield Press.

Petrescu, I. and Adès, D. (eds) (2002) *Friendly Street Poetry Reader 26*. Adelaide: Friendly Street with Wakefield Press.

JUDE AQUILINA

Published poetry books
Knifing the Ice, Wakefield Press/Friendly Street, Adelaide 2000
On a Moon Spiced Night, Wakefield Press, Adelaide forthcoming

Biographical note
Jude Aquilina was born in Adelaide and grew up in Magill in the City's eastern suburbs. Jude graduated from Norwood High School and married Daniel Aquilina in 1987. She began writing poetry at the age of thirty after her second child was born, and subsequently published a collection of poems, *Knifing the Ice,* which was launched at Writers' Week 2000. Jude's poetry has been published in newspapers and journals across Australia and in the UK. She also writes short stories, reviews and articles. She is a regular reader at Friendly Street and often performs her work at festivals, schools and other venues. Jude conducts poetry workshops for students and adults. She now lives with her family on a farm in the Adelaide Hills.

(Compiled by Kirsty Lubcke)

Interview with Jude Aquilina

by Adriana Timpano and Kirsty Lubcke

Adriana Timpano (AT): What inspired you to start writing poetry?

Jude Aquilina (JA): I was surrounded by poetry from an early age because my father had a large collection of old English poetry. He would read to me from small suede-bound books. I remember him reading 'The Sands of Dee' by John Drinkwater, a poem about a young girl who drowned while herding her cows. My brother introduced me to poetic singers such as Leonard Cohen and Bob Dylan and their words inspired me. I didn't start writing poetry until after my children were born. I went to a group run by Jeri Kroll and she introduced me to contemporary poetry, and more importantly, contemporary women's poetry (most of the poetry I'd read until then was by men).

Kirsty Lubcke (KL): When you are not writing poetry, how do you like to spend your time?

JA: I live on a farm at Cudlee Creek so there is always plenty to do. I keep geese, chickens, ducks and rabbits. They give me a lot of pleasure and provide a balance for my other work. I work part time in a music shop, so I tend to do most of my writing at night. I also give poetry workshops in schools and attend poetry festivals, and readings such as Friendly Street. I've recently been a mentor for a young SA poet who has gone on to publish her first book. This is very rewarding. And I have been mentored by WA poet Andrew Taylor as part of the Australian Society of Authors' mentorship program.

AT: How do you record your inspirations?

JA: I am a notebook person. I find inspiration comes from my everyday life and if I don't jot down a note or idea, I may forget it. Later, when I have some spare time, I take my notebooks to my study, start the computer and try to turn the notes into poems. Some poems work, others do not. I never run out of ideas. I also keep a dream diary. Dreams can make you feel emotions you may never experience in real life. I record my vivid dreams and I sometimes use elements of them in my writing. I once tied a pen to my bed-head hoping to wake up with brilliant ideas and jot them down. Most of the time the pen didn't work and when it did, I couldn't read my scrawl.

KL: Whose poetry do you most admire?

JA: I admire many poets, especially Margaret Atwood, Marge Piercey, Gwen Harwood, Oodgeroo, Judith Wright. There are also a number of SA poets whom I hear read their work and am inspired by.

AT: How would you describe your poetry?

JA: My poetry is contemporary, non-rhyming, and sometimes humorous. My poems vary in style and subject matter. I let a poem find its own form and am not bound by strict poetic rules, although I have written sonnets and used rhyme at times. I have no taboos and will write about any issue.

KL: How did you first get published?

JA: When I began writing poetry, Jeri Kroll suggested going to Friendly Street to hear other poets read their work. This was enlightening, nerve-racking, and inspiring. I learned that many of these poets were sending their work out for publication. This encouraged me to do so. I joined the SA Writers' Centre and began sending poems to newspapers and magazines. After some publishing success, I submitted a manuscript to Friendly Street and it was accepted. My first poetry collection, *Knifing the Ice* was published as a single collection by Wakefield Press/Friendly Street Poets and launched at Adelaide Writers' Week 2000.

AT: Are you currently working on any projects?

JA: I am working on my next poetry collection titled *On a Moon Spiced Night*. I am currently doing the final edit. The book has four sections: *Habitat, Love's Dream, Seeds,* and *Creature Acts*. It will be published by Wakefield Press in 2004. I also write articles, reviews and short stories. So there are always a few projects on the go. I would like to write a novel one day.

KL: What was your first poem?

JA: 'Older Brothers' was my first poem. It is a factual record of my upbringing. I was the youngest in the family and the only girl, and was consequently somewhat spoilt. This poem is about the devious teasing my brothers put me through. The poem went through about twenty drafts before I was happy with it.

AT: What do you hope to achieve through your poetry?

JA: I hope that my poems might make people think/laugh/cry—this is an achievement, to have other people share your words and become moved in some way. I'd also like my work to reach a wider audience. I recently had poetry published in the United Kingdom. I'd like to travel, and hope my next book might enable me to do so. I'd like to get a writer's residency in another state or country.

KL: What is your background?

JA: I am part Yugoslav, Scottish and English. My husband is part Maltese. It is great to have such diverse heritage. I am interested in family history and do a little research in my spare time. I was born in suburban Adelaide and I always wanted to live in the country. My dream came true when I married Daniel and moved to the Adelaide hills.

AT: What was your inspiration for 'Cheese', 'To a Black Fridge' and 'The Lonesome Cowgirl Blues'?

JA: 'Cheese'—at the time of writing this poem, I worked at the Adelaide Central Market in a cheese boutique. I was surrounded by cheese. This poem came easily and it won the Satura Poetry Prize.

'To a Black Fridge'—the poem is based on a university party, a black and white party. I met my husband there in the kitchen next to a fridge, which someone had painted black. Party life always seems to revolve around the kitchen and the fridge. I wanted to capture this phenomenon.

'The Lonesome Cowgirl Blues'—at the time of writing this poem, I was president of the Barossa Writers. Our monthly writing topic was 'a line of seduction'. I'm afraid I got carried away!

KL: What is your process for writing poetry?

JA: I usually have a lot of poems going at once. Then, when I get time, I work on them. I've always believed that you can see what needs to be done to a poem after an interval or a week or so. Having poems in various stages of completion means that I don't get too close to or precious about any single poem. My friends and family rarely read my poetry. However, I am in a poetry workshop group called First Draft. This group of Friendly Street poets has been meeting for over a decade. There are ten members and we all bring copies of our work and give constructive criticism to each other. I also use Friendly Street as a forum for trying out new work.

AT: What does poetry mean to you?

JA: It means capturing a truth. Poetry is a very truthful art and I've learnt many things about people and life from reading poetry. I like the way you can say more in a short space with poetry than with prose. You can write about a subject from obscure angles, from different personas; you can be strange; and you can capture the essence of something in very few words. My poems are often written from personal experience, so they provide a record and help me understand myself and my surroundings. The act of writing poetry is also an escape from the busy modern world. For me, self-expression through poetry provides an exciting journey which I hope keeps changing and offering surprises.

Talking to Jude Aquilina

by Adriana Timpano

Browsing the poetry section in Borders, a bright azure coloured book caught my eye. I flicked through the pages to find the interesting, fresh and unique poetry of Jude Aquilina. It was after reading the multi-faceted 'To a Black Fridge' that I found my project-perfect South Australian poet. I was not surprised whenanother colleague shared this interest. We united as Jude devotees and began our journey immediately.

On the interview morning, we met to distribute our tasks in the discussion. Half an hour later, we wandered up the stairs to the SA Writers' Centre, a scene that was unfamiliar yet, as we were to find out, vital to our future as writers. We were directed to a conference area with a large table. As the entrance doors to the centre opened, we kept wondering 'is that her?' After seeing a diminutive picture of Jude in her book *Knifing the Ice*, we expected a dark haired lady with a retro aura. She appeared on time with a colossal smile, and greeted us with enthusiasm. She was everything I had expected in appearance right down to her deep red lipstick and black outfit.

From the moment Jude entered the room, there were no difficulties in initiating conversation. Her fervent answers showed her appreciation of our partiality to her work. She spoke eloquently as she does in her poems, and with a gentle voice. She ensured each word she uttered expressed perfectly her opinions, and therefore appeared a cautious speaker. However, she was not restrained in revealing information that exhibited her effervescent personality. The interview focused on how Jude began, the motivation behind her works and the aspirations she holds for her poetry. I discovered that Jude the person is almost identical to Jude the poet. Both are optimistic, humorous, and inspired by people and life. Incidentally, Jude believes that poetry allows you to reveal more truths and express them directly. Honesty is a trait of both Jude the poet and person, as revealed by the realistic ideas in her poems and her answers to our questions. Jude also told us that many of her poems have sentimental value. 'Older Brothers' is about the problems she experienced when she was younger, having two bossy brothers. It is her first poem and she considers it one of her 'treasures.' Jude's fervour for poetry based on personal experience has inspired me to write poetry from my heart.

Reading the poems

by Adriana Timpano and Kirsty Lubcke

It has been said that 'a poem may be read as a conjectural means of access to the hidden depths of the author's personality' (Preminger 1965, p. 170). This is evident throughout the works of Jude Aquilina, which endorse personal views and sentiments through a contemporary free-form approach. Aquilina's poems 'Cheese', 'To a Black Fridge', and 'Mrs Doom' each represent a different stage in her life, and use rhythm, metaphor and simile to offer an insight into the world of the poet.

While working at a cheese stall in Adelaide's Central Market, Aquilina wrote an ode to her beloved cheese. The use of similes and metaphors is prevalent throughout Aquilina's work, none more infatuating than in the third stanza of 'Cheese':

> How many odes to a cow are sung?
> More honour is bestowed on the moon,
> that languid autumn Gouda
> eaten by hungry shadows.

Aquilina's poetry is not just that of personal accounts, as a deeper underlying notion of cultural significance can be felt. The first and fifth stanzas, written in third and first person respectively, signify cheese as the unsung hero of the marketplace. The poem does not employ any set rhythms, and changes between first, second and third person perspectives. Readers set their own rhythm and feeling to a poem making different qualities of the text attract separate audiences.

'To a Black Fridge' is a symbolic poem of the night Aquilina first met her husband. Through two specific metaphors the fridge is personified. In the first stanza, the fridge is observed as a robot whose 'delightful' human qualities provoke feelings of adoration from the speaker. The rhythmic words 'stranger', 'corner' and 'longer' at the end of lines four, five, and six respectively hypnotise the reader, demonstrating how the speaker is spellbound by the black fridge as if it were human:

> You robot of the party you
> You delightful little dalek
> Tattooed in greenpeace and 5MMM
> Oh dark and silent stranger
> Luring me into your corner
> I can't resist you any longer
> Here hold my drink while I lean

The second metaphor envisions the fridge as a flirt through adulterous images (Preminger 1965, p. 363). The fridge is labelled a 'tart' for its tendency to lavishly dispense alcohol. The two metaphors illustrate the speaker's varied emotions. At the beginning of the poem, she is passionate towards the fridge, now a robot, suggesting it is alluring because it is black rather than the conventional white like the 'other squares'. The attitude turns bitter at the end of the second stanza when it is discovered that the fridge is an unlawful 'tart'. The line 'don't push me away like that' gives the image of the fridge door thwacking the speaker out of the way as it opens for others. When the truth is discovered, the speaker seeks revenge by picking off the tacky stickers with which the fridge is 'tattooed'.

The free verse style is suggestive of the casual atmosphere of the party. As Hirsch (1999) suggests, free verse allows the reader to 'participate in the making of poetic thought' (p. 283). In 'To a Black Fridge', this refers to the reader's participation in the speaker's abrupt change in attitude in stanza two. The reader does not predetermine this transformation. There is no recognisable structure in the poem as in a limerick where the nonsensical ending is a structural characteristic the reader has predetermined.

Similar to 'Cheese' and 'To a Black Fridge', 'Mrs Doom' focuses on a personal aspect of Aquilina's life. The protagonist is Aquilina's aunt, who after reading the poem was oblivious to the resemblance. As with every poem, the author writes for a specific reading from the audience (Preminger 1965, p. 160). Aquilina aims for the reader to form an image of her aunt as eccentric. The intended representation of Mrs Doom is provoked early in the first stanza. The reader is informed that she 'prefers wakes to weddings' and 'gets a certain high from the smell of hospitals'. Such partialities are associated with the notions of death, illness, and with the label 'doom':

> Mrs Doom is six foot two
> Towers above her husband
> Thrives on illness
> House is spotless
> Knows how germs breed
> Prefers wakes to weddings
> Cough-lollies to alcohol
> And gets a certain high
> From the smell of hospitals.

The first two stanzas produce an image of a hospital. The word 'spotless' is used to describe Mrs Doom's house, perhaps suggesting it is disinfected or infirmary-like. Another of Mrs Doom's peculiarities is her interest in devastation as she 'points out weeds, aphids and rust,' perhaps as evidence of the destruction of life. The speaker suggests in the final stanza that Mrs Doom's odd fascination may be a result of the shingles breakout she suffered on her wedding day. Her 'tackle-box' of pills has since been her saviour.

As in 'To a Black Fridge' and 'Cheese', there is no structured rhyming in 'Mrs Doom'. However, the use of alliteration gives the poem a similar pulse to that of rhyme. The phrases 'slowly sits', 'seeing the specialist' and 'wakes to weddings' initiate rhythm through phonic echoes and give truth to Tsvetaeva's (1999) notion of comparing lyrical elements to the waves of the sea (in Hirsch 1999, p. 306). Although the interpretation of the poem may vary for each reader, the intended image of Mrs Doom's eccentricity will be recognised.

The combination of varying first and third person perspectives, as well as line structure and rhythms within each of Aquilina's works, complement her free verse approach. Metaphors, similes and imagery both of the romantic and practical nature are predominant throughout. The themes of the poems are consistent as is the idea of the poet's desire to recognise the tenor for each poem as a significant phase of her life, and that of the consequent personal accounts.

References

Buchbinder, D. (1991) *Contemporary Literary Theory and the Reading of Poetry*. Melbourne: Macmillan.

Hirsch, E. (1999) *How to Read a Poem and Fall in Love with Poetry*. New York: A Harvest Book, Harcourt Inc.

Preminger, A. (1965) 'Imagery' and 'Practical Criticism' in *Encyclopaedia of Poetics*. New Jersey: Princeton University Press.

STEVE EVANS

Published poetry books

Edison Doesn't Invent the Car, Wakefield Press/Friendly Street, Adelaide 1990
Algebra, Wakefield Press, Adelaide 1992
Bonetown, Wakefield Press, Adelaide 1994
Useful Translations, Picaro Press, Warners Bay 2003
Luminous Fruit, Bookends Publishing, Adelaide 2003
Taking Shape, Five Islands Press, Wollongong, forthcoming 2004

Biographical note

Steve Evans grew up in the country of South Australia and eventually moved to Adelaide, where he now resides. After a career as an accountant and business manager, Steve undertook an MA in Creative Writing at Adelaide University.

Steve's first collection of poems was published while he was still working as an accountant, however, after he gained his degree in creative writing, poetry became his number one occupation. Steve now teaches at Flinders University, after having taught at TAFE, within the community, and at other universities.

(Compiled by Fleur Holmes)

Interview with Steve Evans

by Fleur Holmes

Fleur Holmes (FH): Please tell us about your first experience with writing and poetry. Did you enjoy writing other genres before you became interested in poetry?

Steve Evans (SE): Poetry came first, though I wrote two novels when I was young. They were awkward, experimental things and I put them in the bottom drawer and left them there.

Poetry was always my first love. At the age of eight or nine I read prose but by about the age of eleven or twelve I was preoccupied by poetry. Pop music influenced this, with the baby-boomer teens discovering the world and freedom, the Beatles, hippies, changing attitudes to work, women's liberation, beat poets, European poetry, and so on.

FH: As an established poet, whom do you see as rising talent within South Australia or elsewhere?

SE: This is where you leave someone out and remember them later! A rising talent is someone like Shen. Aiden Coleman is very good; he hasn't got a book out yet but is very good. Other local writers that should get more notice are people like Jude Aquilina. What I like about what's happening in South Australia is not just to do with individual poets, but the scene that is developing—like Friendly Street, the pub scene and the alternative readings. That is where a lot of our rising talent comes from. It's the core. If I think of any more names I'll let you know!

FH: Who do you most admire as a poet and why?

SE: What we had available to us when I was younger was largely World War Two school stuff, then poets such as Judith Wright and Bruce Dawe, which was okay. But I found that it was so familiar that I couldn't get out of it what I could from, say, Thomas or Levertov or Dickey. Dickey's work was so narrative-driven with strong characters; it was very visual writing. Denise Levertov, her writing was superb, and Sylvia Plath of course. Dylan Thomas, I guess for the music in the language and a very strong sense of tradition and passion. The people in Australia that I started to read after that were people like Robert Gray and Geoff Lehmann. I'm just trying to picture my bookshelves. For a little while it was Vicki Vidiikas, and Peter Goldsworthy; he has a nice sardonic edge. It's like there's two camps. There are the foreign, more established poets, and the fine local ones. There's Kate Llewellyn, a woman born in Tumby Bay. She has a lovely feel, a nice sense of touch; she writes about a woman's life. Richard Tipping is a very funny, edgy writer. Christine Churches is a lovely writer, but she basically gave it up to study becoming a historian. To come back to the present—I've grown to love Csezlaw Milosz,

Wislawa Szymborska, Charles Simic for that European sensibility. Can't overlook Seamus Heaney or Eavan Boland, and Billy Collins amuses. Where do you stop?

FH: Where does most of your inspiration for your poetry come from? You've mentioned music—what about work or family?

SE: It comes from everywhere. The specifics or the situations that help me to write vary, but the best one is often reading poetry itself. The first step is finding the time to read and in a sense this allows you to pull yourself away from other things, practical things such as cleaning dishes or marking papers. If you can do this you're halfway there, halfway to getting into that frame of mind for writing. That's not to say that you can't find some little slice of time somewhere to write—but for me, if I want to write my best, it means making the time. The moments can come anywhere—in meetings, doing spreadsheets, during news broadcasts. Suddenly I think, 'where's the pen?' It can be one word that does it; a piece of dialogue or, quite frequently, it can be a twist on something. I might think, what if I change the role of a person, or what if I tweak the situation and make it absurd—can I write about it? One of the most frustrating things is not to have pen and paper. I always try to carry them for those moments in the day when you can find that slice of time. People may say to me after a meeting, 'Gee, you jotted a lot down while so-and-so was talking!' when really I've been off in my own world of poetry, scrawling.

FH: When do you write most of your work? You have answered some of this already. Is there any more you would like to add? What about the editing process?

SE: The start of writing poetry is as I've just said, but the drafting and re-drafting of poems take place at more set times and stages. The re-working of my poems usually takes place at night. I have a folder of poems that I will occasionally go back to, and sometimes I look at what's there and think, 'what was I thinking?' But there is the flip side of, 'oh, I wrote that!'—a pleasant surprise now and then. Some people say they've got the genesis for a poem scribbling on the back of their cigarette pack, it's almost like that. I write on advertising brochures, napkins, margins of newspapers, whatever is there at the time.

One of the worst things that can happen is if you're out somewhere and someone who is not a writer desperately needs a piece of paper and you give up yours—you sort of think, 'Oh no, I'm losing my piece of paper! My lifeline!'

FH: What do you feel is the hardest part of writing a poem? The start, editing or shortening of a much-loved poem?

SE: The starting of a poem is when you'll know where it's heading, hopefully. If I've just got a scratch of poetry and it doesn't seem to be going anywhere then I just put it aside. It really depends what mood I'm in. I will know if a poem has legs pretty early on.

Reworking a poem later is not always that difficult because I always like to walk away from a poem and then come back and see how it reads. Sometimes I can go over drafts and not like any of them, and it may be that it's just a bad time to be working on poetry.

I enjoy finding titles. That can be a lot of fun and provide you with other inspiration.

FH: You have just mentioned that you enjoy titling your poems. I really enjoyed the titles of many pieces in your most recent book, *Luminous Fruit,* such as 'Why Guns Are Different from Oranges'. How do you come up with the titles of your poems?

SE: I have a computer file at home full of titles. I am a very organised person, very structured, but mainly because I'm always on the brink of total chaos, and always trying to fend it off. So I categorise a lot of stuff—one of my folders is just for titles for poems. In 'Why Guns Are Different from Oranges', I took two things that wouldn't usually be compared, and compared them. The title is descriptive, but it's that surrealism of conjunctions. The poem was initially just a title but the rest of it was already inside that title; I knew what I would write. If that title was transparent, in other cases, if the title is more cryptic, then I would have written the poem and come back and titled it later on. If I have a title but don't know what's in it, so to speak, I'll come back later and unpack it. Other times, the title will reflect the mood of the poem or the sound. The title is almost the key to the poem, and that might not be obvious until the second to last line—the title shouldn't necessarily spell out where the poem's going.

FH: In your book *Luminous Fruit* you explore many aspects of life that have obviously intrigued you. Did 'The Piano in the Horse Float' come from a real-life experience?

SE: I have actually seen a piano in a horse float, but I don't own a piano. It was just one of those things where you start with something and you ask yourself ,'what if? … what if I can extend and expand it?' What comes next ought to be in a direction that is slightly unexpected, otherwise it's boring. I just thought, here's a horse float; now there's a piano in there—where's the horse gone?! Haven't we got this weird fusion going on?

FH: Where have you put all of the awards you've received? Which one is most significant to you?

SE: Well, on Sunday I painted one of the toilets and my wife said, 'Don't hang your awards in the toilet!' But that's where most of them go. You've got to give people something to look at in there—captive audience!

FH: Which ones are most significant?

SE: The one that comes to mind is Warana, that's the Queensland Premier's Prize for Poetry, and I was short-listed for the John Bray Award. This year I was co-winner of the New England Review Prize, and actually the first book I wrote was either winner or co-winner of the Jessie Litchfield Award, and it was the runner-up for the Anne Elder Award. There's the Gawler Poetry Prize and the Union Art Prize, and a few other ones.

FH: If you could receive any award in the world what would you choose? Athlete of the year, father of the year, a literary prize?

SE: Life is changing so fast that if you can define your very own skills and find your niche, that should be about enough, a recipe for serenity. Anyone who has their aura of peace is a winner—well that's my politically correct answer. The incorrect answer is that on a local scale, I'd love to win the John Bray Award and, internationally, the Nobel Prize for Literature, to stand in the shadows of some really great writers.

FH: Have you seen where your work has been displayed in Canberra?

SE: Yes. They put some of the winning works up in shop windows and I heard about that just before I was going to Canberra, so I found out which place my poster would be in. When I went there the owner said, 'Oh no! We took all of those down last week!' So I thought, 'Oh well, fair enough.' Then about three months later a friend of mine was over there and he said that he'd seen my plaque. I said, 'What?', and he said, 'You know, your poem. They've put your poem in the ground.' So, the next time I was over there I found my poem in the ground of the main shopping district—a nice brass plaque for people to walk on, or stop and read.

There was actually another one that was supposed to be put in the ground along the North Terrace pavement here in Adelaide but the council thought the surface would be too slippery. So my poem ended up on a pole outside of Hungry Jack's! Adelaide Railway station also has some of my poetry on a billboard, and there are poems on buses at the moment.

FH: That's all of our questions, thank you for your time. Did you have anything else you wanted to add?

SE: Being a teacher, I am mostly involved with students. I find that there's often a stage where people are involved in writing, but they don't necessarily know what the poetry scene is like. The Writers' Centre is a wonderful way to learn about lots of different genres. There are a lot of poetry venues in Adelaide and there are more small publishers now. There's no need to feel lost or alone with poetry. The obverse of that is it doesn't mean anything goes; it's a craft that people underestimate. It is much more than just deciding on a structure and having an ability to write in short lines; aspiring to improve the craft is always a wonderful thing. It's just so exciting seeing someone's piece of writing where you can tell they've weighed up all of the subtleties, and put their heart into it.

Talking to Steve Evans

by Fleur Holmes

Steve Evans is a well-known poet, however, I had not heard of him until I entered Wakefield Press searching desperately for a South Australian poet to interview. One of the first books that caught my eye was Evans's latest collection of poems titled *Luminous Fruit*. I flicked through the book and finding the text easy to read and with many quirky poems, I bought the book. In class the next week, Alison and I compared notes. She had found a different poet but when I told her the title of Evans's book she immediately jumped on board the Steve Evans bandwagon.

When we first met Steve Evans, a friendly man who looked exactly like his *Luminous Fruit* front-cover photo, greeted us. Evans showed us into the staff room at Flinders University and we chatted for a while before starting the interview, with high hopes the tape recorder was in working order.

The interview that followed lasted for about thirty minutes and not only gave me an insight into Evans's poetry, but also an insight into his sense of humour and motivations. Steve is very well read and spoke highly of his colleagues and up-and-coming poets. Since the interview I have borrowed a few books by the authors he mentioned and now know what he means when he talks of their passion for words.

The most fascinating part of the interview was actually when we had finished the 'official' part and Evans showed us his office to prove what a mess it was. As Evans had been away sick the previous week, he said it was messier than usual but personally I think the mess went a little deeper than a mere week. The reason I found this part of the interview so enjoyable was because I could see all of the texts that he used for his classes, and personally. The shelves were covered in books of all sorts. Evans showed us a couple of art books and said he used them to inspire some of his writing classes. It was good to know that we too had used this method of inspiration in our poetry classes.

Steve was a lovely person to meet. I was very humbled to meet him, especially after he spoke of all the awards he had received for his writing. My grasp of poetry has benefited from meeting him. I can't say that I write any better, but I do know that I read more extensively since the interview. I found the experience of interviewing Steve Evans a pleasure and an interesting and colourful way to learn about poetry. Most of all, the interview gave me a wider sense of the sort of opportunities available to poets in South Australia.

Reading the poems
by Alison Kiesau

Steve Evans's first poetry collection, *Edison Doesn't Invent the Car*, was written in 1990 while he was working as an accountant and business manager. He has since had four other collections published, he completed an MA in Creative Writing, and is currently lecturing in English at Flinders University, as well as completing a PhD.

Evans's interest in poetry began when he was a child. By the age of twelve, influenced by pop music, European and beat poets, as well as the changing world of the 1960s, Evans was writing poetry. His latest collection, *Luminous Fruit*, begins with '10,000 Poems'. This poem is about the ten thousand poems that were to be sent to the Prime Minister, who committed Australian troops to the war in Iraq. The first stanza describes the scenario the poets would have been hoping for. The Prime Minister is completely absorbed in the poems,

> answering no calls
> refusing visitors
> biting his lip,
> misty-eyed

The second stanza relates the most probable fate of the poems—they are unread, discarded, dismissed. The third stanza refers to a haiku, which has been 'smuggled in' and slips 'under his guard'. This tiny poem causes him to

> … startle
> at his own tears
> his heart wide open

This poem captures the power of something as small as a haiku, crafted by a single person, and through this shows the power of the individual. It also speaks about the power of poetry to touch people deeply.

Evans's poetry in *Luminous Fruit* is thought-provoking, poignant, and sprinkled liberally with his own brand of quirky humour. Many of the poems deal with everyday domestic life and family relationships. There are several poems about children, right from conception ('Beginning'), feeding and bathing ('Feeding You' and

'Siren'), to the tender account of his young daughter's artistic perception ('Naïve'):

the snake in her garden is smiling
completely without irony
it is a happy snake …

… she will learn not to do this
she will learn to paint less from
the heart than the head …

… if I could stop this
I would not

'Notes', 'Stomach' and 'This Bed' are examples of poetry dealing with the relationship between husband and wife. It is in this poetry about relationships close to the poet's heart, that the 'spontaneous overflow of powerful feelings' (Wordsworth & Coleridge 1965, p. 10) is most apparent. The playfully humorous 'Notes', detailing the mix-up of a love note and a shopping list, is bolstered by a strong feeling of love:

peaches
pears
nectarines
passionfruit
how could I write her anything
more delicious
more full of love?

In the poem titled 'Stomach', Evans describes a mother being concerned about her stomach after giving birth to another child:

you worry about your stomach—
I don't …

… I put my lips to the stretchmarks
soft as a watermark on expensive paper …

The father in the poem is completely in awe of the mother's body and the fact that the 'stomach' is where the life of their daughter began:

the precious clusters of your eggs
me no size at all
witnessing the store
finite, irreplaceable
looking and looking at where she began

Other poems in *Luminous Fruit* ask (and answer) the question 'what if?' The poem 'Luminous Fruit' draws upon an example of genetic modification where pigs were implanted with jellyfish genes, resulting in them having noses that glow in the dark. Evans takes this a step further, envisaging a world in which fruit is used as a source of light:

and the ceiling in my bedroom's hung
with satsuma plums
their fleshy glow just right
for an erotic novella.

'Rise and Fall: Nine Ways of Looking at Lake George' is a resonant poem that stays with the reader.

4.
Lek Jo is the ancient name
for a virus in all of us
that multiplies in conversations
and takes over anthologies

In 'Why Guns Are Different from Oranges' Evans wryly explores this juxtaposition: 'Oranges don't need instruction manuals', or 'Guns make undrinkable juice.'

'Uncommon Sense' is a hilarious comment on the resurgence of ridiculous superstitions:

if no-one celebrates your birthday
walk once around your house backwards
and leave the front door open …

… if the phone stops ringing
before you reach it
call a number at random and ask for Ted

Evans's musical influence is obvious in the beautifully lyrical 'She'.

she's the obscure script
in margins of a borrowed book
the one who looks you in the eye
and when you relax just enough
lets you fall
knowing you've wanted for years
to fall like this

ghosts and angels
one of them
here now

With this interesting blend of the everyday, and the quirky answers to 'what if?', one must agree with Peter Goldsworthy's praise of Steve Evans: 'Even in the world of the very ordinary, Evans finds extraordinary poetry' (Evans 2003).

References

Evans, S. (2003) *Luminous Fruit*. Unley: Bookends Books.
Wordsworth, W. and Coleridge, S.T. (1965) *The Lyrical Ballads 1798–1805*. London: Methuen & Co. Ltd.

THOMAS SHAPCOTT

Chapter by Naomi Brewer

Published poetry books

Time on Fire, Jacaranda Press, Brisbane 1961
The Mankind Thing, Jacaranda Press, Brisbane 1964
Sonnets 1960–3, Officina Donohoena, Brisbane 1964
A Taste of Salt Water, Angus & Robertson, Sydney 1967
Inwards to the Sun, University of Queensland Press, St Lucia 1969
The Seven Deadly Sins, Queensland Opera Co., Brisbane 1970
Finders at Air, The author, Ipswich 1970
Begin with Walking, University of Queensland Press, St Lucia 1972
Shabbytown Calendar, University of Queensland Press, St Lucia1975
Seventh Avenue Poems, Angus & Robertson, Sydney 1976
Selected Poems, University of Queensland Press, St Lucia 1978
Turning Full Circle, New Poetry, Sydney 1979
Make the Old Man Sing, Coach House Press, Toronto, Canada 1980
Welcome! University of Queensland Press, St Lucia 1983
Travel Dice, University of Queensland Press, St Lucia 1987
Shapcott: Poetry Bilingual Edition, English/Macedonian, Golden Wreath, Struga, Macedonia 1989
Selected Poems 1956–1988, University of Queensland Press, St Lucia 1989
In the Beginning, National Library of Australia, Canberra 1990
The City of Home, University of Queensland Press, St Lucia 1995
Chekhov's Mongoose, Salt Publishing, Applecross 2000

Biographical note

Thomas (Tom) Shapcott (born 1935) is a well-known Australian poet who has been published in a number of countries. Translations of major selections of his work have been published in Hungary, Romania and the Republic of Macedonia. He has published eighteen collections of poems in Australia, as well as six novels and other prose works. He is the inaugural Professor of Creative Writing at the University of Adelaide, in South Australia. Shapcott has received many literary awards and was awarded the Order of Australia in 1989. His latest published volume of poetry is *Chekhov's Mongoose.*

Interview with Thomas Shapcott

Naomi Brewer (NB): In his book *How to Read a Poem,* Edward Hirsch says that he was 'initiated into the poetry of trance' when he was eight years old—he knew it was raining and a Saturday afternoon in October. Do you have such a vivid recollection of your first meaningful encounter with poetry?

Thomas Shapcott (TS): Yes, I probably do. My first poem was written when I was ten years old, but that is best forgotten. When my older brother finished primary school in Queensland (1946) I helped him burn all his textbooks. One was an English primer and as I tore the pages out, one particular page seemed to stick to my hand. It had a poem on it—Gerard Manley Hopkins's 'The Windhover'. I read it and it made a sudden and dramatic impact on me. Something changed, really changed my life. It was such a powerful poem. I'd never read anything in my life like it. The intensity, the use of language, its shocking strangeness was magical. I always count that as the moment when poetry suddenly became a subject of discovery, revelation, a sort of magic.

NB: How old were you then?

TS: Bob was thirteen so I was eleven. Then, when I went to secondary school (for only two years) I discovered, accidentally, another quite different poem that had a similar effect—of discovery, of new possibilities. That was Matthew Arnold's 'Dover Beach'. A melancholy poem, but in free verse. It showed other possibilities. These two poems were my first cornerstones. I really wanted to be a composer back then. When I was nineteen, in 1954, I did National Service training in the army, and that really was the end of my musical aspirations. But, you know, in camp you can always carry a notebook around in your pocket and in that notebook I started writing poetry in earnest. When I came out of National Service, I decided seriously to be a poet. At that stage the

Bulletin, based in Sydney, was the only national weekly paper and they published about eight or nine poems a week. I started buying it and reading the poems. I started sending my poems to the *Bulletin* and it took two years before they accepted my first poem. That was in 1956. It was nice to see my poems in print.

NB: It must have been fantastic to see them actually in print with your name on them.

TS: Yes, yes it was all that. Not that anyone at home took any notice. I showed that first poem to my parents and Mum said, 'Yes dear, that's nice' and Dad said he didn't understand it.

NB: Well a prophet has …

TS: Yes—so that was the beginning.

NB: I can vaguely remember studying poetry in primary school but my most pleasant memories of learning/studying poetry were in high school. Do you have any memories (good or bad) about studying poetry when you were at school?

TS: The school readers in primary school in Queensland were actually very good and gave a wide range of literary examples from English, Irish, Scottish, American, European as well as Australian material. A lot of people in my generation were influenced and can still remember their poetry lessons and so I absorbed all that sort of stuff. It was at secondary school, though, when I became much more selective even though I spent only two years there. In the library there I came across the *Oxford Book of Modern English Verse* edited by W. B. Yeats and that was very exciting. It made me aware that poetry could be experimental, not simply conforming to a pattern. Just after I left school someone gave me Eliot's *Four Quartets* and that was the clincher for me. I didn't really become familiar with Australian poetry until I did National Service—and at that time I decided, 'Yes, that is what I am going to try to do'. I had to see what my peers were doing, so I went into a Brisbane bookshop and bought eleven books of Australian poetry. That was the beginning of my career, and my own first book was published in 1961. So between 1956 and 1961 I was beginning to be published in magazines. I guess you could say I was self-taught. Back then we were told we were lucky to have two years secondary schooling—my father left school at thirteen, and only about six of my final primary class (forty five pupils) went on to secondary school. By the time my younger brother came along though, the whole attitude to education had changed and he went on to tertiary level, just like that. Bob Menzies, the Prime Minister at the time, had pushed the need for higher levels of education.

NB: Were you already writing your own poetry then or did you begin when you were a lot younger?

TS: Ipswich was a mining industrial town with a big Welsh population and the annual Welsh Eisteddfod was a big thing. They had a literary section and in 1945, at the end of the war, the Queensland Eisteddfod was held in Ipswich. My father was secretary. The judge for the literary section came up from Sydney. He was Frank Clewlow, from ABC Radio, and he was the founder of the ABC Children's Session, the Argonauts Club, which was enormously important in those days before TV: it encouraged writing, music, art, botany, all sorts of things. I was a regular listener. The Argonauts Club was very, very important to a whole generation of Australian people who moved on to become artists, musicians, writers etc.

NB: Did your father give your poem to Frank Clewlow?

TS: Yes, dad showed it to him and he said, 'Very nice, but if you gave it a little more thought you would find a proper rhyme for the last verse'. So I went away and thought almost immediately of a better word. In other words that was my first attempt at craft.

NB: Do you find that you have a specific time of day that is good or creative for poetry writing?

TS: I don't think so—I mean, morning is my best time for writing, definitely, but that would be mainly when I'm writing my novels. Poetry is something that can come at any time. I was, for many years, an accountant. I had my own accounting practice and I would quite often be working on a poem when clients came in and I would shove the poem under 'Form A' and do their income tax. When they left I would pull out my poem and do a bit more work—so I think that there is the aspect of mobility in writing poetry. That is why I wrote virtually only poetry in the early 1970s. The demands on my time over that period were pretty intensive, and yet, though the months July to December are the most stressful doing tax lodgements, and the period February to June is easier, I found I wrote more in the busy period. Adrenalin, I suppose. It wasn't until I sold the accounting practice in 1978 and I had a three-year writing grant from the Literature Board, that I started writing fiction because writing novels really involves a nine-to-five activity. It demands constant work over a long period, whereas poetry could be concentrated in short bursts.

NB: Do you carry a notebook around with you in which to jot down any poetic thoughts that come to you during the day?

TS: At various times, yes. I have carried a notebook and jotted down various things. In that period when I had the accounting practice I had lots of little bits of paper just anywhere, so not only notebooks but the backs of envelopes...

NB: Serviettes at restaurants?

TS: I have actually done that on occasions, yes. I always carry a pencil/biro and a piece of paper.

NB: What sorts of things inspire you to write poetry? Do you get inspiration from newspaper articles or politics?

TS: An enormous range of things inspire me—I suppose my first book of poems was essentially the work of a young writer responding to the environment which was Ipswich in Queensland; a sub-tropical, industrial, mining town, set in a rural district reasonably close to Brisbane. Brisbane itself was a bit distant. But I did spend a year, in 1958, living in Sydney and that year provided me with extraordinary stimulus—I wrote city things, and in that period I fell in love with and married my first wife. So that first book includes nature poems, poems about country, city poems and love poems. The second book relates to the time when I decided to do a university degree, and at uni as a part-time student in the 1960s the biggest influence there was the fact that I did three years of French. This opened up a whole new world of history and other languages. It gave me a broader sense of society and the dynamics of political influence, and things like that. So the second book certainly expands on those sorts of issues. Then by the late 1960s, though I was still living in Ipswich, I broadened my range of contacts and became very involved in a lot of contemporary literary affairs so I suppose my political interests in that period are probably what grew—and I went to the United States in 1972. That again made me much more aware of what Americans were writing, and that acted on me and broadened my interests. I published an anthology, *Contemporary American and Australian Poetry* in 1976, which was considered a groundbreaking work. Then by the late 1970s I became very involved in a project based in Hungary, which came out eventually as a novel, *White Stag of Exile*, and that began my interest in Central European cultures. It was translated successfully into Hungarian.

NB: Do you speak Hungarian?

TS: No, but I can understand a little. But I became deeply involved in Hungarian culture. As a language it is different from any other European language—other than Finnish.

NB: Do you ever wake up in the middle of the night and think, 'I've got a marvellous idea for a poem'?

TS: That has only happened very rarely and one extraordinary example of that was a poem called 'The Litanies of Julia Pastrana'. She was a 19th century Mexican bearded lady and I'd read a biography of her and I thought it was so bizarre and extravagant, what could I do with it? It's far too exotic! And then one night I was at home, looking after the kids actually. My wife had gone to organise the theatrical group she was the president of, and I suddenly had to pick up a piece of paper and I started writing and it was as if I was the medium and what came out was in the first person of Julia Pastrana and about five different sections. This took me until about half past ten—it just came out! By which time I was exhausted, so I didn't even stay up until my wife came home. I went straight to bed and when I woke in the morning I thought, 'Oh, that's going to be rubbish', and I came down to rewrite it but only altered three words and added a tiny little postscript of five lines. So that is an example of a poem just simply coming out like that.

NB: That's how I imagined that people wrote poetry.

TS: Ideas come in all sorts of odd places and sometimes you know exactly what it's going to be but at other times you start off without knowing how it will end. I have had one other example of middle of the night writing. A poem came to me, which I jotted down on a piece of paper in the dark and the next morning that curiously was the central passage of a long historical poem called 'Portrait of Captain Logan'. All in strict rhyme too, that section. It was the only rhyming section of the sequence. Captain Logan was the commandant of the convict settlement in Brisbane in 1824. The poem is a portrait, political, historical and social and this one section in the middle (the one I wrote in the middle of the night) is in the form of an official letter. In rhyme. But otherwise, poetry can come at almost anytime. Sometimes the subject matter springs up out of something you've read, talked about, seen on TV, very often it hovers around in your sub-conscious mind for a while, and then I think it forces itself out. Then, when you have a line or an image which you've got to jot down, you find out what's going on. It's like a seed germinating, or a burr burrowing.

NB: I have read some of your work in *Chekhov's Mongoose*. Some of the poems seem to be conversations with yourself (e.g. 'The Letters', p. 9). Are the poems records of your personal experiences or did you write about another man's experiences as if you had had them yourself?

TS: Poetry is a personal experience. I mean, in one sense, yes it is all personal experience but in other senses you adopt distancing devices. I've actually written quite a number of poems which are first person monologues. Robert Browning, the English poet, was the one who really established that sort of portrait, which I, a long time ago, found very powerful as a means of expressing, in dramatic form, all sorts of emotions and feelings. The monologue poem is a non-lyrical form and that can be a useful contrast to shorter, more lyrical sorts of expression. In my writing I often like to work in as many ranges of form or structure as I can, so I really write lots of sonnets and sestinas and other structured verse forms, and then I turn to free verse, dramatic monologues, even concrete poetry and more experimental approaches. That's just one way I myself find very stimulating and challenging.

When you're writing a poem, which is a portrait poem, you have to put yourself into that person's mind and sometimes many strange things come out. It is moving poetry to its edges and getting close to drama or performance.

NB: How did you choose the poems for *Chekhov's Mongoose?*

TS: When I get to the stage when I've got a whole pile of poems, I start to sort them into some sort of order or shape. With *Chekhov's Mongoose*, I juggled them completely at least three different times to see how poems sat next to other poems. Sometimes they'd clash; sometimes they might work up the detail in another poem like a picture on the wall might bring out the orange spot on this painting, which you might not notice otherwise. Also, to a certain degree, I often link the poems thematically. But you have to be careful that you don't get repetitive and monotonous when you do that sort of thing. Sometimes it's a very useful way, a very stimulating way, to get you to fill in the blanks—the book's nearly there and you suddenly feel you should do something else. So I suppose with *Chekhov's Mongoose*, the poem for my mother, which ends the collection, became a central point. I actually started that poem in 1996 when I was visiting my son in England and I did the first section then. And it just stayed there for a couple of years and I didn't quite know what to do with it.

It wasn't complete in itself. It seemed to be leading somewhere. Then, at about the time I was thinking about shaping it again, I looked through a lot of bits and pieces that I had been writing and I came across the draft opening again and I suddenly saw what I wanted to do with it. When I first started writing it, my mother had only been dead a year or so. Sometimes it takes a few years before you are able to get a meaningful perspective on it.

NB: I noticed that you included three sonnets on death in the last section of your book. Did you deliberately sit down one day and decide to write the sonnets or did they just happen?

TS: The three sonnets on death: they were really written for Geoffrey Dutton, the poet originally from Adelaide. When he died I read his obituary in the paper. I'd known Geoff for many years, and they were prompted by that. I think he would have enjoyed them. I can't consciously remember writing a poem before about death, and so I sat down and wrote the first one thinking of Geoff. Then I realised that there was more I wanted to say so I ended up writing three sonnets. It was personal, although to anyone else, the poems exist by themselves; Geoff's name is never mentioned. The poems were in the sonnet form. Often, when I write down the first line I can immediately tell if it is going to be workable as a sonnet, or free verse, or if it's going to be workable as something else. This doesn't always happen. In one of my other poems, one that has been widely anthologised, called 'Flying Fox', I initially wrote that as 4 four-line stanzas and I thought it was going to be a kind of narrative poem. It describes a woman waiting at home in bed for her husband to come, and outside there is a flying fox in the papaw tree. That much I had put down, and then stopped. It was written on green paper and I shoved it in a wardrobe. Months later, cleaning out the rubbish up there, I discovered the piece of green paper, read it, and suddenly realised the poem was virtually all there. It only needed two more lines to finish it off. Another sonnet!

NB: How long do you spend re-working, re-writing or editing each poem? Do you ever just write one down and not have to touch it?

TS: Almost none. Apart from 'The Litanies of Julia Pastrana'. I could write up to a dozen drafts with a poem, sometimes involving big changes, but not always. The important thing in the first draft is to get the general shape and the main ideas. Then the polishing begins. It is a good idea to put it aside for a while and come back to it later. Judith Wright recommended that to me—but I was often too impatient when I was young. Judith Wright mentioned to me another useful device when drafting a poem. That is, to look back over the first draft and see at what point the real poem begins. She said she would often cut off the first four or five lines—they had been 'warming up' lines before she got into the full stride of the poem itself. It is something I have often noticed with drafts of poems I have seen over the years.

Talking to Tom Shapcott

When I first decided to ask Tom Shapcott for an interview I had no idea just how famous and how decorated this man was. And it is just as well, because I would have been much more nervous about approaching him than I was already. I started by researching poets on the Internet. I am not sure why I chose Tom Shapcott's name first to key into the search field—I think it was because his name looked solid and down-to-earth.

I printed his biographical notes from the Adelaide University website. The first step in arranging an interview was not as easy as it sounds. I was given his email address and told to send him an email asking if he would mind talking to a student from UniSA. I spent a long time composing that email. I wanted to sound 'academic' and intelligent, and in the end sent a very long email to Tom. Tom's reply was very short and to the point—obviously a very busy man. He said:

Dear Naomi,
Would next Thursday sometime suit? My room is 605, Napier Building. Tom S.

He suggested in a further email that I should send him the ten questions I planned to ask him before our interview so that he could prepare some answers ahead of time—probably so he would not waste too much time over the interview. I realised he would have had many interviews over the years and would have answered the same questions many times over, so I tried to make them a little bit more interesting and maybe different because they were coming from my point of view.

Armed with a notebook and pen and a very old portable tape recorder I presented myself at Tom's office door a few minutes before the time we had agreed on. I had purchased Tom's latest book of poems, *Chekhov's Mongoose*, and had read a few of his poems. I particularly liked the section entitled 'For Dorothy My Mother', and one other poem called 'The Letters'. I had wondered about the title of the book and thought I might ask him about it during the interview.

While I was waiting outside his office I perused the glass book cabinet in the corridor. The cabinet displayed books that had been written by the English Department's staff and students and I noticed that Tom had written a book about the research he had done on twins. I asked him about it before we started on the interview and he told me that he had a twin brother and he was very interested in the study of twins.

Tom was very welcoming and put me at my ease immediately. He asked me to test the tape recorder before we started—he had obviously had experience with this type of interview before. I tested it and we began the interview, which consisted of Tom speaking very fluently about his life. He is a softly spoken man and has lived an extremely full and interesting life. His love for poetry has led him overseas to Europe where he became very involved in the Hungarian culture, and where he gleaned many ideas and much information for several of his poems.

The hour and a half that I spent with Tom went very quickly—I was fascinated with what he told me about his life and how he wrote his poetry—as well as by his amazingly accurate memory. Dates came to him very easily as well as the titles of the poems he read when just a small boy. I made a mental note to look up the poems that had inspired him to write poetry to see if they had any effect on me. One of them, 'The Windhover', by Gerard Manley Hopkins, would have made no sense to me at eleven years of age—in fact I am not quite sure what it is about even now. I looked up the poem when I got home and after reading it wondered what Hopkins meant when he wrote,

> My heart in hiding stirred for a bird,
> —the achieve of; the mastery of
> the thing!

I doubt very much that I would have been encouraged by that poem to write poetry myself.

I did not get a chance to ask Tom about where the title for his book of poems, *Chekhov's Mongoose*, came from. We filled both sides of the tape with the answers to my questions—in fact, I think Tom gave me much more than I expected from the interview. He came across as a very kind man and this was demonstrated when he gave me a copy of one of his earlier books of poetry, *Travel Dice*, that he signed especially for me.

After the interview I transcribed the tape recording and sent the transcription to Tom for editing. He edited the text and had it back to me in a very short time. I realise that I was extremely privileged to spend time with such a wonderful Australian who has done an amazing amount of good for the Australian literary world, and not just here in Australia but overseas as well.

Reading the poems

Aristotle wrote that poetry in general seems to have sprung from two instincts within humankind's nature—the instinct for imitation and the instinct for harmony and rhythm (*Poetics*). It is these two instincts that poets have allowed to direct their writings from the time of the Mesopotamians, who wrote their love poems in 'cuneiform', writing on clay tablets, to today's poets who can record their poems electronically on the Internet and reach an audience of millions both locally and globally. It is also true that rhymes in early literature provided vital clues for linguists to determine the correct pronunciation of words. Shakespeare's rhymes assisted them to reconstruct 'the sound system of Elizabethan English' (Fromkin et al.). Hirsch states that 'poems breathe deeper meaning into our lives, and that we in turn breathe deeper life into poems' (1999).

Poetry has survived through the history of the world until this present day. It is evident in human writing in religious contexts (e.g. Song of Solomon and the Psalms in the *Holy Bible*), plays (e.g. Shakespeare) and operas. In the third century AD, ivory covered booklets filled with poems were given as gifts by the Romans. Poetry has been used to record wars, great moments in history and everyday occurrences from births to deaths. Its popularity has waxed and waned. Plato banned poets from his ideal republic because he believed that the artistic nature of poets appeared to be founded in a kind of 'inspired madness' and they lacked genuine knowledge of what they were doing.

In Australia there has been no shortage of poets. Henry Lawson and A. B. 'Banjo' Paterson are still popular poets, as was seen when Paterson's 'The Man from Snowy River' was read at the opening of the Sydney 2000 Olympics. Bush poetry is synonymous with the Australian outback. *The Age* newspaper published an article that said 'poetry is an international art form that works to make the world smaller and more understandable, as well as giving us a still potent realisation of events down the ages' (July 2000). Poetry operates in Australia in several arenas—song lyrics, working class verse, performance poetry, rap, newspaper poems, and even graffiti.

Page (1995) states that there was a general agreement among anthologists that 'Australian poetry in the early to mid-1960s was duller than it should have been' and the radical poets of the late sixties emerged as the new contemporary Australian poets. A general 'loosening up effect' on poetry after the sixties was said to have been the result of cheaper ways for poets to publish their poetry and a general move away from the American style of poetry writing (Page 1995). These days contemporary popular poetry is operating in society locally as well as globally. *The Age* newspaper runs a weekly poem on its books pages, Radio National attracts 40,000 listeners to its weekly *PoeticA* program and poetry readings are mainstream events at writers' festivals (*The Age* July 2000).

A brief visit to popular bookshops will reveal the many books of poetry that are available today, as well as anthologies, volumes of Shakespeare, Keats, Browning and Whitman, and thick tomes of critical analysis. If one can judge poetry's popularity in the 21st century by researching websites on the Internet, it could be safely assumed that poetry is still very popular today. There are hundreds of poetry sites, review sites and discussion sites that the poetry enthusiast can visit to satiate their thirst for this genre.

In defence of contemporary poetry, Tranter wrote in 1970 that it was only in the late 1960s that it was accepted in Australia, but it is now read with 'keen anticipation' by thousands of Australians and by 'millions throughout the world'. Tranter also stated that the *Poetry Australia* magazine had one of the largest circulations of any poetry magazine in the country. At one time in the history of Australian poetry, it could be said that it was very conservative in subject matter and the way in which it was written (McAuley 1975).

Poets have changed from the early 1940s, when some appeared to reject 'Australianity', but now 'no recent Australian poet seems bothered by it' (1975). With the advent of multiculturalism and the ease of overseas travel has come a change in Australian poetry. The poets have drawn on their experiences overseas and their interaction with people of other nationalities to change the subject matter and style of their writing. Even though novels are a more popular genre than poetry, which can be seen by the number of novels for sale in any bookshop, poetry still has a presence in South Australia. Postmodernist thinking has been absorbed into today's poetry and many experimentalist poets are being published, even though, according to Leonard (2001), Australian poetry has taken 'longer than most to successfully accommodate (with a few notable exceptions) any sort of modernistic techniques'. Poetry festivals are held regularly, and more and more poets are reading their poetry to audiences in anticipation of being published or, in anticipation of selling their books if they have already been published.

Poetry readings are held on a regular basis at various venues throughout South Australia. Friendly Street Poets and the SA Writers' Centre are two organisations that provide evenings for writers to read and perform their poetry in public as well as encouraging them to submit their poems for publication. Most bookshops in Adelaide have a small section that promotes South Australian poets.

It is in a popular bookshop in Adelaide that Tom Shapcott's *Chekhov's Mongoose* (signed copy) is available for purchase. Shapcott, originally from Queensland and now resident in South Australia, has been a published poet since 1961. He has written many books of poetry as well as novels and libretti.

As an editor he has been responsible for the publication of several books on Australian poetry and is the inaugural Professor of Creative Writing at the University of Adelaide. Like Hirsch (1999), who said he was 'initiated into the poetry of trance' when he was eight years old (p. 61), Shapcott began his poetic life at the young age of eleven when he read Hopkins's poem 'The Windhover'. Shapcott said that reading that particular poem had a dramatic influence on him and it changed his life. Poetry 'suddenly became a subject of discovery, revelation, a sort of magic' (see interview p. 216). The magic worked on Shapcott's creative mind and lead him in the direction of literature and in particular to the poetic genre.

It is interesting to note that Leonard did not include Shapcott in his anthology of contemporary Australian poetry in 2001. He says that he favoured poetry with 'a rich music of syllable and rhythm' as well as poems in which 'the pentameter is worked with subtlety' (2001). It is a pity that Shapcott's works have not been included in this anthology because his work displays all that and more.

What is it about Shapcott's poetry that makes it award winning poetry? One reviewer of Shapcott's *Selected Poems*, says that he has been 'indefatigably prolific for more than thirty years' and is 'conventional in lifestyle, diverse in subject and technique' (Wallace 1990). Wallace lists Shapcott's strengths as 'self-scrutiny, observation of domesticity and locality, and dramatic monologues that are enriched by his imagination.' Again his skill in representing family life, children and growing up is applauded by Warrick Wynne, when he reviewed Shapcott's *Shabbytown Calendar*.

It is obvious from Shapcott's poetry that he has an interest in people and in his book *Travel Dice* his love for the people he writes about and his affinity for the countries he has travelled in shines throughout his work. He said that 'physical travel forced me to see the relativity of things, my own feelings and my otherness' (Kinsella 2002).

It has been written that 'Shapcott's own work demonstrates the liberating influence of US models' (McLaren 1989) but he has developed his own particular model and he has experimented with syntax and metre and visual structure. Shapcott takes us travelling the world in his book of poems, *Travel Dice*, through history as well as countries, from Australia, around the world and back again to the mundane business of living, moving house, going to the beach and picking flowers in the garden.

While the majority of his poems are free verse, in some he experiments with structure. In 'Life Taste (VI)' Shapcott recreates the ebb and flow of the waves at the beach:

Sand
        ready to be plunged into surf
                and then saved
sand sunning itself
        The dunes roll
                under the smallest wave

Visually, the reader is transported to the beach to join the poet as he watches the waves and the swimmers, then scrambles into the shade of an overhanging cliff to eat melon slices with his friend.

In both *Travel Dice* and *Chekhov's Mongoose*, Shapcott has included a poem for Gwen Harwood, an unpredictable poet who was an inspirational figure to many young poets and 'a yardstick of technical accomplishment and emotional involvement' (Page 1995). His poem 'Strelitzia (for Gwen Harwood)' in *Travel Dice* speaks of that beautiful orange and purple flower that can be seen in many Australian gardens, the writer's fear of sunshine, and a girl who competes with the sun and the strelitzia while dancing in a cemetery in Toowong. It is a poem that reveals a very intense range of images, all the more potent to any reader who has experienced them in reality.

The poem 'Letters from Gwen Harwood' published in *Chekhov's Mongoose* is not so carefree. Shapcott's words portray his grief in their sombre tone and hint of bitterness as he recalls their delight in sharing the riches that they uncover with the 'scratches of words done by hand'. With the one word 'scratches' he links the two verses. Shapcott reveals the pain he feels at her passing and as he reads her 'perky letters' his eyes are 'scratched with grief' with the words that 'lead to an empty shell'. Once more we are convinced by his words and feel his sorrow at the passing of his friend.

Chekhov's Mongoose contains a great many poems written in free verse that recall the 'lost images of childhood experience and discovery' that Shapcott is skilled in recreating in his work. He says that the four sestinas in his collection are the pillars that hold the book together (Kinsella 2002). A sestina consists of six stanzas of six lines apiece with a final stanza shorter than the preceding ones. In Shapcott's sestinas, the *envoi*, or final stanza, is made up of three lines. The rhyming scheme has the same six end-words appearing in each stanza in a different but fixed order.

It is said that Arnault Daniel (c. 1200) invented the sestina and it has been used by Kipling, Pound, Eliot and Auden (Cuddon 1999). Shapcott's sestina rhyming pattern is abcdef, faebdc, and so on for the rest of the verses. It is a very complex way of writing but Shapcott has obviously mastered it as can be seen in his four sestinas. There is a story behind the writing of the sestinas. Shapcott asked his students to write sestinas in a class exercise and he saw it was such a rewarding exercise that he tried it for himself.

Sonnets are another feature in *Chekhov's Mongoose*. Shapcott said that his sonnets on death were written on the passing of his friend and fellow poet, Geoffrey Dutton (see interview page 222). Once again we see Shapcott's very human side, reaching out to his friend, to stay connected, even after Dutton's death. Shapcott's sonnets seem to follow the French model of twelve syllables to each line. Each sonnet contains fourteen lines and Shapcott develops the theme of death in all three, but each one could stand alone. All three sonnets are linked with the one idea of death which he likens to computers or machines. He says that 'Death is the simple thump of an average drum', and he demonstrates that by using alliteration in the fourth line of the second part of his first sonnet: 'Death is the debt-collector come.' These words pound out a simple message, sounding like drum beats as that machine of death approaches the door and calls us 'each by name'. In place of 'temples and monuments to death'

Shapcott uses imagery to liken death to computer failure—all the screens blank, no breath, 'no trace of smell, no memory of earth.'

The poem, 'For Dorothy My Mother', was started before Shapcott's mother died and then put away in a cupboard to be found several years later. He has said that he needed some time to pass after her death before he could finish the poem he had started. His eye for detail and incredible memory conjure up wonderful images of Australian family life in the Depression. He takes us on a journey through his own life within the realm of his mother's kitchen, her domain, and laments that:

> It is only now that I remember things she valued
> other than family, all those clamorous selves.

He calls her the queen of the kitchen, that important room where they grew up, where they were given treats, recited their homework, and where they took her for granted.

> That is our greatest tribute:
> granting her the security of our need,
> asking, asking and never conscious of giving.

He admits that the poem was written to record his own need rather than hers, but it is still a tribute to her love for her family and the obvious love for her that Shapcott still felt. It is a testament to Shapcott's great skill in painting a picture so rich and full of real and tangible images, that he has won so many awards over the years for his great contribution to the Australian poetry scene.

When reviewing *Chekhov's Mongoose*, Barry Hill, poetry editor of the *Australian*, wrote, 'this is one of Shapcott's strongest collections, with birds in the trees all around it.'

Thomas Shapcott is truly one of Australia's great contemporary poets. He is a convincing storyteller whose 'European consciousness' (Wynne 2002) causes his poems to be extremely popular in Australia and overseas. He has a descriptive talent that has the ability to breathe abundant life and brilliant colour into everyday happenings. His poetry is highly regarded and he has been the recipient of many poetry awards both here in Australia and internationally. His poems elevate the reader's soul because he takes the time to craft and construct them to fulfil that purpose. He has made an enormous individual contribution to the development of contemporary poetry in Australia, not only by his own writings but by the wholehearted encouragement and support he has shown for Australian literature. He believes that the new writers who are emerging now will find it tough going, but not as tough as the new writers had it during the 1950s and 1960s (Kinsella 2002). In the words of Page (1995) he has remained, 'in his own work and in his promotional activity, an important contact with more recent Australian past.'

References

Aristotle *Poetics*

Cuddon, J.A. (ed.) (1999) *The Penguin Dictionary of Literary Terms and Literary Theory*, 4th edn, Blackwell Publishers Ltd.

Fromkin, V. et al. (1997) *An Introduction to Language*. Marrickville, NSW: Harcourt Brace & Company.

Hill, B. (2001) 'Maestro Fires up Metrical Magic', *The Weekend Australian*, p. 14, 19 May 2001,[viewed 21 October 2002], *Academic SearchElite*: EBSCOhost. AN 200105191R14700128.

Hirsch, E. (1999) *How to Read a Poem and Fall in Love with Poetry*. New York: A Harvest Book, Harcourt Inc.

Kinsella, J. (2002) *Interview with Thomas Shapcott*, Thylazine's electronic interview archives, [viewed 19 October 2002], http://www.thylazine.org/archive2/tsinterview.html

Leonard, J. (ed.) (2001) *New Music: An Anthology of Contemporary Australian Poetry*. Wollongong, NSW: Five Islands Press.

Manguel, A. (1997) *A History of Reading*. London: Flamingo.

Marsh, L. (ed.) (1995) *The Wordsworth Book of Sonnets*. Hertfordshire: Wordsworth Editions Ltd.

McLaren, J. (1989) *Australian Literature: An Historical Introduction*. Melbourne: Longman Cheshire Pty Ltd.

Page, G. (1995) *A Reader's Guide to Contemporary Australian Poetry*. St Lucia, Qld: University of Queensland Press.

Poe, E.A. (1846) 'The philosophy of composition', *Graham's Magazine*, April 1846, [viewed 28 August 2002], http://www.eapoe.org/works/essays/philcomp/htm

Shapcott, T.W. (1987) *Travel Dice*. Melbourne: Globe Press.

Shapcott, T.W. (2000) *Chekhov's Mongoose*. Applecross, WA: Salt Publishing.

The Age 23 July 2000, 'Poetry, the Undying Art'.

Tranter, J. (1970) 'In Defence of Poetry', University of Sydney, [viewed 3 November 2002], http://setis.library.usyd.edu.au/tranter/docs/pearlrk-jt.html

Wallace, A. (1990) 'Reviews: Literary & arts', *Social Alternatives*, vol. 8, issue 4, p. 69, [viewed 21 October 2002], Academic Search Elite:EBSCOhost. AN 9610110020.

Wynne, W. 'Of Here and Now', *The Australian Book Review*, [viewed 19 October 2002], http://poetry.alphalink.com.au/selected.htm

Bibliography

Abrams, M.H. (1999) *A Glossary of Literary Terms*, 7th edn, Fort Worth, Texas: Harcourt Brace College Publishers.

Adès, D. (2002) 'The Work of My Face' in *SideWaLK*, issue 9.

Andrews, R. (1991) *The Problem with Poetry*, Philadelphia: Open University Press.

Aristotle *Poetics*, translated by S.H. Butcher, [viewed 14 October 2003] http://classics.mit.edwAristotle/poetics.html

Aristotle, *Poetics*, translated by I. Bywater (1954) New York: Random House.

Aristotle *Poetics*, [viewed 1 September 2002], http://libertyonline.hypermall.com/Aristotle/Poetics.html

Aristotle *Poetics*, Internet Classics Archive, University of Melbourne, n.d., Asialink, [viewed 12 September 2002], http://www.asialink.unimelb.edu.au/arts/residencies/Litrescurrent.htm

Ashbery, J., Harwood, L. and Raworth, T. (1971) *Penguin Modern Poets 19*, UK: Penguin.

'Australian Poetry' (1998) Department of Communications, Information Technology and the Arts, [viewed 26 October 2002], http://www.acn.net.au/articles/1998/08/poetry.htm.

Bizzaro, P. (1993) *Responding to Student Poems*, Urbana, Illinois: National Council of Teachers of English.

Bogen, N. (1994) *How to Write Poetry*, New York: Macmillan.

Bolton, K. 'To generalise', from *Ten Australian Poets Series 5* [viewed 23 September 2003] http:// www.thylazine.org/archive/thyla5/kb.html

Bolton, K. (1999) blurb of *Around Here* by Cath Kenneally. Adelaide: Wakefield Press.

Bolton, K. (1997) *Untimely Meditations*, Adelaide: Wakefield Press.

Braune, B. (2000) 'Musing on Chaos: Two Books of Poetry', *Australian Women's Book Review: Online*, volume 12. Available online at http://emsah.uq.edu.au/awsr/recent/7.html

Braune, B. (1998) 'Stephen Lawrence, Beasts Labial', *Cordite*, no. 4, pp. 19–20

Breton, A. (1936) *What is Surrealism?* http://www.shaviro.com/Classes/Surrealism.html

Brewster, A and Johnson, R. (eds) (1982) *Friendly Street Poetry Reader No. 6*. Adelaide: Friendly Street with Wakefield Press.

Brower, R.A. (1963) *The Poetry of Robert Frost: Constellations of Intention*, Oxford: Oxford University Press.

Buchbinder, D. (1991) *Contemporary Literary Theory and the Reading of Poetry*, Melbourne: Macmillan.

Bywater, I. (ed.) (1954) *Aristotle's Rhetoric and Poetics*, New York: Modern Library.

Campbell, P. (1991) *Wordsworth and Coleridge Lyrical Ballads*, London: Macmillan.

Carpenter, B. (1997) 'Wislawa Szymborska and the importance of the unimportant', *World Literature Today*, vol. 71, no. 1, pp. 9–14 [viewed 2 November 2002] Available: EBSCOhost; Academic Search Elite.

Carpio, B. (1998) *Form*, [viewed 8 September 2002], http://litera1no4.tripod.com/form_frame.html#imagism

Catt, G. and Mann, K. (2003) *Blue. Friendly Street 27*, Adelaide: Friendly Street with Wakefield Press.

Cohen, J.M. (1966) *Poetry of this Age*, UK: Hutchinson.

Cuddon, J.A. (ed.) (1999) *The Penguin Dictionary of Literary Terms and Literary Theory*, 4th edn, Blackwell Publishers Ltd.

Evans, S. (2003) *Luminous Fruit*, Unley: Bookends Books.

Felinghetti, L. (2000) *What is Poetry?* Berkley, California: Creative Arts Book Company.

Fraser, G.S. (1970) *Metre, Rhyme and Free Verse*, London: Methuen and Co. Ltd.

Frazer, C. and Westburg, B. (eds) (1989) *Friendly Street Poetry Reader No. 13*, Adelaide: Friendly Street with Wakefield Press.

Fromkin, V. et al. (1997) *An Introduction to Language*, Marrickville, NSW: Harcourt Brace & Company.

Furbank, P. and Kettle, A. (1975) *Modernism and Its Origins*, Milton Keynes: Open University Press.

Gardner, H. (ed.) (1957) *The Metaphysical Poets*, UK: Penguin.

Garnett, M. and Groff, M. (2000) 'Editor's blurb', *Vernacular*, volume 2, Adelaide.

Garnett, M. and Groff, M. (eds) (1999) *Vernacular*, vol. 1. Adelaide: Vernacular.

Germain, E. (ed.) (1978) *Surrealist Poetry in English*, UK: Penguin.

Ginsberg, A. (2000) *Deliberate Prose*. London: Penguin Books Ltd.

Goldsworthy, P. (2002) 'Death and the Comedian', [viewed 15 August 2002], http://www.mja.com.au/public/issues/17311041200/goldsworthy/goldsworthy.html.

Goldsworthy, P. (2001) *New Selected Poems*, Sydney: Duffy and Snellgrove.

Goodfellow, G. (1989) *Bow Tie & Tails*, Adelaide: Wakefield Press.

Goodfellow, G. (2001) *Poems for a Dead Father*, Melbourne: Vulgar Press.

Grant J. (2003) *Good Reading*, 'Views of Ordinary Life', Odana Editions.

Haynes, J. (2002) *An Australian Treasury of Popular Verse*, Melbourne: ABC Books.

Hill, B. (2002) *The Australian*, 27–28 July, pp. 2–3.

Hill, B. (2001) 'Maestro Fires up Metrical Magic', *The Weekend Australian*, p. 14, 19 May 2001, [viewed 21 October 2002], *Academic SearchElite*: EBSCOhost. AN 200105191R14700128.

Hirsch, E. (1999) *How to Read a Poem and Fall in Love with Poetry*, New York: A Harvest Book, Harcourt Inc.

Hirsch, E. (1997) 'After the End of the World', *American Poetry Review*, vol. 26, no. 2, pp. 9–13 [viewed 4 November 2002] Available: EBSCOhost; Academic Search Elite.

Jacobus, M. (1976) *Tradition and Experiment in Wordsworth's Lyrical Ballads*, Oxford: Oxford University Press.

James, B. (2002) *Poems for a Dead Father: Study Guide*, Adelaide: Vulgar Press.

Johnson, M. (2002) 'Fragility Is the Poet's Strength' in *The Bunyip*, 28 August.

Jones, P. (1972) *Imagist Poetry*, Middlesex, England: Penguin Books Ltd.

Jones, R. (1986) *Studying Poetry: An Introduction*, London: Edward Arnold Ltd.

Jones A.R. and Tydeman W. (eds) (1972) *Wordsworth Lyrical Ballads*, London: Macmillan Press Ltd.

Kazemek, F.E. and Rigg, P. (1995) *Enriching Our Lives: Poetry Lessons for Adult Literacy Teachers and Tutors*, USA: International Reading Association Inc.

Kenneally, C. (1999) 'Tonight This Headache', *Around Here*, Adelaide: Wakefield Press.

Kinsella, J. (2002) *Interview with Thomas Shapcott*, Thylazine's electronic interview archives, [viewed 19 October 2002], http://www.thylazine.org/archive2/tsinterview.html

Koch, J.L. (2002) *Each Goldfish Is Hand Painted*, Adelaide: Wakefield Press.

Ladd, M. (2001) 'Untitled', in M. Garnett and M. Groff (eds), (1999) *Vernacular*, vol. 3, Vernacular, Adelaide.

Ladd, M. (2000) *Close to Home*, Wollongong: Five Islands Press.

Lawrence, S. (2002) *How Not to Kill Government Leaders*, Adelaide: Wakefield Press

Leonard, J. (ed.) (2001) *New Music: An Anthology of Contemporary Australian Poetry*, Wollongong, NSW: Five Islands Press.

Leonard, J. (ed.) (1990) *Contemporary Australian Poetry*. Victoria: Houghton Mifflin Australia Pty Ltd.

Lloyd, P. (2002) *Collage*, Adelaide: Wakefield Press.

Lowell, A. (1917) *On Imagism*, [viewed 2 October 2002], http://www.english.uiuc.edu/maps/poets/g_l/amylowell/imagism.htm

Macneice, L. (1968) *Modern Poetry: A Personal Essay*, Oxford University Press.

Manguel, A. (1997) *A History of Reading*, London: Flamingo.

Marsh, L. (ed.) (1995) *The Wordsworth Book of Sonnets*, Hertfordshire: Wordsworth Editions Ltd.

McFarlane, P. and Harris R. (1997) *Doing Bombers off the Jetty*, Melbourne: Macmillan Education Australia Ltd.

McFarlane, P. and Mansutti, E. (eds) (1992) *Friendly Street Poetry Reader No. 16*, Adelaide: Friendly Street with Wakfield Press.

McLaren, J. (1989) *Australian Literature: An Historical Introduction*, Melbourne: Longman Cheshire Pty Ltd.

Monaco, R. and Briggs, J. (1974) *The Logic of Poetry*. New York: McGraw-Hill.

Morris, H. and Ribner, I. (1962) *Poetry: A Critical and Historical Introduction*, Chicago: Scott, Foresman and Company.

Morisson, M. (1997) *Poetry and the Public Sphere*, from the Conference on Contemporary Poetry April 24–27, 1997, http://english.rutgers.edu/morisson.htm, [viewed 2 September 2003].

Murdoch, G. and Sexton, R. (1997) *Fluorescent Voices. Friendly Street Poets No. 21*, Adelaide: Friendly Street with Wakefield Press.

National University of Singapore (2000) *Imagism*, [viewed 2 October 2002], http://65.107.211.206/post/modernism/imagism.html

Nowottny, W. (1962) *The Language Poets Use*, London: Athlone Press.

Page, G. (1995) *A Reader's Guide to Contemporary Australian Poetry*, St Lucia, Qld: University of Queensland Press.

Parrott, E. (1990) *How to Be Well-versed in Poetry*, UK: Viking Press.

Petrescu, I. and Adès, D. (eds) (2002) *Friendly Street Poetry Reader 26*, Adelaide: Friendly Street with Wakefield Press.

Poe, E.A. (1846) 'The philosophy of composition', *Graham's Magazine,* April 1846, [viewed 28 August 2002], http://www.eapoe.org/works/essays/philcomp/htm

Porter, P. (ed.) (1996) *The Oxford Book of Modern Australian Verse,* Melbourne: Oxford University Press.

Powell, B. (1967) *English Through Poetry Writing,* Sydney: Ian Novak Publishing Co.

Preminger, A. (1965) 'Imagery' and 'Practical Criticism' in *Encyclopaedia of Poetics,* New Jersey: Princeton University Press.

Reeves, J. (1965, 1970) *Understanding Poetry,* London: Heinemann.

Rice University (2002) *Generations,* [viewed 27 May 2003], http://www.cs.rice.edu/~ssiyer/minstrels/poems/102.html

Roberts, P. (2000) *How Poetry Works,* London: Penguin.

Rowlands, G. (1992) *Selected Poems,* Adelaide: Wakefield Press

Rowlands, G. (1988) *On the Menu,* Adelaide: Friendly Street Poets.

Rózewicz, T. (date unknown) *Selected Poetry,* [viewed 2 November 2002] http://www.geocites.com/Paris/6170/poetfeat2.html

Shapcott, T.W. (2000) *Chekhov's Mongoose,* Applecross, WA: Salt Publishing.

Shapcott, T.W. (1987) *Travel Dice,* Melbourne: Globe Press.

Shapcott, T.W. (1970) *Australian Poetry Now,* Melbourne: Sun Books.

Shen (2001) *City of My Skin,* Wollongong: Five Islands Press.

Shen, 'Certifying the Dead', in J. Dally and G. Kemp (eds) (1996) *Friendly Street Reader No. 20,* Adelaide: Friendly Street Poets with Wakefield Press.

Spurr, B. (1997) *Studying Poetry,* Sydney: University of Sydney.

Stead, C.K. (1964) *The New Poetic,* UK: Pelican.

Strachan, J. and Terry, R. (2001) *Poetry: An Introduction,* New York: New York University Press.

Taylor, A. (1987) *Reading Australian Poetry,* Melbourne: The Book Printer.

The Age 23 July 2000, 'Poetry, the Undying Art'.

The Bunyip (28 August 2002), Bunyip Print, Gawler, South Australia.

Tranter, J. and Mead, P. (eds) (1991) *The Penguin Book of Modern Australian Poetry,* Victoria: Penguin Books Australia Ltd

Tranter, J. (1970) 'In Defence of Poetry', University of Sydney, [viewed 3 November 2002], http://setis.library.usyd.edu.au/tranter/docs/pearlrk-jt.html

Tunnicliffe, S. (1984) *Poetry Experience: Teaching and Writing Poetry in Secondary Schools*, USA: Methuen & Co

Wallace, A. (1990) 'Reviews: Literary & arts', *Social Alternatives*, vol. 8, issue 4, p. 69, [viewed 21 October 2002], Academic Search Elite:EBSCOhost. AN 9610110020.

Warburton, A. (2003) 'Geoff Goodfellow: poet for hire' in *ABC Tasmania*, 8 May 2003.

Wilde, W.H., Hooton, J. and Andrews, B. (1994) *The Oxford Companion to Australian Literature*, 2nd edn. Melbourne: Oxford University Press.

Wordsworth, W. and Coleridge, S.T. (1965) *The Lyrical Ballads 1798–1805*. London: Methuen & Co. Ltd.

Wright, J. (ed.) (1957) *New Land, New Language, Anthology of Australian Verse*, Oxford University Press.

Wynne, W. 'Of Here and Now', *The Australian Book Review*, [viewed 19 October 2002], http://poetry.alphalink.com.au/selected.htm

Lythrum Press Pty Ltd
1st floor, 128 Hindley Street
Adelaide
South Australia 5000

Telephone: (08) 8415 5150

www.lythrumpress.com.au

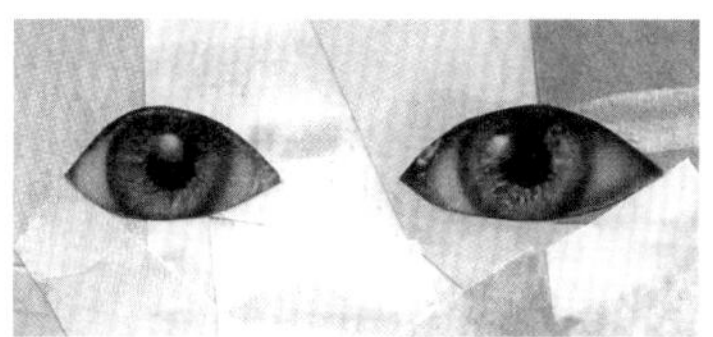